D1031803

GHOSTS OF THE SOMME

GHOSTS OF THE SOMME

*Commemoration and Culture War
in Northern Ireland*

JONATHAN EVERSHED

UNIVERSITY OF NOTRE DAME PRESS

NOTRE DAME, INDIANA

University of Notre Dame Press
Notre Dame, Indiana 46556
undpress.nd.edu
All Rights Reserved

Copyright © 2018 by University of Notre Dame

Published in the United States of America

Title page image: "The Road to the Somme Ends,"
https://extramuralactivity.com/2013/01/11/the-road-to-the-somme-ends/.
Image courtesy of Extramural Activity.

Library of Congress Cataloging-in-Publication Data

Names: Evershed, Jonathan, 1989– author.
Title: Ghosts of the Somme : commemoration and culture war in
    Northern Ireland / Jonathan Evershed.
Other titles: Commemoration and culture war in Northern Ireland
Description: Notre Dame, Indiana : University of Notre Dame Press, [2018] |
    Includes bibliographical references and index. |
Identifiers: LCCN 2018011948 (print) | LCCN 2018012581 (ebook) |
    ISBN 9780268103873 (pdf) | ISBN 9780268103880 (epub) |
    ISBN 9780268103859 (hardcover : alk. paper) |
    ISBN 0268103852 (hardcover : alk. paper)
Subjects: LCSH: Somme, 1st Battle of the, France, 1916—Centennial
celebrations, etc. | World War, 1914–1918—Northern Ireland—Anniversaries,
    etc. | Great Britain. Army. Division, 36th. | World War, 1914–1918—
    Ireland—Influence. | Collective memory—Northern Ireland. |
Group identity—Northern Ireland. | Political culture—Northern Ireland. |
    Ireland—Politics and government—21st century.
Classification: LCC DA962 (ebook) | LCC DA962.E84   2018 (print) |
    DDC 940.4/272—dc23
LC record available at https://lccn.loc.gov/2018011948

∞ *This paper meets the requirements of ANSI/NISO Z39.48-1992
(Permanence of Paper).*

For Ray Silkstone

Who taught me about arguments:

how to make them and how to hear them

The future to come can announce itself only as such and in its purity only on the basis of a *past end*. . . . The future can only be for ghosts. And the past.

J. Derrida, *Spectres of Marx*

CONTENTS

FOREWORD

The use of the poppy as a symbol of commemoration can be dated to the years following the First World War. In Australia and New Zealand, the United Kingdom and Canada, the practice of wearing the poppy and laying wreaths at cenotaphs serves as an annual reminder of those who have given the "ultimate sacrifice." The political power of the poppy places it at the center of the nation's story, a story that is physically structured in cenotaphs and memorials at the center of city, town, and village and is worn close to the heart by citizens every November in an apparently simple and universally agreed on statement of remembrance.

A closer examination of the narratives surrounding the avowedly simple poppy, however, reveals a distinct lack of agreement, great inconsistency, and, often, contention. In each country in which the poppy is worn the narratives about it differ significantly, as the particularities of each nation's relationship with war and sacrifice demand more nuanced readings of its symbolism. Very often it is a particular battle around which the national narrative is structured. In Australia, it is the stark story of the Battle of Gallipoli that provides the focal point. The narrative encompasses a scathing critique of Britain's incompetent and clumsy handling of the invasion of Turkey in 1915, while it simultaneously asserts Australia's rightful place among the nations and profiles a white, masculine (and increasingly contested) ideal-type for the Australian citizen.

In the United Kingdom, the design and prevalence of the poppy has become considerably more pronounced in the twenty-first century. The simple flower has become larger, more embellished, and even jewel-encrusted. Prominent British sports teams now have their array of international players wear an embossed poppy on their shirts during the month of November, and the few who refuse to do so are widely and roundly condemned. The international football teams of England, Scotland, and Northern Ireland have demanded the right to wear the poppy at international matches, defying the rules of FIFA, the football world's governing body, about the display of political symbols. Commemoration has become both more enforced and more controversial.

The complex and conflicted symbolism of the poppy is nowhere better illustrated than in Ireland. The same years that saw it first worn as a symbol of remembrance also saw Ireland divided into two states. Northern Ireland became a devolved region of the United Kingdom, while the other twenty-six counties took dominion status before eventually becoming the Republic of Ireland. The First World War did not provide a suitable narrative, nor the poppy a suitable symbol, for the southern state, where the 1916 Easter Rising delivered the story of sacrifice around which national identity was structured. But in Northern Ireland, a story of sacrifice for Ulster and for the empire sustained relationships with the British "mainland." Like the Australian soldiers at Gallipoli, the soldiers of the 36th (Ulster) Division at the Battle of the Somme came to symbolize a gallant and foundational sacrifice for King and country.

This sophisticated and detailed book by Jon Evershed offers us real insight into the contemporary politics and poetics of commemoration. In particular, it examines the narratives and practices of commemoration by groups of working-class Unionists in Northern Ireland. It explores how and why, in Belfast, the poppy has migrated from its traditional habitat on lapels and at the foot of memorials in the early weeks of November to appear year-round in "Loyalist" paramilitary murals and on the uniforms and instruments of marching bands during the parades of the summer months. It helps to explain why it is not uncommon to see people in Northern Ireland wearing a poppy at any point throughout the year, or even to see etched in people's skin as part of a tattoo. In Northern Ireland, the sacrifice of which the poppy is symbolic belongs to complex narratives and divisive claims about British sovereignty, citizenship, and identity on the island of Ireland.

And yet, as Jon Evershed maps, the 1998 multiparty Agreement has helped to create a new environment in which the poppy and its story have increasingly been salvaged and reclaimed in the Republic of Ireland

and, consequently, in which a narrative of common sacrifice by Protestant *and* Catholic, British *and* Irish, on the fields of France and Flanders has been constructed and rehearsed. This narrative has been encouraged by both the British and Irish states in the name of peace-building, to the point that it appears to threaten the particularity of the loyalty—and the identity—of some of the Unionists of Ulster.

Conflicting narratives, driven by the politics of group identity, are plotted throughout this book. Importantly, it captures a moment in time, "a decade of centenaries," by and through which these politics are currently framed and negotiated. As a work of anthropology, people and their practices are central to the analysis. What people say and what people do when they commemorate are captured through Evershed's ethnography, and he provides a challenging commentary on the social, cultural, and political role of remembrance. This volume is therefore an important case study of commemorative practice, of the will to commemorate, and of the politics of remembering.

Dominic Bryan
Belfast, July 2017

ACKNOWLEDGMENTS

This book was born of my PhD research, which—with the generous support of an Arts and Humanities Research Council scholarship for which I am immensely grateful—I was privileged to undertake at the Institute of Irish Studies, Queen's University Belfast. For more than fifty years, the Institute has continuously sought to interrogate and broaden the boundaries of Irish Studies scholarship, and my research benefited immeasurably from the encouragement and support I received from my colleagues at Queen's. I feel very lucky to count so many leading scholars not only as peers, but as friends. They have helped to make Belfast a second home.

To my former supervisors, Dominic Bryan and Evi Chatzipanagiotidou, my sincerest thanks. I could not have asked for better, more thorough, or—when it mattered—more motivational support and guidance. My examiners, Neil Jarman and Eric Kaufmann, contributed significantly to polishing and refining the manuscript. The work presented here also profited from the encouragement, collaborative spirit, and critical eye of, among others, John Barry, Guy Beiner, Kris Brown, Marie Coleman, Oona Frawley, Fearghal McGarry, Richard Grayson, Roisín Higgins, Sophie Long, Tony Novosel, Michael Pierse and Joe Webster. I am grateful to Pawel Romanczuk for some of my earliest introductions to Belfast, its complexities and idiosyncrasies. Thérèse Cullen, Órfhlaith Campbell, and Ray Casserly were great craic and provided many laughs along the way. Kristen and John Donnelly always made their home open, and their emotional support was invaluable and greatly appreciated. Special thanks are due to two friends and colleagues: Erin Hinson, for the enduring friendship that has meant so much; and Stephen Millar, for the many unforgettable days and nights spent together "in the field." Here's to many more to come.

To Mum, Dad, and Dai, for whose unconditional love and support I have always feared I am insufficiently appreciative, from the bottom of my heart, thank you for teaching me always to try and not to give up. To Dad, in particular, I am so grateful that you took the time to teach me the importance of the political, and helped me to find my voice. Thank you too for being a sounding board and for your expert proofreading. Maia, I hope you know how much your passion, your patience, your belief in me when I find it hard to find any, and, of course, your unmatched insight continue to mean to me.

The publication of my first monograph was a prospect made less daunting by the help and support of the University of Notre Dame Press. I would like to record my thanks to my two reviewers and to the editorial board for their unanimous support of this project. Particular thanks are due to Eli Bortz, Rebecca DeBoer, and Sheila Berg for so adeptly supporting this newcomer through every step of the publication process. I would be remiss not to acknowledge that certain of the ideas contained in this book represent the new use of material and the development and expansion of arguments previously presented in "From Past Conflict to Shared Future? Commemoration, Peacebuilding and the Politics of Ulster Loyalism during Northern Ireland's 'Decade of Centenaries,'" *International Political Anthropology* 8, no. 2 (2015) (on which the opening vignette in chapter 3 and parts of chapter 6, in particular, draw extensively); "Ghosts of the Somme: The State of Ulster Loyalism, Memory Work and the 'Other' 1916," in Richard S. Grayson and Fearghal McGarry, eds., *Remembering 1916: The Easter Rising, the Somme and the Politics of Memory in Ireland* (Cambridge University Press, 2016) (to which parts of chapters 3, 4, and 6 owe their genesis); and "A Matter of Fact? The Propaganda of Peace and Ulster Loyalist Hauntology during the 'Decade of Centenaries,'" in Fiona Larkan and Fiona Murphy, eds., *Memory and Recovery in Times of Crisis* (Routledge, 2018) (from which parts of chapters 3 and 7 draw key themes and arguments). My appreciation to the editors and publishers of these volumes.

My greatest thanks are reserved for the many people who helped to transform the field into a home. I am indebted to my colleagues at Cooperation Ireland, particularly Barry Fennell, Alan Largey, and Corinna

Crooks, for showing me the ropes. I am enduringly thankful and deeply humbled by the generosity of all of those who allowed me to share in their lives—in the highs and the lows. I hope that the work I have presented here stands as a fitting tribute to it. There are some to whom special thanks are due. I am grateful to Iain Elliott for his hospitality, forthrightness, and honesty and his company at eleventh night bonfires. Nev Gallagher always had my back, went out of his way to support me and my work, and did perhaps more than anyone to make me feel welcome. This research would simply not have been possible without him. I feel privileged to call Philip Orr my friend and mentor; his dedication, intellect, and integrity have been a great source of inspiration. Finally, to my friend Jason Burke, for walking with me on every step of this journey and the many jokes we shared, I will be forever grateful.

In the end, responsibility for the work presented (and any mistakes, omissions, or errata contained therein) is my own.

ILLUSTRATIONS

ABBREVIATIONS

ACT	Action for Community Transformation
BCC	Belfast City Council
CRC	Community Relations Council
DCAL	Department of Culture, Arts and Leisure
DETI	Department of Enterprise, Trade and Investment
DUP	Democratic Unionist Party
GPO	General Post Office
HIU	Historical Investigations Unit
HLF	Heritage Lottery Fund
ICIR	Independent Commission for Information Retrieval
INCORE	International Conflict Research Institute
INLA	Irish National Liberation Army
IPP	Irish Parliamentary Party
IRB	Irish Republican Brotherhood
IRG	Implementation and Reconciliation Group
IRSP	Irish Republican Socialist Party
ISPS	International School for Peace Studies
LAD	Loyalists Against Democracy
LCC	Loyalist Communities Council
LOL	Loyal Orange Lodge
MLA	Member of the Legislative Assembly
MP	Member of Parliament
NIE	Northern Ireland Executive
NIHE	Northern Ireland Housing Executive
NIO	Northern Ireland Office
NISRA	Northern Ireland Statistics and Research Agency
OFMDFM	Office of the First Minister and Deputy First Minister

PIRA   Provisional Irish Republican Army
PSNI   Police Service of Northern Ireland
PUL   Protestant/Unionist/Loyalist
PUP   Progressive Unionist Party
SDLP   Social Democratic and Labour Party
T:BUC   Together: Building a United Community
TD   Teachta Dála (Deputy to the Dáil)
TUV   Traditional Unionist Voice
UCC   Unionist Centenary Committee
UDA   Ulster Defence Association
UDP   Ulster Democratic Party
UDU   Ulster Defence Union
UFF   Ulster Freedom Fighters
UKIP   United Kingdom Independence Party
UPRG   Ulster Political Research Group
UUC   Ulster Unionist Council
UUP   Ulster Unionist Party
UVF   Ulster Volunteer Force

Introduction

Younger Pyper: The temple of the lord is ransacked.
Elder Pyper: Ulster.
(Pyper reaches towards himself.)
Younger Pyper: Dance in this deserted temple of the Lord.
Elder Pyper: Dance.

> F. McGuinness, *Observe the Sons of Ulster*
> *Marching Towards the Somme*

At 7:30 a.m. on 1 July 1916, the whistle blew and the men of the 36th (Ulster) Division emerged from Thiepval Wood at a quick jog, making their way swiftly towards the heavily fortified German position on the crest of the hill opposite. Under a hail of machine-gun fire they had not been expecting, more than five thousand of them would be killed, wounded, or missing by the end of their assault on the German trenches. Nearly one hundred years to the day—on Saturday, 18 June 2016—to the sound of flute and drum, thousands of men and women marched from the four corners of the city of Belfast, converging on Woodvale Park at the north end of the Shankill Road, bearing flags and banners and many sporting period costumes. At 1:30 p.m. the deafening boom of artillery split the air, and we watched as—accompanied by an ominous sound track overlaid with the crack and rattle of imitation machine-gun fire—one hundred men in khaki uniforms advanced across "no-man's land" from

1

replica trenches, to take the "German" position at the opposite end of a repurposed football pitch. Their leader bore aloft a large Union flag, and when he "fell" amidst the pyrotechnic bomb blasts, it was picked up and carried by another. A loud cheer erupted from the crowd as the flag bearer hoisted it above the German bunker. Over the bodies of tens of "casualties" a gaudy rendition of "God Save the Queen" boomed from the speakers. It was so loud that the sound was distorted, splitting the air like a thunderclap as it reverberated around the park.

In 1973, Clifford Geertz published his seminal essay, "Deep Play: Notes on a Balinese Cockfight," in which he examined the layered meaning and the dramatic role of cockfighting in the (re)production of Balinese culture. As the pageantry, ritual, and ceremony of Geertz's cockfight revealed the intricacies of cultural, political, and socioeconomic relationships in Bali, so I seek to demonstrate in this book how the commemoration, reenactment, and genealogy of 1 July 1916—a day marked by greater loss of life than any other in British military history, and the first of 1916's grinding, bloody, and (to this day) controversial Battle of the Somme (Faulkner 2016)—reveal the complexity of the conflicted relationships and lifeworlds that define the so-called Protestant/Unionist/Loyalist (PUL) community in Northern Ireland. In what follows, I explicate the conflicted role(s) of the Battle of the Somme and its commemoration in the "postconflict" politics of the "new" Northern Ireland. In particular, this book addresses how Ulster Loyalist commemoration during what has come to be called the Decade of Centenaries functions as a site of conflict, negotiation, and the *hauntological* reassertion of Loyalists' "knowledge" or "truth" in a historical and political moment defined by *ontological* crisis.

THE CULT OF THE CENTENARY

In his influential *Sites of Memory, Sites of Mourning*, Jay Winter (1995, 93), argued that the scale and horror of the First World War—theretofore unprecedented in human history and surpassed to date only by the Second World War—lent its commemoration across Europe and beyond a certain apolitical quality. According to Winter, memorialization of the war provided "first and foremost a framework for the legitimation of individual and family grief," becoming politically significant only "now that the moment of mourning has long past" (93). However, it is difficult to see the labeling of Britain's war dead as "Glorious" on Lutyens's Whitehall cenotaph as ever having been less than intrinsically political. War commemoration is, fundamentally, "a practice bound up with rituals of national identification, and a key element in the symbolic repertoire available to the nation-state for binding its citizens into a national identity" (Ashplant, Dawson, and Roper 2000, 7). As Benedict Anderson (2006 [1983], 50) intimates, "No more arresting emblems of the modern culture of nationalism exist than cenotaphs and tombs of Unknown Soldiers. . . . [V]oid as these tombs are of identifiable mortal remains or immortal souls, they are nonetheless saturated with ghostly *national* imaginings."[1]

What Quinault (1998) has called the "cult of the centenary" is likewise a characteristically modern feature of the Andersonian (2006 [1983]) "imagined community." According to Quinault, the evolution of the centenary was one aspect of what Hobsbawm (1983) termed the "mass production" of traditions in European nation-states during the nineteenth and early twentieth century. The decimalization of historical consciousness in this period served to frame the centenary as a neutral or even natural position from which to comprehend the events of the past, such that the special significance of hundredth anniversaries now seems intuitive. However, as Quinault (1998, 322) suggests, "the cult of the centenary reflect[s] not just a detached interest in the past, but also very contemporary preoccupations" (see also Grundlingh 2004; Boyce 2001, 256–59; Cook 2007; cf. Bryan 2016).

Significantly, a centenary locates the event(s) being commemorated just beyond the realm of living memory. The biological fact of human life expectancy makes it extremely unlikely that there is anyone left alive with any meaningful firsthand memory of events. "Memory" is thereby conclusively opened to reinterpretation, negotiation, and contestation, with a minimized risk of intervention or contradiction from those who had direct experience of the event being commemorated. Insofar as any meaningful separation actually exists between them, a centenary marks the final translocation of memory from the realm of the psychological or cognitive to that of the cultural and political (cf. Ashplant, Dawson, and Roper 2000). Far from being monolithic, a centenary therefore represents a discursive and ritual space in which a "struggle for different groups to give public articulation to, and hence gain recognition for, certain memories and the narratives within which they are structured" takes place (Ashplant, Dawson, and Roper 2000, 16).

In a speech at the Imperial War Museum in October 2012, then Prime Minister David Cameron revealed the U.K. government's £50 million plan for what he called "a truly national commemoration" to mark the centenary of the First World War. "There is something about the First World War," the prime minister argued, "that makes it a fundamental part of our national consciousness. Put simply, this matters not just in our heads, but in our hearts; it has a very strong emotional connection. . . . The fact is, individually and as a country, we keep coming back to it, and I think that will go on." "I want a commemoration," he continued, "that captures our national spirit, in every corner of the country, from our schools to our workplaces, to our town halls and local communities. A commemoration that, like the Diamond Jubilee celebrated this year, says something about who we are as a people . . . and ensure[s] that the sacrifice and service of a hundred years ago is still remembered in a hundred years' time" (*Guardian* 2012).

If ever there had been any hope of escaping it (Reynolds 2013; Furedi 2014), then its centenary seems to have ensured that the First World War is something to which return is now inexorable. However, the Great War's emotional, cultural, and political significance and its place in the consciousness of the plurinational United Kingdom is more ambiguous and contentious than Cameron acknowledges (Mycock 2014a, 2014b). Nowhere is this more so than in Northern Ireland. While the commemorative parade and reenactment I watched in Woodvale Park in June 2016 were laden with the symbols of the "national spirit" advocated by the prime minister in 2012, their place in this "corner of the country" is divisive and disputed. "Who we are as a people" is an essentially contested question in Northern Ireland, and the politics of its twentieth and early twenty-first century have been defined by deep and violent division between two national spirits, in which commemoration of the First World War has had a vital function. Crucially, in Ireland—North and South—the centenary of the First World War is located within a broader and contested Decade of Centenaries that marks the hundredth anniversaries of the events that gave birth to the two states on the island (Coleman 2014).

The moniker "Decade of Centenaries" was coined by then Taoiseach Brian Cowen during his address to the 2010 Institute for British-Irish Studies Conference at University College Dublin, in which he stated, "The events of the decade between 1912 and 1922 were momentous and defining ones for all of the people of this island, and indeed for these islands. This was the decade of the covenant and the gun, of blood sacrifice and bloody politics, a time of division and war, not only on this island but across the world. It was the decade that defined relationships on these islands for most of the last century" (Quigley and Cowen 2011, 4).

Though they had earlier antecedents and long-term consequences that extend far beyond it,[2] broadly, the decade's points of reference are the events of the eleven-year period that opened with the Home Rule, Crisis of 1912–14 and closed with the surrender of Anti-Treaty Forces and the end of the Irish Civil War in 1923. The year 1916 is the pivot around which the decade hinges, and in 2016 the centenaries of two foundational events were marked, each representing the apex of (avowedly) divergent memorial trajectories: the Easter Rising for "Catholic" Nationalists and the Battle of the Somme for "Protestant" Unionists.

"1916 AND ALL THAT"

For Ulster Loyalists, the affective significance and cultural-political resonance of the First World War is reducible to a single signifier: the Somme. This significance is a function of the relationship of the Battle of the Somme (and its commemoration) with events that both preceded and followed it. What the historian Philip Orr (2008) has termed "the road to the Somme" began in 1912 with the introduction of the Third Home Rule Bill in the House of Commons by Liberal Prime Minister Herbert Asquith. Home Rule, which would have granted power to a parliament in Dublin to legislate for Irish affairs, was supported by the largest political party in Ireland, the Irish Parliamentary Party (IPP), led by John Redmond. Ulster Unionists were fiercely opposed to the bill. Their antipathy hinged on the dual claims that Home Rule was equivalent to Catholic, or "Rome," rule and that it represented a threat to the economic interests of the industrial capital concentrated in Ireland's northeastern corner (Doherty 2014).

Unionist opposition to Home Rule was coordinated by the Ulster Unionist Party (UUP); its leader, the charismatic Dublin-born lawyer and Member of Parliament (MP) for the University of Dublin, Sir Edward Carson; and his more taciturn but politically astute deputy, James Craig, MP for the East Down constituency. Inspired by the covenanting tradition of his Scottish Presbyterian ancestors, on 28 September 1912 (Ulster Day), Craig masterminded the ritual mass signing of Ulster's "Solemn League and Covenant" in ceremonies across the province, including in Belfast's iconic city hall. Signatories to the Ulster Covenant pledged to resist Home Rule by "all means which may be found necessary." It was signed by 218,206 men, and an equivalent declaration was signed by 228,999 women (Fitzpatrick 2014, 243).

As the Home Rule Bill continued its passage through Parliament, just what the Covenant meant by "all means necessary" became clear. In January 1913, the UUP's governing council announced the formation of the Ulster Volunteer Force (UVF), a militia organization charged with resisting Home Rule, including—in extremis—through force of arms. The UVF attracted some 100,000 recruits, all of whom had signed the Covenant in 1912. They drilled on the estates of landowners and industrialists across Ulster (Bowman 2007). In response to the formation of this Unionist militia, a coalition of Irish Nationalists called a meeting in Dublin in November 1913 to announce the formation of a rival organization, the Irish Volunteers. At the organization's height, the Irish Volunteers claimed a membership of 200,000 (Ó Corráin 2018). Gun-running operations in 1914 saw both the UVF and the Irish Volunteers successfully smuggle large consignments of German-bought rifles into Larne, Co. Antrim, and Howth, Co. Dublin, respectively. In 1914, with two (now armed) rival armies preparing to face each other and the British Army, bloody and complicated civil war in Ireland seemed inevitable. However, when, in July and August 1914, the European empires awoke to the great conflagration into which they had "sleepwalked" (Clark

2012), the gathering storm in Ireland was quickly overtaken by events, and the political landscape was rapidly and radically transformed. By the time the Home Rule Bill passed into law in September 1914 (with an amendment that delayed its implementation until the end of hostilities in Europe) it was on its way to becoming a political relic of a bygone era, a footnote in the history of Ireland's violent twentieth century.

Carson quickly committed the UVF to supporting the war effort, though only after seeking assurance that the British government would not institute Home Rule in their absence. Many Ulster Volunteers were already reservists in the British Expeditionary Force and were recalled to barracks with immediate effect (Grayson 2009). However, the bulk of UVF members who took the "King's shilling" enlisted in their thousands in what would become the 36th (Ulster) Division of Lord Kitchener's "New Army." In May 1915, after training in camps across the north of Ireland, including at Clandeboye estate in Co. Down (which had also provided training grounds for the UVF), the volunteers of the 36th (Ulster) Division made their way to Belfast. There, large flag-waving crowds cheered them onto the boats that would take them first to Seaford, in East Sussex, and then on to France. For many it was the first and last time they would ever leave the island of Ireland (Bowman 2007; Orr 2008).

Redmond too committed himself to Britain's war effort, in part because he hoped this would prevent the Westminster government from reneging on its promise to institute Home Rule at the end of the war. In a speech at Woodenbridge, Co. Wicklow, in September 1914, he called on the Irish Volunteers to go "wherever the firing line extends." He continued, "Remember this country is in a state of war, and your duty is two-fold. Your duty is, at all costs, to defend the shores of Ireland from foreign invasion. It is a duty more than that of taking care that Irish valour proves itself on the field of war, as it has always proved itself in the past" (Century Ireland 2014).

The Irish Volunteer movement split, with the majority heeding Redmond's call. Those who remained loyal to Redmond and the IPP were renamed "National Volunteers," and thousands of them enlisted in the British Army, particularly in the volunteer 16th (Irish) Division (Ó Corráin 2018). Of the remaining 13,500 Irish Volunteers who renounced Redmond's leadership, 1,000 would go on to play a key role in a rebellion planned and led by the Irish Republican Brotherhood (IRB) in Dublin during Easter Week, 1916. This Easter Rising would fundamentally and forever change the face of Irish Nationalist politics.

On 24 April, despite countermanding orders from senior figures in the Irish Volunteers, Republicans captured several key buildings in Dublin, including the iconic General Post Office (GPO). Padraig Pearse, a leading member of the IRB, proclaimed an independent Irish Republic outside the GPO on behalf of the seven members of its provisional government. For five days and nights there was fierce fighting between the rebel forces and the British Army, which called in reserves to crush the rebellion. The gunboat *Helga* sailed up the River Liffey into the heart of Dublin and opened fire on rebel-held positions. On 29 April, Pearse signed an unconditional surrender. Following their courts-martial, fifteen leaders of the Rising—including the seven signatories to the Proclamation—were executed by firing squad in the breaker's yard of Dublin's Kilmainham Gaol.[3] While the Rising had initially been met with ambivalence and even hostility in Dublin and beyond, these executions contributed to a decisive swing in public opinion in favor of its leaders and their Republican project. In the wake of the Easter Rising and the "terrible beauty" (Yeats 1916) to which it had given birth, those Irish soldiers who returned from the battlefields of France, Belgium, and the Middle East found themselves in a country "changed utterly" (Yeats 1916; McGarry 2010).

As the executions of the Rising's leaders were sounding the death knell of Home Rule, "constitutional" Irish Nationalism, and John Redmond's IPP, final preparations were being made by British and French generals for a big push at the River Somme to end the stalemate with the Germans on the Western Front. In March 1916, the 36th (Ulster) Division had been moved up to the front lines between the villages of Beaumont Hamel and Thiepval. After a week of sustained (and largely ineffective) artillery bombardment, the Somme offensive began on the morning of 1 July. Of the divisions that went over the top on 1 July 1916, the 36th (Ulster) Division was uniquely successful in achieving its objectives, capturing the heavily fortified Schwaben Redoubt. However, the devastating losses sustained by the divisions on either side meant that the 36th faced enfilading fire on both flanks, and they were eventually forced to retreat under heavy fire. By 2 July, of the 9,000 men from the

36th (Ulster) Division who went over the top the previous day, more than 5,000 were reported killed, missing, wounded, or taken prisoner, of whom some 2,000 were dead (Orr 2008).

The process of commemorating the 36th (Ulster) Division began almost immediately after news of its appalling losses on the Western Front began to arrive on Ulster's doorsteps. In large part, early commemoration of the 36th was organized at the local level and orchestrated by grieving families, church congregations, and communities for whom the loss was profoundly personal, emotional, and prepolitical (see Switzer 2007). However, this commemoration was also unambiguously politicized from the outset. Ulster Unionists were "unique in the extent to which historical myth and the unresolved dilemma of their constitutional future provided an interpretative framework within which the meaning of the [First World] War was defined" (Loughlin 2002, 136). Following the Armistice of 1918, the sacrifice of Ulstermen during the war, and in particular at the Somme, was invoked by Unionists to justify and guarantee the partition of Ireland.

In the wake of the Easter Rising and—perhaps more significantly—the execution of several of its key protagonists, the volatile years between 1918 and 1923 were marked by the ascendance of Republicanism as the dominant political force in Nationalist Ireland, and by the violence of first the War for Independence (the Tan War) and then the Irish Civil War. During this period, as Loughlin intimates,

> some of the most dangerous phases of the Anglo-Irish struggle for Ulster unionism coincided with war commemorations, allowing unionists the opportunity to counterpoint any tendency of Westminster to 'betray' Ulster with a powerful reminder of the province's sacrifice in the British national interest, and, accordingly a debt owed by Britain. . . . [I]t allowed them simultaneously to share authentically in a profound British experience, and to address their own political concerns. (2002, 137–41)

As part of the renewed efforts to resist any attempt by the British government to "sell" Ulster to a Dublin parliament,[4] the symbolic reduction of the service of all "Ulstermen" during the First World War to that of the 36th (Ulster) Division at the Somme was a deliberate strategy on the part of the Unionist political elite. The Somme's utility for Ulster Unionists was expressed in their sponsorship of the construction of the Ulster Memorial Tower at Thiepval, which was completed in 1921. Modeled on Helen's Tower—which overlooks the Clandeboye estate on which first the Ulster Volunteers and then the 36th (Ulster) Division had trained and drilled—the Ulster Memorial Tower was the first permanent memorial to be constructed on the former battlefields of the Western Front. "In a clear and unambiguous form," it symbolized "the contribution of the North to the defence of Britain and an empire of which it was strenuously asserted Ulster formed an integral part" (Officer 2001, 182; see also Switzer 2013).

The 36th (Ulster) Division had provided the Girardian (1977) blood sacrifice—equal and opposite to that of the martyrs of Easter Week—on which in 1921, amid ongoing violence and civil strife, the "Orange State" (Farrell 1980) was founded in Northern Ireland: the new political entity awkwardly carved out of Ireland's northeastern corner under the terms of the Government of Ireland Act. The ghosts of the Somme were the exemplars and guarantors of the (militarized) masculinity of the ideal Ulsterman, which would become central to the Ulster Unionist state- and nation-building projects in the years following partition (McGaughey 2012). These ghosts were recalled annually in ceremonies of state, including by the Orange Order in its parading traditions, symbols, and regalia (Bryan 2000; Kaufmann 2007). From 1965, they were also invoked by a newly (re)formed Ulster Volunteer Force. As Northern Ireland descended into the violence and bloodshed of the prolonged confrontation that has become known as the Troubles, the ghosts of Ulster's Volunteers continued their haunting.

In the 1980s, as the Battle of the Somme began to pass from the realm of living memory, it looked as though its ghosts might be allowed, finally, to rest. However, the profound political, social, and cultural changes that have taken place in Ireland, North and South, since the advent of the "peace process" have conspired, instead, to raise them anew. As Queen and Uachtáran stood together at the new Island of Ireland Peace Park on the outskirts of the Belgian village of Messines in November 1998, these ghosts were called on to consolidate a hard-won peace—signed at Stormont's Castle Buildings just months before. The ghosts of the 36th were joined there by those of the "Nationalist" 16th (Irish)

Division—whose war record had previously been "forgotten"—to tell a new reconciliatory parable about a shared sacrifice. An emerging new official mythology, which maintains that there was no Orange and Green in the trenches, has seen one of the bloodiest conflicts in human history come to be not merely remembered, but celebrated as a parable for peace-building: a war that stopped a war. Where they were once conjured by the architects of the Orange State, now the Somme's ghosts are raised by those whose "propaganda of peace" (McLaughlin and Baker 2010) seeks to dismantle it.

Despite the radical changes that ongoing processes of peace-building have wrought on the character of the political, cultural, and economic establishment in post-Agreement Northern Ireland, the ghosts of the Somme are still figures of it. But they are also agents provocateurs, providing succor and guidance to those for whom these changes represent a deep, existential dilemma. For Ulster Loyalists, rapid deindustrialization, a crisis in educational attainment, the legacy of a brutal and bloody conflict and the so-called and ongoing culture war have rendered the present out of joint. As Loyalism charts its way through choppy and unfamiliar political, cultural, and economic waters, the ghosts of Ulster's Volunteers are called on to help steer the ship. Battle cries and costumes have been borrowed from the Golden Age (Brown 2007), as Ulster Loyalists seek to reassert their quavering voices in a society they perceive as refusing to listen.

MEMORY WORK AND THE STATE OF
ULSTER LOYALISM

Like all signs, the Somme's meaning for Ulster Loyalism (and scholars thereof) is in large part a function of what it does not signify. Much of its symbolic potency is derived from the implicit rejection of its opposite: the Easter Rising and its legacy and the Irish Nationalist and Republican politics to which its (contested) meanings are central (see Jarman 1999; Graff-McRae 2010; Higgins 2012). The Somme is a vital part of a memorial cartography (see Zerubavel 2003) that maps the Ulster Protestant experience across time—from the Plantation of the seventeenth century to the present day—as one defined in equal measure by perennial conflict with a hostile "other" and the duplicity of the "Perfidious Albion" to which Loyalists claim their fealty. In ways that this book examines, it is fundamental, therefore, to Loyalism's complex political economy of "identity" (Reed 2015) and "community" (Bryan 2006).

In postconflict Northern Ireland, where particular forms of (identity) politics pose a (perceived) threat to the prevailing social, political, and economic order, Loyalists' symbolic (over)burdening of the Somme has come to be labeled by the architects and guarantors of that order as an illegitimate exercise in manipulating history for divisive ends. For example, during a speech in Belfast in June 2016, in advance of her attendance at the centenary commemoration at the Ulster Tower, then Secretary of State for Northern Ireland Theresa Villiers claimed:

> At the beginning of the so-called 'decade of centenaries' in 2012, the UK and Irish Governments both recognised the potential for sensitive events like the Ulster Covenant, the Easter Rising or the Somme to be *hijacked* by those seeking to use them to re-open old wounds and promote discord and division. . . . After all that has been achieved both here in Northern Ireland, and in UK-Irish relations, we therefore determined to work closely together in an effort to prevent this. (NIO 2016; emphasis added)

This delegitimization of particular commemorative forms is emblematic of an epistemological, ethical, and profoundly political conflict over what we may legitimately call "history," which hinges on the accusation that Loyalists' use or "hijacking" of the Somme (and, for that matter, Republicans' use of the Rising) as a signifier is insufficiently based in historical fact. Official commemoration during the Decade of Centenaries is presented as an exercise in rescuing the truth of (Northern) Ireland's past from those who would abuse it for unofficial ends (cf. Papadakis 1993). And it is professional historians who have been charged with this process of truth recovery. In the Republic of Ireland, the official commemorative program for the Decade of Centenaries has been steered by an expert advisory committee, consisting exclusively of academic historians. A similar Centenaries working group has been convened in the North by the Northern Ireland Community Relations Council (CRC) and the Heritage Lottery Fund (HLF) and also contains a number of professional historians. Historians have also provided advice and guidance to the Northern Ireland World War I Centenary Committee, which is responsible for coordinating the official, state-sponsored program of First World War commemorations in Northern Ireland.

In her 2016 speech, Theresa Villiers commended the role of historians in reorienting official commemoration in Ireland, North and South:

> Much of the credit for this changed tone is, of course, down to professional historians, uncovering new facts and providing fresh interpretations of past events. . . . While it is never easy to view history with complete objectivity and impartiality, both administrations have been clear that we seek to put historical accuracy and mutual respect for different perspectives at the heart of our approach. . . . We have seen all too well how history can divide. Our ambitious goal throughout this decade is seek to use history to unite. To build on the political progress that has been made here. (NIO 2016)

However, many Ulster Loyalists regard the "political progress" heralded by the secretary of state and the "objectivity and impartiality" on which it is ostensibly founded as anything but. For them, the official commemoration during the Decade of Centenaries has risked (or is even founded on) the distortion of their authentic memorial tradition. Further, Loyalists see this distortion as part of an ongoing culture war for which peace-building and claims to "parity of esteem" provide a cover. Loyalists' claims to the authenticity of their commemorative tradition, and its place in the (perceived) culture war are the subject of this book. I examine ethnographically the relationship between loyalty, commemoration, and peace-building in Northern Ireland. I have sought to determine and understand commemoration's role in Loyalists' confrontation with the political and economic settlement and the official historiography of the "new" Northern Ireland. In particular, I aim to deconstruct "the Somme" as a signifier, revealing its function in the construction and reproduction of "unofficial" history or "dominated" social memory, through which Loyalists mediate relationships between self, community, other, and the state.

"LEST WE FORGET"

In *Spectres of Marx*, Jacques Derrida added a corollary to Marx's (1852) famous proposition that "the tradition of all the dead generations weighs like a nightmare on the brains of the living." Derrida (2006 [1993], 18) argued that "tradition" is not merely or passively inherited: it is "never gathered together, never at one with itself. Its presumed unity can consist only in the injunction to *reaffirm by choosing*" (emphasis added). Commemoration proceeds precisely from the (re)affirmative injunction upon which Derrida insisted: "Lest We Forget." Appearing on war memorials, in commemorative text, eulogy, and ritual performance, "Lest We Forget" is the command through which the tradition of the dead generations is *made* to weigh on the brains of the living.

Derrida (1986, 71) also claimed, "The very condition of a deconstruction may be at work in the work, within the system to be deconstructed. It may already be located there, already at work. . . . [D]econstruction is not an operation that supervenes afterwards, from the outside, one fine day. It is always already at work in the work." Deconstruction is already at work in the work of commemoration. "Lest We Forget" has myriad potential meanings: the injunction that is at the very heart of the commemorative system is susceptible to forms of semiotic slippage that can be put to work to destabilize and deconstruct that system.

Resisting any claims to the contrary, we must not forget that commemoration is intrinsically political. What and how groups, societies, or communities remember are political choices with political consequences. Attempts to establish official commemorations are often—even generally—predicated on attempts to forget particular sectional or oppositional memorial forms (cf. Ashplant, Dawson, and Roper 2000). Recovery of unofficial narratives and practices is important for locating and contesting (state) power, as well as for understanding how intracommunal relationships and patterns of power are shaped or challenged. In particular, I contend that the state-sponsored hermeneutic of peacebuilding represents an attempt to forget the politics that gave rise to the conflict in and about Northern Ireland and, thereby, the political as such. However, conflicting ideologies (as well as intragroup debate and conflict) at opposing Loyalist and Republican extremes are not, and ought not to be, so easily forgotten. Finally, Loyalists perceive themselves as forgotten—economically, politically, and culturally marginal— and, as revealed in the so-called flag protests of late 2012 and early 2013,[5] if we do not actively seek to remember them, then this may carry risks for the fragile peace in Northern Ireland.

In light of this deconstructive reading of the commemorative injunction, "Lest We Forget," this book seeks to address four interrelated questions:

- What is the current state of Ulster Loyalism—in a political context defined by ongoing processes of peace-building—as understood by Loyalists engaged in commemoration of the Battle of the Somme?
- How is commemoration of the Battle of the Somme by Loyalists during the Decade of Centenaries shaped by this political context?
- What intra- and extracommunal conflicts are reflected and reproduced in Loyalists' commemoration of the Battle of the Somme during the Decade of Centenaries?
- What (potentially) transformative role does commemoration of the Battle of the Somme play in Loyalist politics?

In chapter 1, I locate these questions within the anthropological tradition and emergent discipline of memory studies. Through a (re)-theorization of the relationship between history, memory, and commemoration, I argue that the practice of history in general, and in deeply divided societies like Northern Ireland in particular, amounts to attempts to discipline the more vernacular "memory." It is therefore an exercise in (state) power. In reasserting the primacy of memory, I nonetheless argue that memory studies scholarship often fails to acknowledge the tension between memory as something that individuals *possess* and commemoration as something that groups or societies *do*. Drawing on the poststructuralist, Derridean (2006 [1993]) concept of haunting, I argue that it is ultimately more useful than history *or* memory for understanding how and why the past is made to intrude into the present to condition particular forms of social and, crucially, political action (see also Brown 2001; Gordon 2008, 2011). Commemoration and its ghost dance are vehicles by which identity and community are constructed and negotiated, and through which history and the disciplinary regime of historiographical "truth" over which it presides can be contested.

In chapter 2, I outline the ethnographic methodology of my encounter with history, memory, and commemoration in Northern Ireland during the Decade of Centenaries in general, and with Loyalist commemoration of the Somme in particular. I demonstrate how "the field" exists in a commemorative social world and my use of participant observation, ethnographic interviews, and material and textual analysis to map it. I also discuss the ethics of my ethnography. I focus on negotiating the contradictions between the anthropological will to empathy and the difficulties of establishing and maintaining it with the Loyalist "other." While Loyalists are enrolled in socioeconomic and political structures in the new Northern Ireland on adverse terms, and this should engender an empathetic approach to understanding their lifeworlds, those lifeworlds are also defined by forms of racism, sectarianism, homophobia, and sexism that cannot be ignored. This dualism, and the ethical questions it raises, has been a defining feature of this research. Revisiting a long-running debate in anthropology, I reassert the central importance of the will to empathy in the ethnographic encounter, arguing that this need not imply communion or affinity.

Chapter 3 examines the construction of the Decade of Centenaries in peace-building and community relations policy and its role in what McLaughlin and Baker (2010) have termed the propaganda of peace. Locating the Decade within broader policy discourses about the past in Northern Ireland and drawing on my theorization of the relationship between history and memory in chapter 1, I argue that as a policy construct, official commemoration and its recourse to historical "fact" represent an attempt to delegitimize particular understandings of the violent past. While it claims to have depoliticized the past, the propaganda of peace as it pertains to the decade of commemorations actually represents a form of "anti-politics" (Ferguson 1990) that seeks to preclude or delegitimize particular contestational political forms. This reorientation of commemoration—which implicitly accepts the divisive politics of commemoration at the same time that it claims to have overcome it—seeks to protect the neoliberal social order of what Conor McCabe (2013) terms Northern Ireland's "double transition." Rather than repudiate it per se, the propaganda of peace actually seeks to elevate particular forms of violence as exemplary. It also attempts to restrict certain narratives on the meaning of past violence from the public commemorative space.

These attempts are experienced by Loyalists as part of what they have termed the culture war. Understanding how and why Loyalists view their position in the new Northern Ireland as defined by this culture war is central to understanding Loyalist commemoration during the Decade of Centenaries: it defines the politico-cultural context in which that commemoration takes place. As such, the culture war, its evolution, nature, and consequences, is examined in chapter 4. I argue that fear, insecurity, and "knowledge" of Republican hatred are definitive of the Loyalist experience. Socioeconomic disadvantage in the aftermath of rapid deindustrialization, educational underattainment, political marginalization, and new prevailing cultural trends are all understood as part of the same (Republican) strategy to take the "Britishness" out of Northern Ireland. Almost all political, cultural, and economic forces—not merely those specific to the peace process in Northern Ireland—are understood as belonging to the culture war. As such, the present is defined by Loyalists in terms of a deep and all-encompassing ontological crisis to which resolution is sought through commemoration.

In chapter 5, I therefore examine how commemoration of the Somme, including through genealogical practice and commemorative ritual, functions as part of attempts to (re)produce a secure identity for the Loyalist self, as a member of the Loyalist community, in a context defined by chronic insecurity and uncertainty. Charting the invention and evolution of what, following Kris Brown (2007), I term Loyalism's "cult of the Somme," I demonstrate that it is intrinsically connected to the evolution of the culture war, and provides the chief means by which Loyalists have sought to fight it. Commemoration is the site at which relationships with both the other and the state are mediated and their alleged rewriting of history contested. This contestation hinges, in the final analysis, on understandings of an imagined past or "Golden Age" (Smith 1996, 1997; Brown 2007), which are themselves contested.

Chapter 6 deconstructs "the Somme" and its commemoration to reveal the complexities and nuances of its role in the construction of the so-called Protestant/Unionist/Loyalist (PUL) community. I show that

the Somme represents the unity of a Golden Age to which that community is implored to return but also reveals the impossibility of such a return. In particular, I dissect the way in which the Somme's ghosts are
invoked both as part of claims to authority, legitimacy, and leadership
and to rebuke these claims. These claims and counterclaims represent
the splintering of Loyalist social memory into a multitude of "unofficial
unofficial" historiographies (cf. Chatzipanagiotidou 2012) and "hidden
transcripts" (Scott 1990), each with a particular understanding of the violence of the past and its relation to the present and the future. These
understandings are central to the intracommunal politics of Loyalism.
Crucially, certain of these understandings reveal a deeper critical ap-
praisal of violence and its consequences than for which the newly hegemonic "public transcript" (Scott 1990) on shared sacrifice allows.

In chapter 7, I return to this transcript to examine the ways in which
it seeks to preclude particular forms of Loyalist knowledge about violence from the public commemorative space, including where those
forms of knowledge—and their expression in commemorative ritual—
function to mediate Loyalist attitudes toward conflict transformation.
Based on a deep and often profoundly personal familiarity with violence,
certain Loyalist commemorative forms and discourses explicitly repudiate it where the propaganda of peace actually (and paradoxically)
vaunts it. Commemoration provides a means of negotiating the tension
within Loyalism between revanchist and progressive politics in a way
that the official historiography of the Decade of Centenaries does not. I
conclude that acknowledgment of—and potentially even expansion of
the official commemorative space to include—forms of Loyalist commemoration of the Somme may ultimately prove less detrimental to
peace-building than is conventionally suggested, and may make a more
valid contribution to ongoing attempts at conflict transformation than
claims about a shared sacrifice.

In sum, in writing this book, the contribution I have sought to make
to ongoing debates about commemoration and its politics in Northern
Ireland's deeply divided society (and beyond) is twofold. First, I propose
that the ethnographic encounter with Loyalist social memory on its own
terms reveals a more nuanced approach to negotiating the relationship
between past, present, and future than for which prevailing norms in
commemorative discourse and ritual practice in the United Kingdom

and Ireland during the Decade of Centenaries allows. Loyalist understanding of the contingency of state power and of the nature of the relationship between state and citizen arguably communes more closely with "the real" (Lacan 1982) than does official memory (what we call history). The affective and political authenticity of Loyalists' unofficial historiography(ies) is perhaps more meaningful or even truer than attempts at discursive reorientation of official history based on contestable claims about the fact of a shared sacrifice for peace, freedom, or democracy. It is fundamental to Loyalists' locating or anchoring themselves in a present that for them is out of joint: defined by economic, cultural, and political insecurity.

Second, in its role in the construction of Loyalist identity and community, commemoration of the Somme represents a (if not the) chief means by which Loyalists are able to participate in the political, cultural, and social life of Northern Ireland and attempts to circumscribe particular commemorative forms risks further alienating Loyalists from processes of peace-building in which they already perceive themselves as having little stake. Contrary to the prevailing logic of the Decade, the potential risks to peace in Northern Ireland, which are represented by censure or circumscription, arguably outweigh those represented by attempts at (empathic) comprehension and even facilitation. In making these claims, it is my hope that the research presented here asks broader questions and challenges particular assumptions about the role of commemoration in deeply divided societies, the relationship (and contradictions) between ethnic dominance (Kaufmann 2004a) and forms of socioeconomic and political exclusion (both real and perceived), and what is to be gained from engaging empathically with those whose politics and lived experiences differ radically from one's own, however critically or uncomfortably. For it is in this engagement that the distance between self and other is both revealed and traversed, and new forms of understanding made possible.

CHAPTER 1

(Re)theorizing Commemoration

Professional historians tend to be ambivalent about one of the prime historical phenomena of our time: the desire to commemorate.
E. Runia, "Burying the Dead, Creating the Past"

Memories help us make sense of the world we live in; and 'memory work' is, like any other kind of physical or mental labour, embedded in complex class, gender and power relations that determine what is remembered (or forgotten), by whom and for what end.
J. Gillis, "Memory and Identity: The History of a Relationship"

In March 2015 I attended a workshop titled "What Is Commemoration?" that took place as part of the Creative Centenaries Resources Fair,[1] held by the Northern Ireland Community Relations Council, the Heritage Lottery Fund, and the creative media and arts organization, the Nerve Centre, at the flagship Titanic Belfast. A colleague—a lecturer in history at Queen's University Belfast—had been asked to facilitate, and she, in turn, had asked me to contribute to the workshop by talking about my experiences as a volunteer with East Belfast & the Great War.[2] "The key starting point, and it may seem obvious," she said, "is that history and commemoration are not the same. But they are connected. History provides the content, whereas commemoration is about form."

Some of those in attendance—representatives from an assortment of community history projects, local authority "good relations" units, and other state agencies—nodded their agreement. I smiled to myself, because we had discussed this point and its significance many times before.

I found it hard to dispute her claim that history and commemoration are different. But does it follow that history has more "content" than commemoration? The implication is surely that we would need therefore to look to history's "content" to properly understand commemoration's "form." As I stood to tell the group about East Belfast & the Great War's digital cataloging project, I was careful to emphasize that I was less interested in the past per se than in the meanings attributed to historical artifacts by their current owners. "What do these meanings tell us not only about our relationship with the past, but about our relationships here and now?," I asked. Is the history of a particular event actually the most useful starting point for understanding how that event is remembered or commemorated? Perhaps commemoration provides its own content, in and of itself providing meaning only loosely related to, or even divorced from, the historical events—the content—from which it purportedly proceeds?

While both "history" and "memory" are categories that themselves encompass multiple and sometimes conflictual meanings, that they are distinct categories that are related but not synonymous has become a more or less established tenet of the "memory boom" in historical and social scientific research since the 1980s (Winter 2000; Assman 2010).[3] Both intra- and interdisciplinary contention remains, however, as to the implications of this assertion. While Clifford Geertz (1990, 322) suggested almost three decades ago that "it has been quite some time now since the stereotypes of the historian as mankind's memorialist or the anthropologist as the explorer of the elementary forms of the elemental have had very much purchase," it remains the case that fundamental differences of emphasis between the two "disciplines" of history and anthropology continue to contribute to ongoing debate about the nature, significance, and utility of knowledge about—and the meaning of—the past. Crucially, "'we' means something different and so does 'they' to those looking back than it does to those looking sideways. . . . The anthropological desire to see how things fit together sits uneasily with the historical desire to see how they are brought about, and [often] the old nineteenth century insults, 'idealist!,' 'empiricist!,' get trotted out for one more turn around the track" (323–32).

Traditionally, the assumed epistemological superiority of history over memory was rooted in its claims to (scientific) empiricism (Collingwood 1961; McNeill 1986). Despite the challenge posed to this knowledge regime in the late twentieth century by postmodern debates on the nature of historical knowledge, including the role of power (Foucault 2002; Zinn 2005 [1980]) and—particularly in the case of the colonial subject—the marginalization or absence of the subaltern's voice (Spivak 1988) in the construction of historical "truth," the historian's point of departure remains that some fundamental or objective truth—unmediated by the vagaries of human subjectivity and fallibility—about what happened in the past is nonetheless ultimately recoverable. A foundational claim that the historian's craft is founded on believing nothing other than that which the evidence compels one to believe has survived the postmodern turn, albeit in more varied, muted, and critical formulations (see Carr 1990; Appleby, Hunt, and Jacob 1994; Evans 1997; Cubitt 2007). History, in a retained if nuanced emphasis on demythologizing, remains "perpetually suspicious of memory" (Nora 1989, 9) and its (assumed) propensity to mystify or otherwise obscure that which is "true" about the past.

Nowhere is this more evident than in deeply divided societies like Northern Ireland, where it is often argued that subjective and partisan (and, therefore, inaccurate) memory is a driver of social and political division to which history can provide a remedy. The tensions between memory and history and the categories of true/false, objective/subjective, real/imagined, and selective/comprehensive continue to motivate debates about "the past" in Northern Ireland. These tensions have therefore defined the Decade of Centenaries as a field site. I examine in more depth how discourses on historical "fact" are mobilized in the arguments about the past and in the construction of a shared history during the Decade of Centenaries in chapter 3. For now, I seek to situate my ethnographic engagement with Loyalist commemoration during the Decade within the emergent discipline of memory studies and the wider anthropological tradition.

I argue that adherence to the historical method can impede our understanding of the ways in which the past is perceived, represented, and experienced in the present. This is a central contention of the totemic memory studies scholarship on which I initially draw. In drawing on this scholarship, there is a risk, as Olick (2008, 26) suggests, of seeking to re-invent the wheel (see also Frawley 2011b, 19). However, I also suggest that there is a key weakness in theorizations of "collective" memory that do not draw an explicit distinction between memory as something that groups or individuals possess and commemoration as something that they do. I argue that key theorizations understate the role of agency in shaping collective memory and come close to suggesting, inaccurately, that it is actually collective memories that possess social groups rather than the converse. Drawing on theories about haunting (Derrida 2006 [1993]; Gordon 2008, 2011), the "ghost dance" (Spivak 1995), and the "Golden Age" (Smith 1996, 1997), I argue that commemoration is a set of performative discourses and practices that require individual and col-lective agency and that both mirror and serve to shape social relation-ships. Properly understood, commemoration therefore has everything to do with politics, perhaps less to do with memory, and (almost) noth-ing to do with history.

HISTORY, MEMORY, AND COMMEMORATION

The present "memory boom" owes much to the work of the French his-torian Pierre Nora, whose seminal work on *lieux de mémoire* brought into sharp relief the ways in which memory diverges from history in its orientation to and role in shaping the present. "Memory," according to Nora (1989, 8), "is a perpetually actual phenomenon, a bond tying us to the eternal present; history is a representation of the past." In the mod-ern era, history has superseded memory as the chief means by which we both know and experience the past. As such, "we speak so much of mem-ory because there is so little of it left. . . . [T]here are *lieux de mémoire*, sites of memory, because there are no longer *milieux de mémoire*, real en-vironments of memory" (7). Thus, according to Ian McBride (2001, 11), "Nora proclaimed that the relentless packaging of history in facts serves as an index of our memory loss." The elevation of history as both aca-demic discipline and a profession is both a cause of and a substitute for the decline in more colloquial or democratic engagements with the past.

A similar assertion was made by Claude Lévi-Strauss (1978; see also Margalit 2002), who argued that both a cause and a consequence of the project of modernization was history replacing mythology as the dominant means by which the past is rendered both knowable and meaningful. As suggested above, this has rested on historians' more or less emphatic claims to dispassionate empiricism.

In his "Theses on the Concept of History", Walter Benjamin rejected these claims as what he derogatorily termed "historicism," which he dismissed as a method of "interpretation whose typically modern 'absolutism of method' misses the 'richness of the layers' in history" (Fritsch 2005, 159). With whom, Benjamin asked, does the historian's empathy ultimately lie? "The answer is inevitable: with the victor. And all rulers are the heirs of those who conquered before them. Hence, empathy with the victor invariably benefits the rulers. . . . Whoever has emerged victorious participates to this day in the triumphal procession in which the present rulers step over those who are lying prostrate. According to traditional practice, the spoils are carried along in the procession" (Benjamin 1968, 256). Given that the subjects of the historian's study are "customarily construed as those who left the most visible traces," their empathy "tends to favour the victors, resulting in a history of rulers and victorious law imposition" (Fritsch 2005, 160). The very act of writing history tends to represent it as possessing an implicitly or even overtly progressive quality.[4] The formation and consolidation of states, for instance, is represented as the logical or inevitable consequence of events and processes that were experienced by contemporaries as anything but—in fact, as violent, unpredictable, and contingent (Tilly 1985; Žižek 1999; Edkins 2003).

In essence, the act of constructing a narrative to make sense of and explain a series of historical facts (even the very ascription of the label "historical fact" itself) relies on asserting the legitimacy of particular testimonies or particular memories of a given event or event sequence over others. As Ricoeur (2004, 278) suggests, "We have nothing better than our memory to assure ourselves of the reality of our memories—we have nothing better than testimony and criticism of testimony to accredit the historian's representation of the past." Who determines the legitimacy or validity of particular memories over others, and for what reasons?

The process of testimonial selection—whose testimony we choose to believe, whose to prioritize and whose to discard, and why—is an exercise in selectivity and, ultimately, in power. Where states are expressly involved in the construction of official histories,[5] this is all the more explicitly the case. While it would evidently be unfair, therefore, to tar all historians with a statist brush, despite the best intentions of the best historians, history is necessarily partial, subjective, and ideological, representing a form of official or sanctioned memory (see Hutton 1993, 9).

Barthes (1981, 65) wrote that history "is constituted only if we consider it, only if we look at it—and in order to look at it, we must be excluded from it." The historicism against which Benjamin (1968) warns is based precisely on this process of exclusion: on the privileging not only of certain accounts of the past over others but also of a particular method by which these events and their significance are or can be known and understood. Through disciplined empiricism, the archive is where history is excavated, and the library or lecture hall is the proper arena for its dissemination or propagation. Other, more vernacular, forms of engaging with or methods for gaining knowledge about the past—including commemorative rituals—that help to shape human experience in the present but that do not adhere to strict historicist norms have been consigned increasingly to the margins, both discursive and physical: to Nora's *lieux de mémoire*. Thus, historicism places restrictions on who may rightfully or legitimately claim knowledge of the past, and how.

But "history" is only one way in which the past is made knowable. And not only, as Benjamin (1968) revealed, does history writing act to constrain our knowledge and understanding of the past on its own terms, but, perhaps more significantly, historicism also places critical limits on understanding the social functions of the past in the present. As Guy Beiner (2007a, 369), quoting Malinowski, indicates, "Myth is not merely a story told but a reality lived. . . . Whether factually erroneous or not, myths [mold] popular outlooks, which influence[s] the course of . . . history." In the final analysis, understanding by whom, how, and for what reasons the past is (de/re)constructed, (re)interpreted, (mis)appropriated, and otherwise experienced or lived is something for which the historical method has been ill equipped.[6] Ethnography and its concern with how things fit together in the creation of social order(s) is a more appropriate means by which to locate these processes in their social, political, cultural, and economic contexts and the patterns of power that define and shape these contexts. In order to do so we are therefore required to leave history per se behind, and to engage instead with what scholars have termed collective or social memory. The nuances (and weaknesses) of these particular theoretical and analytical categories receive further treatment below, but for now it is sufficient to say that they are more properly a matter for the anthropologist or sociologist than the historian.

The term "collective memory" was coined by the French sociologist Maurice Halbwachs. Halbwachs's (1950, 44) premise is that memory is the product of an "intersection of collective influences." Collective memory as a "repository of tradition" (78) is greater than the sum of its parts; it is more than a simple accumulation of the memories of the individuals that constitute a given social group. In fact, the memories of a given individual are in large part shaped by the memory of the group as a whole. Insofar as social groups—families, communities, or even entire nations—exist, their identity is determined by what they remember. A group's collective memory is therefore central to defining the group as a group: it is a group because it has a collective memory. In turn, what individuals remember, and thereby their identity, is framed or even determined by their membership of a given group (or groups). According to Paul Connerton (1989, 36) in his rendering of Halbwachs's theory, "Every recollection, however personal it may be, even that of thoughts and sentiments that remain unexpressed, exist[s] in relationship with a whole ensemble of notions which many others possess: with persons, places, dates, words, forms of language, that is to say with the whole material and moral life of the societies of which we are a part or of which we have been part."

Collective memory, thus conceived, functions as a framing or structuring device through which members of a given group experience the world. The inference is that collective memory can therefore act to determine or constrain the behavior of group members. In Halbwachs's theory, memory is regarded as diachronic and, in essence, as the agent to which the group or individual that remembers becomes subject (cf. Bryan 2016). Thus, while it acknowledges the primacy of the social in the attribution of meaning to past events in a way that the historical method does not, the definition of memory as "collective" risks failing to adequately account for the place of both group and individual agency in shaping it (Viggiani 2014, 12–13). Crucially, such a conception of memory arguably downplays or denies the central role of individual cognition in what might meaningfully be called remembering. And as Frawley (2011, 22) argues, "If we approach memory in *culture* without an inkling of how memory functions in mind, we cannot possibly hope to shape a theory that reflects the complexities in mind." While Frawley draws on psychological and neuroscientific studies to demonstrate the relationship between the cognitive act of *remembering* and the cultural practice of *remembrance*, she also suggests that there is a distinction between these two phenomena for which scholars of memory often fail to account. Rather than seeing groups as possessing collective memories, it is actually collective memories that are seen to possess groups and their members. This has contributed to what Berliner (2005, 202–3) has called "a diffusion of the problem of memory into the general process of culture. . . . By a dangerous act of expansion, memory gradually becomes everything which is transmitted across generations, everything stored in culture, 'almost indistinguishable' then, from the concept of culture itself."

Susan Sontag (2003, 76) argued that memory, as distinct from culture, can only properly be thought of as the irreducible property of the individual: "What is called collective memory is not a remembering but a stipulating: that *this* is important, and this is the story about how it happened, with the pictures that lock the story in our minds." The central importance of a particular event to a group's collective memory does not proceed irresistibly from the event itself but is conditioned by more or less explicit and ongoing assertions as to its importance. The more this event recedes from living memory, the farther it moves from the realm of what might truly be called the "remembered." In her work on what she termed "postmemory," Marianne Hirsch (2008, 107) demonstrated how the memory of the Holocaust, in its transference from the generation for whom it was an actual lived experience to their descendants (for whom it was not), is no longer "mediated by recall, but by imaginative investment, projection and creation." To the realm of postmemory belong normative assertions about why and how a particular event ought to be commemorated and, more important, the forms of social action that its commemoration necessitates.

If the (diachronic) demands of collective memory determine individual and group identity, it is at least as much the case that the (synchronic) demands of identity determine collective memory (Bryan 2016). In each act of commemoration, a given group reaffirms itself as a group and makes certain claims about the nature of that group while individual members restate their particular claim to membership of it. While the norms of remembrance that govern commemoration have an important function in defining the group, they are also reshaped in each act of commemoration. These norms are not static or unchanging and have histories of their own, which are defined as much by change and rupture as by permanence and continuity. The outward manifestation of "tradition"—of apparent continuity across time and space—belies that these are complex structures and sets of rules that are not natural, timeless, or innate and are subject to ongoing processes of evolution, adaptation, and change (Hobsbawm and Ranger 1983; Bloch 1986; Bryan 2000). Ultimately, memory cannot act as an agent in its own right, as both its transference and its reception require forms of human action and interpretation. And forms of human action belong definitively to the realm of the present and its patterns of social, cultural, and political interaction.

In their work on social memory, Fentress and Wickham stress that individual and group agency play a decisive role in determining what is remembered and how:

> Social memory is a source of knowledge. This means it does more than provide a set of categories through which, in an unselfconscious way, a group experiences its surroundings, it also provides that group with material for *conscious* reflection. . . . The way memories of the past are generated and understood by given social groups is a direct guide to how they understand their position in the present. . . . Social memory seems indeed to be subject to the law[s] of supply *and* demand. (1992, 26, 126, 201; emphasis added)

As Connerton (1989, 4–5) suggests, "If there is such a thing as social memory . . . we are likely to find it in commemorative ceremonies; but commemorative ceremonies prove to be commemorative only in so far as they are performative" (see also Tilmans, van Ree, and Winter 2010). Performance is conditioned by inherited tradition, but it also serves to shape it. In each performative iteration of a given memorial trope, in each commemorative act, we do not simply remember, but re-member, imagining the commemorated event anew and reestablishing it as central to our individual and group identities in new ways. Diprose (2006, 239) neatly surmises, "As a finite, mortal, historical being who, by definition is neither omnipresent or omniscient, my reception of the customs and norms I inherit will be partial and my expression of them, through speech or action will not be entirely faithful, and so will be in that sense unique and extraordinary."

Commemoration is defined by its taking place predominantly in public spaces and by its symbolism and ritual.[7] Its ritual forms exist in a relationship with wider discourses, material, and textual memorial cultures and with more "private" forms of both remembering and remembrance in ways that I examine in later chapters. The more obviously or overtly ritualistic forms of commemoration include parades or wreath-laying ceremonies, but commemoration can also take the form of a religious service, a talk or lecture, genealogical research, or an exhibition. These other types of commemoration often incorporate the symbols and semiotics of the more ritualistic forms, or include forms of performativity that function ritualistically in their own right. Commemorations are rituals in the sense that they involve actions that are established and bound by rules that render them comprehensibly "commemorative": what Humphrey and Laidlaw (1994) term "apprehensible." "That is, they are available for a further assimilation into the actors' intentions, attitudes or beliefs" (Humphrey and Laidlaw 1994, 89).

In a cognitive sense, it is often (and during a centenary, usually and perhaps always) the case that most of the participants in a given commemoration don't remember at all the original or foundational event that is the ostensible subject of the ceremonials. It is common to commemorate events that fall outside of living memory by at least one generation and often by several. Over the course of my fieldwork, it became clear that insofar as individual participants in a commemorative ritual are really engaged in "remembering," what they are remembering is previous experiences of the commemoration, not the event itself (see also Giesen 2006, 339). Participants were as likely to remember a deceased friend as they passed the street corner on which that friend would have stood to watch the parade in years gone by, to reflect on their relationship with their own parents as they laid a wreath at a grave in Flanders, or to feel nostalgic about their childhood as they watched a marching band pass by as they were to imagine themselves in the shoes of their forefathers in Derry, at the Boyne, or on the Somme.

This suggests that commemoration's relationship to the past is more ambiguous than for which either historians or scholars of memory have traditionally accounted. It does not simply provide form to history's content, nor is it merely an expression of the dull, diachronic compulsion of "collective" memory. Commemorations are events with substantive and intelligible content of their own. Each public, performative act of commemoration is at some level a choice on the part of those actors engaged in it. This choice is conditioned ultimately by the demands of identity and the need to maintain boundaries between "us" and "them," "self" and "other" (Bryan 2014), as well as by perceptions of the spiritual or material needs of the community (Cohen 1989; Jarman 1997) and one's perceived place or role in it. Commemoration does not simply reflect a community's group memory, but actively (re)constructs it. Quite simply, "we" do not commemorate our collective past. Who "we" are, what our collective past is, and what actions this is deemed to necessitate are constructed through commemoration. As such, any act of commemoration is not (merely) an act of remembering; it is an act of world-making, which is to say, of contemporary politics.

As Kertzer (1988, 95) indicates, "Political reality is defined for us in the first place through ritual, and our beliefs are subsequently reaffirmed through collective expression." Commemorators are "embedded in collective representations . . . working through symbolic and material means. . . . [They] implicitly orient others as if they were actors on a stage seeking identification with their experiences and understandings from their audiences" (Alexander and Mast 2006, 2). Commemorative ritual, as perhaps the ultimate or definitive form of symbolic activity (Connerton 1989; cf. Giddens 1996), "far from simply projecting the political order onto the symbolic plane[,] propagates a particular view of the political order" (Kertzer 1988, 87). Commemoration thus mirrors Geertz's Balinese cockfight:

> What sets [it] apart from . . . the ordinary course of life, lifts it from the realm of everyday practical affairs, and surrounds it with an aura of enlarged importance is not, as functionalist sociology would have it, that it reinforces status discriminations. . . . Its function, if you

want to call it that, is interpretive: it is [the community's] reading of [the community's] experience; a story they tell themselves *about themselves*. (Geertz 1973, 26; emphasis added)

This story is often disputed, and commemorative rites are sites at which it is not simply represented, but asserted, contested, and negotiated. As Edkins (2003, 56) suggests, these contests are not, fundamentally, over what or who should be remembered and how: "the struggle is not just over what memorial should be built, but over the much larger issue of what form social and political institutions should take." Through mobilizing a particular form (or forms) of what Bourdieu (1986) called cultural capital or by invoking and manipulating what Turner (1995) termed communitas, commemoration is the means by which different actors make claims—both implicit and explicit—to moral and political authority to create, challenge, or defend the social and political order(s). Throughout my research forms of commemorative political negotiation were in evidence at various and often overlapping levels. From the level of the household and the familial through to the high politics of international diplomacy, commemoration forms a central part of properly political conversations about how the social order should be shaped.

Commemoration thus has functions, meanings, and political implications that transcend a given commemorative ritual itself. In particular, as Jarman (1997, 9) suggests, "as the scale of the event expands, so does the overall importance of the ritual outside the formal ritual time. In this way the ritual creation of memory begins to collide with other media, such as oral narratives or the routine contact with memorials. In some cases the ritual process seems to be in danger of becoming a total way of life, rather than constrained by liminality." In *Remembering and Forgetting 1916*, Rebecca Graff-McRae (2010, 15) proposes that "commemoration functions as a fulcrum point, a hinge, in the discursive construction of conflict and the political—in ways which serve to re-produce, re-write and deconstruct its accepted and acceptable boundaries." It is the means not only, or even chiefly, by which the past makes claims on the present—by which "history" or "memory" makes its inescapable claim on members of a group—but also by which members of a group make a claim on the past. As Graff-McRae (2007, 221) indicates, "Commemoration is not merely an event, a parade, a statue, a graveside oration: parades can be disrupted and re-routed; statues defaced or bombed; speeches repressed or re-written. Commemoration simultaneously inscribes, reinscribes and transgresses the borders between history and memory, between memory and politics and between politics and history. It is not an act or a word, nor is it inaction or silence. Commemoration is itself constantly under negotiation."

Mirroring wider transatlantic academic trends, insofar as poststructuralism ever obtained much credence in the arts, humanities, and social sciences in (Northern) Ireland,[8] claims about its "jargonism," obscurity, and even conservatism and intellectual laziness (Ó Seaghdha 2011) have seen its fairly conclusive fall from grace. These claims are not without validity. However, it is my contention that certain poststructural ideas, particularly those of *différance* and *hauntology* (Derrida 1976, 2006 [1993]) may yet play a useful role in interpreting and intervening in Northern Ireland. They can help us to understand the ways in which commemoration both defines and is defined by the politics of a place that itself continues to frustrate attempts at rigid structuration or definitive categorisation (Graham 1997, 1998). In particular, poststructural analysis reveals that "the 'problem' of Northern Ireland is not something around which politics spins, with agents proffering varied solutions to it, but is exactly what political actions are concerned with and derived from" (Finlayson 2008, 67). In my analysis I have sought to mirror Edkins's (2008, 26) deconstructivist insistence that "we should look not at what causes conflict, but what does a particular conflict do? Who does it benefit and how? How does constituting 'the conflict' as an object of study produce certain effects?"

I follow Graff-McRae (2007, 219–22) in proposing that "commemoration reproduces the ways in which all politics (and their relationship to the political) are antagonistic. . . . Each version of commemoration seeks to establish its own relationship between truth, remembrance and liberation." Methodologically, however, Graff-McRae defers primarily (indeed, almost exclusively) to a type of Foucauldian discourse analysis to critically examine the politics of commemoration, conflict, and the political. Others have noted the particular weaknesses of an approach that fails to account for or consider actually existing commemorative practice in this examination (see, e.g., Beiner 2011). To understand how commemorative discourse is mirrored, represented, and (re)produced in wider societal relationships and social practices requires deeper forms of ethnographic engagement—participant observation and ethnographic interview—the use of which I elaborate in chapter 2.

"A PRAYER TO BE HAUNTED"

In 2012, the Northern Ireland Community Relations Council organized a flagship lecture series in Belfast to mark the beginning of the Decade of Centenaries.[9] The series was given the title "Remembering the Future." Whether intentionally or not, in so naming their series the CRC invoked an intriguing and characteristically counterintuitive poststructural irony that is at the heart of what Derrida called hauntology: that we imagine the past in order to remember the future (see also Jameson 2005; Kirkby 2006). "Haunting," as Avery Gordon asserts,

> is a constituent element of modern social life. It is neither pre-modern superstition nor individual psychosis; it is a generalizable social phenomenon of great import. . . . The ghost is not simply a dead or missing person, but a social figure, and investigating it can lead to that dense sight where history and subjectivity make social life. . . . Following the ghosts is about making a contact that changes you and refashions the social relations in which you are located. It is about putting life back in where only memory or bare trace was visible to those who bothered to look. (2008, 7–22)

Social life never simply *is*: "the social order is not natural, it doesn't exist unless it is produced continually." Crucially, "we never *are*, we only ever *will have been*. . . . Things can 'be' in our modern western sense only in the context of [linear] temporality. They 'are' because they have a history in time, but they are at the same time separate from that history" (Edkins 2003, 12). Ghosts or specters occupy the spaces between "was," "is," and "ought to be," which are constitutive of the social order: they are the very substance of political discourse (Jameson 1999). They exist somewhere between the real and the imagined, structure and agency, signifier and signified. They carry messages from the past that can act to compel particular forms of individual or collective action, but they also require forms of action in order that these messages might be received. Both forms of action combine to (re)produce social life and the social order.

The figure of the ghost or specter is therefore useful in thinking about how social groups are "haunted" by rather than involved in re-membering their (imagined) past(s) and how this haunting manifests in forms of social action in the present. To talk of ghosts and haunting, I contend, is ultimately more useful than to talk of history or even of memory in understanding commemoration: how the past is imagined, interpreted, and represented by whom, how, and for what reasons.

"Haunting always harbours the violence, the *witchcraft*, and *denial* that made it, and the *exile of our longing*, the utopian" (Gordon 2008, 207). Ultimately, therefore,

> the issue of memory is always linked to the question of a future promise, or perhaps even a utopia, in the broadest sense of the word, despite the fact that our times appear to have liberated themselves from the great historical narratives that project themselves onto a goal in the future. . . . [We] remember the dead only if this memory is also, at the same time, a memory and a promise of the future that is not a future present, but a future otherness "in" the past no less than in the present: "the past as absolute future." (Fritsch 2005, 183)

In particular, the act of repetition or (re)iteration that defines com-memorative ritual "reaches out to return the future to the past, while drawing on the past also to reconstruct the future" (Giddens 1996, 15; see also Tonkin and Bryan 1996).

Like Spivak (1995, 78), I do not "applaud Derrida because he has said hello to Marx." Derrida's failure to grapple with the materiality of Marx's political economy as well as the limits—to which I have already alluded—of Derridean deconstruction in both theory and transforma-tive political practice are well rehearsed (see, e.g., Callinicos 1990). Nonetheless, if *Spectres of Marx* enabled Spivak to "read 'Far from Me-dina' as a ghost dance, a prayer to be haunted, a learning to live at the seam of the past and the present, a heterodidactics between life and death," so it allows for a reading of Loyalist commemorative discourses and practices. Commemoration is, quite literally, "a ghost dance, a prayer to be haunted" (Spivak 1995, 78): "an interpretation which transforms what it interprets" (Derrida 2006 [1993], 63).

According to Walter Benjamin (1968, 254), "The past carries a secret index with it, by which it is referred to its resurrection. . . . [I]t has been given us to know, just like every generation before us, a *weak* messianic power, on which the past has a claim." Hauntology is concerned both with the transmission of this "weak messianic power" and with its reception by actors in the present. Representing a promise of a corrective or even redemptive future, this power in some sense obliges or compels the receiver to testify or, more important, to act. However, it is weak precisely because it requires first to be received in order then to be transformed into political action, and this requires that groups and individuals choose to become receivers or conjurers: that they engage in a prayer to be haunted.

Ghosts are conjured as part of a process of contestation, to justify present actions as part of historic struggles and simultaneously to represent the present as a deviation from the authenticity of heritage. As Brown (2007, 709) suggests, the ghost is no mere or "insubstantial will o'the wisp[], clinging to recent tombstones or dog-eared history books; [it] can be effectively conscripted into the shaping of communal identity." The same ghost may play a variety of roles, depending on who has conjured it and for what reasons. The ghost can be an establishment figure—providing support or justification for the status quo—or it can be an agent provocateur—working either overtly or implicitly to undermine the established order. In other words, ghosts play a vital, intrinsically contestational and at times unpredictable or disruptive role in defining the political present. This is not to say, as Jameson (1999, 39) indicates, that "spectropolitics" of this sort necessarily involves "the conviction that ghosts exist," or that the past is "still very much alive and at work, within the living present: all it says, if it can be thought to speak, is that the living present is scarcely as self-sufficient as it claims to be, that we would do well not to count on its density and solidity, which might under exceptional circumstances betray us."

Haunting is distinct from trauma in that it calls for a something-to-be-done. "The something to be done feels as if it has already been needed or wanted before, perhaps forever, certainly for a long time, and we cannot wait for it any longer" (Gordon 2011, 5). Further, "haunting is not the same as being exploited, traumatized or oppressed, although it usually involves these experiences or is produced by them" (2). It is undoubtedly the ghosts of the Middle Passage, of Sobibor, Soweto, or Srebrenica, that are most demanding—and deserving of—our attention. The hauntology of Benjamin and Derrida, however, seems to assume that a ghost must, of necessity, be the bearer of a message for future action that is concerned with reversing that which is self-evidently oppressive, with righting that which is incontrovertibly wrong or unjust.[10] But it is not the case that all ghosts are unequivocally counterhegemonic.

As Graff-McRae (2010, 28) indicates, "The return of the ghost, the figure of the ghost itself, is neither hegemonic nor subversive; rather it produces a rupture even as it lays claim to continuity." If politics is a process of world-making animated by past promise, then this is no less the case for the projects of hegemony as for those that are counterhegemonic. In other words, the construction of hegemony is surely just as motivated by the ghosts of its imagined past and remembered future as are movements that define or construct themselves in opposition to it. Furthermore, at the "end of history" (Fukuyama 1992; Jameson 2004), the very distinction between hegemonic and counterhegemonic (insofar as it ever meaningfully existed) is itself blurred.[11] Simply put, "resistance can be regressive. That is, resistance doesn't have to be counterhegemonic to be resistance" (Gallaher and Shirlow 2006, 150).

In ways that I explore in more detail in following chapters, at one level the resistance that both defines and is given shape by Loyalist commemorative discourses and practices represents a form of incomplete mourning (or melancholia) for the demise of the Unionist hegemony that was at the heart of discrimination against Catholics and Nationalists in Northern Ireland's Orange State (see Farrell 1980). More fundamentally, however, it demonstrates that this hegemony probably was never actually experienced as such. Whether or not they are justified in so doing, Loyalists nonetheless experience the present political moment as out of joint. In this moment defined by cultural-political, economic, and ontological crisis, the ghosts of the Somme that haunt the politics of Ulster Loyalism are the bearers of the eschatological promise of redemption that inheres in the glorious past—what Smith (1996, 1997; Brown 2007) called a Golden Age—which exists properly only in a remembered future. As such, they are central to the dialectics—pride/shame, winning/losing—that underpin the political economy of Protestant/Unionist/Loyalist identity in so-called postconflict Northern Ireland. Commemoration, particularly of the Battle of the Somme, is Loyalism's Geertzian cockfight. It is work that Loyalists undertake to tell themselves a story about themselves. This story defines a particular political and cultural project that is ongoing and contested and reaches far beyond the commemorative moment itself. Seeking to understand this story and this project requires engaging with it on its own terms.

In this chapter, I have revisited a long-standing debate within and between the disciplines of history and anthropology to argue that "history" represents an attempt to delegitimize, circumscribe, and discipline particular, popular (and dissident) forms of engaging with the past: what we conventionally term memory. History, therefore, is ultimately a more or less explicit exercise in (state) power (cf. Fentress and Wickham 1992, 127; Bryan 2016) that cannot adequately explain the function of the past in social action in the present. Although I have reasserted the primacy of memory in the ethnographic engagement with the relationship between past and present, I have also suggested that memory studies scholarship often fails to acknowledge the differences and tensions between the individual, cognitive act of remembering and commemoration as a social and political process. I have argued that Derridean (2006 [1993]) ideas about ghosts and haunting help to address this tension, bridging the spaces between structure and agency, inheritance and (re)invention, and the reception, interpretation, and reiteration of the past's message for social action in the present. It is precisely these spaces that the discipline of history seeks to police.

Drawing on and guided by the Derridean concept of hauntology, my ethnographic research has sought to determine how and why, during the Decade of Centenaries, the ghosts of the Somme are willfully conjured and their message for social action received, represented, and contested by Ulster Loyalists. This has been about "situating [Loyalists] in relation to their own traditions, asking how they interpret their own 'ghosts' and how they use them as a source of knowledge" (Fentress and Wickham 1992, 26) to confront a particular vision of a shared future for Northern Ireland, which is promoted as part of what McLaughlin and

Baker (2010) have termed the propaganda of peace, and which is built on a particular (contestable) regime of historiographical truth. In this confrontation, I argue, Loyalist commemoration (and the forms of knowledge it both represents and works to reproduce) acts to disrupt the project of peace building, perhaps for good as well as for ill.

CHAPTER TWO

"What does it mean to follow a ghost?"

Locating "the Field" and the Ethics of Empathy

Deconstructive ethnography . . . takes as its starting point not the frame 'is this fact?' . . . but the consideration 'how could this come to be considered as fact?' and 'what are the consequences of treating this as fact?'

S. Linstead, "From Postmodern Anthropology
to Deconstructive Ethnography"

John Brewer (2000, 6) defines ethnography as "the study of people in naturally occurring settings or 'fields' by methods of data collection which capture their social *meanings* and ordinary activities, involving the researcher participating directly in the setting, if not also the activities, in order to collect data in a systematic manner but without meaning being imposed on them externally." This conventional view of ethnography sees "the field" as a singular, bounded, and, above all, corporeal place. And in a sense I have adhered to this convention. Although it has on occasion led me to other parts of Northern Ireland, to the British "mainland," the Republic of Ireland, and even the battlefields of France and Belgium, the locus of all the relationships that defined my fieldwork was the city of Belfast. However, in ways I have already hinted, these relationships actually have roots that are less physically mappable. They

40

have all been defined, in one way or another, by a mutual interest or involvement in the discourses, practices, and politics of commemoration. In many respects, it is the Decade of Centenaries itself that served as my field site.

This is a "fuzzier" field than is typical (Nadai and Maeder 2005, 2009). Its extent is determined not by the bounds of either physical or political topography per se. It exists, rather, in a social world determined by "sets of common or joint activities or concerns bound together by a network of communications" (Kling and Gerson, cited in Strauss 1984, 123). It is the "processes, actions and ideas and their protagonists" that define this social world and its particular community(ies) of practice that are the focus of the ethnographic study (Nadai and Maeder 2005; see also Wenger 1998). In other words, "identifying adequate sites, which add up to an ethnographic field requires a theoretical clarification of the object of study first. Such a theoretical framework then serves as the compass for the search of a field" (Nadai and Maeder 2005).

The Decade of Centenaries is constructed across multiple spaces by those engaged in its discourses, practices, and forms of material production. Since 2013 I have variously observed and participated in this process of construction through academic conferences and workshops, peace-building and local history projects, exhibitions, Northern Ireland Assembly debates, television and radio programs, social media, policy papers, committee meetings, and commemorative events and parades. In particular, through my involvement with both East Belfast & the Great War and Co-operation Ireland's Entwined Histories project,[1] I played explicitly participatory roles in the Decade's social world. Both roles were important in gaining and maintaining access to the groups and individuals with a stake in the politics of the Decade. This includes those involved in defining its terms of reference through academic and policy discourses, as well as those involved in its forms of embodied practice. At different stages and dependent on the setting, I occupied different roles, through more traditional forms of participant observation at academic conferences and policy workshops to what might more accurately be called the "observation of participation" (Tedlock 1991) at commemorative parades. The aim was to explore how commemoration is constructed at and across various sites through action, interpretation, and meaning. To this end, the ethnographic interview was an important way in which respondents were able to discuss and explain how, when, and why they participate in the Decade's social world.

Over the course of my fieldwork, I conducted thirty-six interviews with thirty-two individuals, as well as two focus groups. These interviews were of varying lengths and intensity, and all were semistructured, open-ended "InterViews" in the Kvalean (1996) mold (the shortest lasting thirty minutes and the longest, just under three hours). Kvale (1996, 14–159) describes an interview as "an interchange of views between two persons conversing about a theme of mutual interest. . . . The interview is a conversation in which the data arise in an interpersonal relationship, co-authored and co-produced by interviewer and interviewee" (see also Skinner 2012, 9–10). I approached my interviews as exercises in knowledge co-creation: as an opportunity not only to investigate the views and perceptions of my interviewees but also to share and negotiate my views on and interpretations of Loyalism and commemoration, their meanings and the relationship between them. Interviews were therefore kept deliberately conversational, involving—sometimes heated—exchanges of opinion, in the belief that "the reciprocal influence of interviewer and interviewee on a cognitive and emotional level is not . . . necessarily a source of error. . . . Rather than seeking to reduce the importance of this interaction, what matters in the research interview is to recognize and apply the knowledge gained in the interpersonal interaction" (Kvale 1996, 36).

As Burgess (1984, 75) attests, "The selection of individuals in field studies is a different procedure from the selection procedures associated with statistical sampling. In field research informants are selected for their knowledge of a particular setting which may complement the researcher's observations and point towards further investigation." While a number of actors, in different ways and with varying political interests, contributed to the shaping of the Decade of Centenaries, it is on those involved in its discourses and practices who view themselves—and, to a lesser extent, are viewed by others—as Loyalist that my research principally focused. In most instances, the chief criteria by which "key respondents" (Burgess 1984, 73–75) were chosen were their self-defined Loyalism and their active involvement in commemoration, particularly of the Battle of the Somme.[2]

The overwhelming majority of my respondents (twenty-seven of thirty-two) were men. Furthermore, with one exception, those women I interviewed tended not to be actively involved in commemoration but had a stake in the Decade of Centenaries by virtue of their roles as political representatives, civil servants, or community relations professionals. Of the Loyalists I interviewed who actively participated in ritual forms of Somme commemoration, only one was a woman. There are several reasons for this. The first, as discussed in greater depth in chapter 6, is the masculine character of Ulster Loyalism in general and its commemorative cultural forms specifically (see McCaughey 2012; Ashe and McCluskey 2015). While women participate in commemorations—and do so in large numbers—the majority of those involved in coordinating Loyalist commemorative activity are men. Second, where snowball sampling (Brewer 2000, 79) was employed to establish relationships with individuals within and across the different groups and organizations involved in Somme commemoration, this tended to result in my being referred to men, by men. This process was fairly haphazard and ad hoc and was one over which it wasn't always possible to assert control (cf. Reed 2012, 209–10). Third, and significantly, was the impact of my own gender on my interactions in the field and the performance—at times more and at others less subconsciously or unreflectively—of my own gender (biases) in selecting and building relationships with my respondents.

In the vast majority of cases, interviewees were individuals with whom I had built long-running relationships through more participatory forms of research. With some exceptions, our interview was neither our first nor our last conversation. As such, the interviews I recorded feel like snapshots, freeze-framing relationships that have endured far beyond the moment of the interview itself. With each interview, I worried that the recorded material did not capture or convey the complexity of my relationships with people whom I have been privileged, in many cases, to call friends (cf. Tonkin 1992; McGuire 1987). In attempting to mitigate some of this concern, I employed ongoing processes of respondent verification (Burgess 1984, 206–7), revisiting interview content with respondents and providing them with opportunities to comment further on both the transcripts themselves and my interpretations of them. Twenty-seven of the interviews and both focus groups were recorded (a total of some thirty hours of recorded material). Where interviewees were uncomfortable being recorded, detailed notes were taken instead. I elected to use direct quotations only from interviews that were recorded and transcribed.

Of course, my interviewees do not exist exclusively or even chiefly in an immaterial, centennial social world. Their lives are not defined solely by the discourses and ritual practices of commemoration. "Loyalism" exists in the material and the mundane as well as in the transcendental, because most of the experiences of day-to-day living are, by definition, prosaic and ordinary. According to Brewer (2000, 59), the aim of participant observation is to "generate data through watching and listening to what people naturally do and say, but also to add the dimension of personally experiencing and sharing the same everyday life as those under study."

While retaining a focus on large-scale commemorative rituals, my participant observation therefore also involved myriad forms of day-to-day interaction—"hanging out" (Geertz 1998; Browne and McBride 2015)—with Loyalist commemorators. Developing and maintaining relationships with key respondents took place not only at parades, but across the multiple everyday spaces they occupy: at work, in the pub or club, going to the shop to buy cigarettes, watching TV at home, and all the spaces in between. My interactions with respondents within and across these multiple spaces built up to create a more comprehensive picture of the experiences and meanings that constitute Loyalism as a lived identity (or set of identities). In fact, following people as they cross back and forth between the ordinary and the ritual—and exploring the extent to which the ritual is everyday and the everyday, ritualistic (cf. Goffman 1972)—also revealed the blurring of the boundary between normal and ritual time, providing valuable insights into the way commemoration and its politics enter into the ordinary, profane activities and meanings of Ulster Loyalism.

This blurring of the normal and the ritual is evident in the documents and artifacts produced, shared, and consumed by Loyalist commemorators, including via social media. A number of Loyalist publications are expressly commemorative. Various Facebook groups are dedicated to the memory of the Somme, and the discussions that take place often center on contemporary political issues. Likewise, many Loyalist Twitter users use handles and profile pictures that are commemorative in nature. As Hammersley and Atkinson (2007, 121–22) suggest, "Documentary sources construct 'facts', 'records', 'diagnoses', 'decisions', and 'rules' that are crucially involved in social activities. . . . [M]ost of the settings in which contemporary sociologists and anthropologists work today are literate and contain a plethora of documents: not only are their members able to read and write, but this capacity is also an integral feature of their everyday life and work." Loyalist meaning during the Decade of Centenaries is constructed not only through verbal discourses or physical performances but also through and in relationship with forms that are, textual, digital, and material. As such, collection, recording, and analysis of texts constituted an important part of my fieldwork, complementing both my participant observation and my ethnographic interviews.

Much of this material, including (but not limited to) articles in magazines or periodicals, leaflets, posters, booklets, and program for commemorative events, constitutes ephemera in the most literal sense. After a particular parade or political moment has passed, these documents are liable to be discarded and forgotten. Their production is haphazard and their precise impact hard to assess. For instance, it has not been my experience that individual articles in either the UVF-aligned magazine, the *Purple Standard* (or its predecessor, *Combat*), or the South Belfast Ulster Political Research Group (UPRG) publication, the *Loyalist*, are widely read, let alone directly referenced. The process by which texts are forgotten even as they are produced and consumed is compounded by the advent of social media (cf. Postill and Pink 2012). Individual posts are quickly buried or superseded by those that follow them, and visceral and often violent arguments can flare up on Twitter or Facebook only to quickly subside as the news cycle moves on. Even material forms that at first appear more enduring, such as murals or memorial plaques, actually belong to symbolic landscapes that are evolving and changeable (McCormick and Jarman 2005).

Arguably, it is the accretion evident in these forms over time and space that makes them important in an ethnographic analysis of Loyalist commemoration. Forms of "hashtag sociality" (Postill and Pink 2012, 9) built through the accumulation and reiteration of images, symbols, and Loyalist texts both on- and off-line mirrors and helps to shape Loyalist constructions of meaning. Perhaps paradoxically, the evanescence of social media and the apparent stasis of the symbolic landscape lend each a similar affective quality. Both provide evidence of the perpetual present that is the experience of modernity (Rushkoff 2013), reflecting the characteristic transience or "liquidity" of that experience (Bauman 2000), and the ways in which documents and objects are readily produced and consumed and then just as readily discarded, forgotten, or abandoned in the construction of meaning and identity. Employing Armstrong's (2010, 247) spectral ethnographic lens to text, place, and materiality "is a way of looking at culture as a network of inter-connected resonances, echoes, presences, and other spectral accumulations. . . . [I]t is possible to see [these] ghosts of culture as accumulations of time and space that work to influence the ways that people move through their lives and understand their associated and accumulated spaces, places, atmospheres and objects."

In short, if the flaneur can come to know Parisian modernity through that which it has produced and then abandoned (Benjamin 2002), then this is similarly true for Loyalist Belfast (cf. Bairner 2006). In the very act of walking through particular spaces, it is possible to experience how Loyalism has inscribed itself on them, transforming them into places imbued with layered forms of material and symbolic signification that are available for interpretation (Ingold and Vergunst 2008). Graffiti, memorial gardens, murals, flags, and painted curbstones and even the sound of particular songs being played through open windows all work to designate space as "Loyalist." The digital flaneur is bombarded with tweets, posts, and videos that combine, coalesce, and overlap to tell particular stories about Loyalism and the Loyalist experience.[3]

Likewise, the meanings people both attribute to and derive from the material, a photograph of a long-dead relative, a flag, or a poppy wreath, form an important part of their social and political experience (cf. Navaro-Yashin 2009). Particularly in terms of how people understand, experience, and demonstrate their genealogy or heritage, materiality provides an importance means by which they feel connected to the past. As Hammersley and Atkinson (2007, 136) suggest, "Objects themselves embody their owner's memories: memory is not a mental state from this perspective, but is inscribed in material objects, and in the autobiographical narratives they evoke. . . . A deceptively trivial place, such as the mantelpiece thus provides a microcosm of everyday domestic, aesthetic and interpersonal arrangements."

AN ETHIC OF EMPATHY

It is generally accepted or assumed that it is the role of the anthropologist to seek, empathetically, to understand and ultimately give voice to the worldview, experiences, hopes, frustrations, and fears of his or her respondents (see Scheper-Hughes 1995; Hammersley 2000). This role is intrinsically political, and it often involves challenging prevailing prejudices or conventions about, for instance, the role of violence in the construction and negotiation of social and political relationships (see Bourgois 1995). The ethnographic exercise is, at least in part, intrinsically about interrogating and antagonizing structures and instruments of power, chiefly as it is exercised by the state (cf. Shah 2010). In short, ethnography is often about identifying with and representing people who are or perceive themselves to be in some sense excluded or economically, culturally, or politically marginalized. In the Northern Irish context—in ways I explore below and in greater depth in chapter 4—to me this means an empathetic engagement with Loyalists and with Loyalism. However, what is meant by "empathy," its pursuit and practice in ethnographic research, particularly where that research takes Loyalism as its subject, is not straightforward.

In a speech to the American Academy of Arts and Sciences in 1974, Clifford Geertz revisited a controversy over Malinowski's field diaries, published posthumously in 1967, in which the latter had noted his (at times quite shocking) disdain for his interlocutors and had thereby, it was argued, rendered "the established image of how anthropological work is conducted fairly well implausible. The myth of the chameleon field-worker, perfectly self-tuned to his exotic surroundings—a walking miracle of empathy, tact, patience and cosmopolitanism—was demolished by the man who had perhaps done the most to create it" (Geertz 1974, 27). The revelations contained in *A Diary in the Strict Sense of the Term* called into question the extent to which any anthropologist could legitimately claim the empathy—understood as "communion"—with the "native" that was held to be central to his or her experience of their lifeworld(s) and, thereby, the key to claiming ethnographic knowledge.

Geertz argued against the (mis)reading of the anthropologist's craft as the seeking of "communion," contending that it privileged the "experience-near" over the "experience-distant," or the "emic" over the "etic," to such an extent that it misrepresented the nature of the ethnographic enterprise. Both, in fact, are of equal validity and importance in the construction of anthropological knowledge and understanding. In essence, "we never really could, nor did we need to feel as our interlocutors felt in order to understand how they inhabited the world. Case in point, you don't have to believe in magic to understand how magic works its magic. . . . Instead of empathy, we needed to interpret the representations [respondents] produced for themselves about themselves" (Gable 2014, 240).

In the wake of the controversy surrounding the publication of Malinowski's *Diary*, the proper role of empathy in ethnographic fieldwork has remained the subject of ongoing debate (see Hollan 2014). This debate is further complicated in studies of extreme otherness, of groups defined by political ideology, forms of identification, or modes of behavior with which the anthropologist profoundly disagrees. Kathleen Blee (1993, 1998, 2003), reflecting on her work with women in the Ku Klux Klan, for instance, has noted the difficulties experienced by researchers who work with Klan activists in establishing rapport, empathy, and intersubjectivity with respondents while simultaneously grappling with the repugnance of their political views.

As Besteman (2015, 282) notes, "Writing with an ethic of love, and understanding oneself to be engaged in a mutual project of imagining a new and better society is challenged when the anthropologist's vision of a good society directly contradicts those of his or her research subjects." In large part, this accounts for anthropologists' reticence to engage with groups or movements on what might broadly be termed the hard political Right (see Edelman 2001). Though I include Ulster Loyalism in this category, in ways that I discuss below, it is not always a neat fit or a useful way of understanding Loyalism's idiosyncrasies. Nonetheless, in my own research, the distance between my views and those of my respondents was notable, and the subject of much internal debate. It also manifested in—at times quite frank—conversations about this fact with my respondents, many of whom recognized and even identified with my political, emotional, or ethical discomfort. In one particularly poignant conversation a respondent told me, "I want to show you my community, warts and all. I've just tried to be honest with you. I just hope you'll represent what you've seen here honestly, warts and all." This is what I have tried to do.

The anthropologist may actively disagree with, perhaps even be disgusted by, the logics or behavior of the respondent whose point of view he or she is seeking to understand, and quite openly so. Indeed, and as Gable (2014, 242) suggests, "some of the best conversations humans have are veiled arguments that seem to go nowhere, that seem to reveal the impossibility of rapport, and therefore lead to recognitions of profound difference." Anthropologists do not have an obligation to agree with or even like their respondents. But the commitment (as) faithfully (as possible) to represent their behavior and worldview on its own terms remains the root of ethnographic claims to knowledge. It is of vital ethical importance that those who are being represented are able to recognize themselves in the anthropologist's representation of them. "A good interpretation of anything," as Geertz (1973, 18) argues, "takes us into the heart of that which it is an interpretation." I have relied on ongoing processes of respondent verification (Hammersley and Atkinson 2007, 181–83; cf. Pilkington 2016, 21) in order to ensure that my respondents are able to recognize themselves in my ethnographic representation.

Whether or not this can meaningfully be called empathy is questionable. Besteman (2015, 283) would perhaps propose "respect" or "sincerity" instead. There is an argument that in my confrontation with the (abject) Loyalist subject, I am actually mislabeling what could more accurately be called sympathy or even pity. But in this confrontation, the will to empathy remains centrally important (cf. Wikan 1992; Svašek 2010). Whatever I may have thought of the actions or views of my respondents, in sharing them with me, they revealed their vulnerability and, often, their pain and even shame. Empathy is more sincere, more nuanced, than sympathy, and it implies a commitment to attempt, as far as possible, to share in the emotion if not the worldview of the other, however extreme the otherness or uncomfortable that experience, in a way that sympathy does not (see Brown 2012). Indeed, my research has revealed that the Loyalist other is actually often, sometimes uncomfortably, familiar (cf. Blee 2003, 16).

Empathy thus construed is not about becoming or communing with the other but about attempting to acknowledge and reflect on the meaning and validity of their lived experience in a way that is "rooted in a range of emotional and sensory experiences that generate affective bonds regardless of whether the researcher shares beliefs, values or behaviours with respondents. . . . [It] requires an *emotional* engagement with respondents which does not simulate friendship but takes a variety of situational forms that may . . . transcend the research context" (Pilkington 2016, 21–25; emphasis added). In the final analysis, I take empathy to be rooted in Nigel Fielding's (1982, 99) foundational question in his research on the National Front: "What would I have to be like to believe as these people do?"

THE DIVISIVE SUBJECT

Loyalism is a much-reviled and, in the wake of the flag protests, even ridiculed sociopolitical label. A subset of the wider Protestant ethnoreligious category, it is the "L" in the abbreviation PUL (Protestant/Unionist/Loyalist), which is at once indicative of a unified ethnonational group or community and of this community's divisive internal structuration. While the ambiguities and nuances of the term receive further treatment in chapter 4, broadly, I follow Ramsey (2011, 5) in that I have chosen to use the term "Loyalist" to describe those involved in this research, "because the associations with the working class, with local communities and with political commitment make it particularly apposite." While the definitively working-class character of the "Loyalist" label is indicative of particular forms of socioeconomic, political, and psychosocial vulnerability (Burgess 2002; Mulvenna 2015), it is conventionally associated with forms of right-wing ethnic chauvinism or dominance (Kaufmann 2004b), paramilitary violence, pro-state terrorism, virulent sectarianism, and, increasingly, racism and homophobia (see, e.g., Bruce 1992; Taylor 2000; Wood 2006; Cusack and McDonald 2008).

As a social, political, and cultural category, there is significantly more to Ulster Loyalism than this characterization allows for (see

McAuley 2010; Burgess and Mulvenna 2015). However, any researcher of Loyalism must contend with the methodological and ethical sensitivities of interacting with a culture defined to a lesser or greater extent by vulnerability and a profound sense of alienation but also by overt hostility to outsiders and the entrenched attitude, "everybody hates us and we don't care" (Reed 2012; McVeigh 2015). This attitude often manifests in forms of political discourse, symbolic action, or behavior that ranges from the upsetting or distasteful to the morally repugnant and threatening.

On one memorable occasion I was told by a Loyalist bandsman, "The only n*ggers I like are the n*ggers in the Orange Order, and I don't like them very much." It is important to stress that this level of overt racism was exceptional and that another bandsman with whom I was also speaking at the time—who had been involved in an antiracism project called "Loyalist or Racist: You Can't Be Both" (McAuley 2013, 96)—was quick to admonish his colleague. However, this outburst was part of a wider trend that permeated much of my fieldwork experience. Hate speech—directed increasingly over the course of my fieldwork at Muslims—hypermasculinity and sexism, and performative forms of racism, homophobia, and sectarianism were a defining part (albeit only one part) of my ethnographic encounter with the Loyalist experience.

For example, over the course of my fieldwork, it was hard to become anything other than contemptuous of the evident and at times visceral delight taken by some bands and their supporters in the playing of the controversial "Famine Song" at volatile interfaces on parade routes in North and East Belfast.[4] Likewise, the practice of burning the Irish national flag and effigies of Nationalist and Republican politicians at 11 July bonfires is one in which it is emotionally and morally jarring to participate, however passively. Of course, Loyalism has been and remains associated with forms of outright and unambiguous violence, including those connected to drug dealing and racketeering (McAleese 2015). It is important to stress that during the course of my fieldwork I did not encounter any of this violence directly or personally, but it would be naive to suggest that I am therefore unaware of its existence. Ultimately, as is well known to all of my respondents, while I have sought to understand it, I refuse to sanitize or justify that which is, in my view, nakedly and indefensibly sectarian, racist, homophobic, or otherwise discursively or physically violent.

But Loyalism is not defined exclusively by forms of reactionary or radical right-wing politics. Many Loyalists I met during my research, including those in the example above, emphatically condemned the racism and sectarianism of some of their peers. Recent scholarship, including Tony Novosel's *Northern Ireland's Lost Opportunity* (2013), has explored the evolution of a progressive, left-wing Loyalist politics during the 1970s and 1980s, particularly in the "cages" of Long Kesh, under the tutelage of Gusty Spence and advanced by his protégés, including David Ervine, Billy Hutchinson, and Billy Mitchell. Loyalist political parties— the Progressive Unionist Party (PUP), formed in 1979 to provide a political voice for the UVF; and the Ulster Democratic Party (UDP), formed in 1981 by the Ulster Defence Association (UDA)—played a key role in coordinating efforts to bring about and maintain the 1994 Loyalist paramilitary cease-fires, as well as in the following talks that culminated in 1998's Good Friday Agreement. Indeed, policy documents and position papers produced by both the UVF and the UDA during the 1980s, including *Sharing Responsibility* (1985) and *Common Sense* (1987), preempted much of what was contained in the Good Friday Agreement itself (see Novosel 2013).

The UDP has since been dissolved, but the PUP remains active in Northern Irish politics. Having never enjoyed resounding electoral successes, it has foundered electorally since the advent of the Agreement and the untimely passing in 2007 of its leader, the charismatic and well-liked David Ervine. However, to date, the party and its brand of "Ervinian" or "new" Loyalism (McAuley 2005, 2010) maintain a token representation on some local bodies, including the Belfast City Council. Its program is one of social democracy, social liberalism, and what it calls civic nationalism. It maintains strong links with the Irish Council of Trade Unions and has campaigned against welfare reform and cuts to health and public services. Of its three sitting Belfast city councilors at the time of writing, one, Julie-Ann Corr Johnston, is a young pro-choice and openly gay woman who is an active campaigner for LGBTQ rights. Many Loyalist former political prisoners from both the UVF and the UDA have taken leading roles in community development, conflict transformation, and cross-community educational projects, in many cases working with former enemies (see Shirlow and McEvoy 2008; Shirlow 2012). Organizations founded by Loyalist former prisoners, such as the community-based restorative justice program, Northern Ireland Alternatives, provide support and guidance to young, working-class people who are politically, culturally, and economically marginalized and educationally disadvantaged.

In ways determined variously by its hostility, intolerance, and even criminality but also its socioeconomic vulnerability and political marginalization, "Loyalism" as a label or ethnographic category represents particular forms of deviance (Hobbs 2001). This, in turn, has rendered at least some of my research sensitive (Lee 1993), in that it has involved (and in a sense continues to involve) particular intrusive and political threats, as well as threats of sanction for both me as researcher and certain of my participants. In all instances it is the ethical duty of the ethnographer, as far as possible, to protect his or her respondents, and this duty is even more acute in instances where a failure to do so could result in sanctions. For instance, even to claim membership of the UVF or the UDA is proscribed under U.K. law and to be revealed to be a current member of either organization carries a potential prison sentence of up to ten years (Home Office 2015). As far as I am aware, none of my respondents were active or current members of a proscribed organization, but this represents only one form of the guilty knowledge I have risked acquiring over the course of my research. Much of this knowledge is, on the face of it, fairly innocuous—who does or does not like whom and for what reasons—but in a close-knit community this kind of information can be extremely sensitive, with potentially damaging consequences when "they" can read what "we" write (cf. Lee 1993, 5; see also Brettell 1996).

Becker (1967, cited in Fielding 1982, 91) has suggested that "one should refrain from publishing items of fact or conclusions that are not necessary to one's argument or would cause suffering out of proportion to the scientific gain of making them public." I went one step further by choosing not to ask questions about expressly illegal activity. These questions were, in any case, unlikely to be answered by respondents fully aware of the legal issues raised by the so-called and ongoing Boston Tapes controversy.[5] For each of my respondents, the specific boundaries of the research were clearly laid out and lines drawn as to what information I was prepared to be privy to and what activities I was prepared to observe and in which I was prepared to participate (cf. Polsky 1971).

Complete anonymity can never be guaranteed, particularly in a context where crucial clues to identity can inhere in information as seemingly innocuous as a street name (Lee 1993, 186). However, all reasonable steps to protect the identity of my respondents have been taken. To this end—and in consultation with respondents—names have been changed and the biographical information pertaining to each interlocutor has been kept to a minimum.

In sum, this research has involved complex ethical and moral negotiations and some compromises on my part that have at times been quite emotionally challenging. The problem of balancing the will to speak out against or challenge forms of intolerance and prejudice against maintaining good relationships with my respondents was often difficult to negotiate. Cassell (1988) has argued that in order to gain access to the field it is possible and even desirable to temporarily adopt the views of respondents, and at the very least, it is often not for the anthropologist to openly condemn particular ideas or actions where they are encountered in their setting. Especially in the early stages of my fieldwork, building relationships with gatekeepers to gain access (Reed 2012, 209), I found it difficult to judge what I ought or ought not to say, how to respond to certain kinds of provocative questioning, or how much of myself—my own views, beliefs, and opinions—I ought to reveal. In the end, however, building and maintaining relationships with respondents or interlocutors in the field is really no different from building relationships more generally, even where those respondents or interlocutors hold views and engage in forms of behavior that are at odds with one's own. Honesty (with the exception of a few white lies that are the stuff of social grace), integrity, flexibility, and, importantly, a good sense of humor and the capacity to both give and take a good "slaggin'" (Rodham 1998) were fundamental to developing reciprocal relationships based on trust, openness, and mutual respect. While I did not come to share the worldview of my respondents, I will always have a profound and enduring respect for their opinions and gratitude for the patience, kindness, and generosity they have shown me.

Ultimately, negotiating the violent division in Northern Irish society (see Knox 2001) and interrogating the forms of Loyalist deviance that condition some of that division were just two processes among many that contributed to making this research both challenging and rewarding. Ethnographic research by its very nature is intense, emotional, and exhausting. In sum, and as Nigel Fielding (1981, 1982) has stressed, research of this type isn't always "nice." But this should not be an excuse not to do it. Devoting too much time to discussing questions of access, field relationships, or the ethics of representation, while these are crucial questions, arguably represents a "reluctance to go out and face those problems by actually entering the field" (Lee 1993, 119). From the outset, my intentions were genuine, and I hope they were recognized as such. I am genuinely interested in how Loyalists understand their place in a world defined by rapid socioeconomic and political upheaval and dislocation.

Mirroring Hilary Pilkington in her *Loud and Proud: Passion and Politics in the English Defence League*, this interest is, above all, representative of and rooted in

> a commitment to the reclamation of 'politics'; the relinquishment of its quest for universal rational consensus through attempts to design institutions capable of reconciling all conflicting interests and values . . . and its reconfiguration as a space for the legitimate expression of such conflict. This comes with real costs; uncomfortable views, and those who express them, have to be treated seriously, academically and politically, rather than dismissed, caricatured or ridiculed. (2016, 1)

As I discuss in greater depth throughout this book, and particularly in chapter 7, I believe that Loyalist voices yet have something to contribute to the politics—properly understood—of ongoing processes of conflict transformation in Northern Ireland. At the very least, their intentional marginalization by the architects of the ongoing peace and political processes, as well as their vilification by its cheerleaders in civil society, is counterproductive, promoting an (un)virtuous circle of Loyalist grievance. Despite the many fundamental political differences that exist between us, and the difficulties this has posed over the course of my fieldwork, it has therefore been my intention throughout to represent the views of my respondents on their own terms, with honesty and integrity.

CHAPTER THREE

Policy, Peace-Building, and "the Past" during the Decade of Centenaries

In Ireland, history repeats itself, the first time as tragedy, the second as farce, and the third as a 'community relations' project.

> R. McVeigh, "No One Likes Us, We Don't Care"

The unnerving confidence displayed when instructing communities on the supposed correct way to remember, relies on a rhetoric of ethics, which under scrutiny can turn out to be little more than a cover-up for political opinionating.

> G. Beiner, "Troubles with Remembering"

On 31 July 2014, the Ballynafeigh and Annadale Cultural and Heritage Society held a parade and service of remembrance to commemorate the twentieth anniversary of the violent deaths of Joe Bratty and Raymond Elder. The two men were both senior members of the largest Loyalist paramilitary group in Northern Ireland, the Ulster Defence Association (UDA). They were killed while walking on South Belfast's Ormeau Road by Provisional Irish Republican Army (PIRA) gunmen, days before the latter announced its 1994 cease-fire. In the years since this cease-fire, the section of the road on which the two men were murdered has been transformed: it has experienced a postconflict renaissance and become one of Belfast's most diverse and cosmopolitan districts. It boasts a number of boutique cafés, an artisanal bakery, a yoga studio, a Buddhist center, up-market restaurants, and pubs specializing in micro-brews. I couldn't help but feel that this parade commemorating two paramilitary deaths, a reminder of a violent past that many who live, work, and play on the Upper Ormeau Road are keen to forget and a symbolic display of particular working-class aesthetic forms and tastes (Bourdieu 1989; Ramsey 2011), must have looked jarring to those watching it across the top of flat whites handcrafted by professional baristas.

Bandsmen quickly buttoned their jackets and hauled their drums hurriedly past us as they made their way to the parade's starting point outside the Ballynafeigh Orange Hall.[1] Many of the bands wore uniforms of black or sky-blue, or carried the standards of the Ulster Defence Union (UDU),[2] and one had attached a toy Womble to its bass drum.[3] A steward stood on the street corner on which Bratty and Elder had been shot and killed twenty years previously. He carried a banner bearing an image of the men's faces. This provided a signal to passing band captains as to where their standards and flags should be dipped and the sound of flutes and drums replaced with a solemn, solitary beat on the side-drum. The bands struck up again as they rounded the corner, leaving the Ormeau Road and proceeding to a memorial garden located in the nearby Annadale Flats, in which the parade was followed by a memorial service.

In the event, this commemoration would be described in terms far stronger than merely "jarring" on what one journalist lauded as the "relaxed, relatively integrated, comfortable in itself . . . village-Main Street-like" Ormeau Road (McDonald 2014). The *Irish News* spoke of "a celebration of the UDA which does nothing to advance or promote community relations in South Belfast" (Hughes 2014). The *Belfast Telegraph* called the commemoration a "disgrace" (Kilpatrick 2014). Much of this critical coverage hinged on a perception that the UDA had illegitimately co-opted—"shameful[ly] hijack[ed]," as it was put in a *Belfast Telegraph* op-ed (2014a)—an otherwise legitimate and innocuous First World War memorial as a locus for its commemorative ceremonials. This memorial garden had recently been installed in the Annadale Flats by the Northern Ireland Housing Executive (NIHE) at a cost of £11,000, as part of a "re-imaging" program.[4]

On 2 August, the NIHE issued a press statement disclaiming the commemoration and insisting, "The garden . . . and commemorative plaque [were] funded by the Housing Executive and designed to commemorate the First World War. . . . There is no sectarian or paramilitary imagery in the garden. . . . The Housing Executive was not aware and had no involvement in the parade, and would not have sanctioned the additional imagery that was placed in the garden" (BBC News 2014a). This "additional imagery" consisted of a small, temporary plaque bearing the red hand insignia of the UDA and its military wing,[5] the Ulster Freedom Fighters (UFF), and the names of Brigade volunteers who had been "killed in action" during the Troubles; an Ulster banner (the unofficial flag of Northern Ireland); and flags bearing the crests of the UDA and the UFF.

Presumably, also included in this category of unsanctioned additional imagery were the red poppy wreaths laid in tribute to Bratty and Elder during the memorial service by the bands and the officers of the (UDA-affiliated) South Belfast UPRG. These symbolic tributes, however, happened to mirror precisely the officially sanctioned imagery in the garden, which is avowedly neither paramilitary nor sectarian. The garden's permanent plaque bears a handful of images, including a red hand and four red poppies (fig. 3.1). The NIHE-sponsored inscription reads, "To remember the fallen is not just to remember how they fell, but to remember why they fell. It is through their courage and sacrifice that we have continued freedom."

Despite the fact that the sanctioned symbolic furniture in the memorial garden therefore shares much in common with that employed by the UDA, and contains no explicit reference to the First World War at all, the incensed op-ed in the *Belfast Telegraph* that spoke of the "shameful hijacking" continued:

> The replacement of a paramilitary memorial in south Belfast by a commemorative garden remembering the fallen of World War One was a project designed to give the area a more positive image. Given that this is the centenary of the beginning of that war it was seen by many as a fitting tribute to the many who had died to guarantee our freedoms.

Figure 3.1. Annadale Garden of Remembrance, Belfast, 31 July 2014.

It is sickening that the garden should have been hijacked by the UDA to commemorate members from the area who were killed during the Troubles. While the official plaque in the garden does not mention World War One by name it is clear that it is not any kind of paramilitary memorial.

> To equate dead terrorists with the heroes who fought at the
> Somme or any Great War battles is to sully their memory. . . . This
> is another issue which falls into the poisoned chalice of dealing with
> the past. (*Belfast Telegraph* 2014b)

The media furor generated by the UDA's use of the Annadale memorial garden to commemorate the deaths of Joe Bratty and Raymond
Elder is illuminating. It reveals some of the semiotic slippages, dual-
isms, and contradictions that define the Decade of Centenaries' politics of commemoration, which involves claims and counterclaims about
who or what may legitimately be remembered, by whom, how, where,
and for what reasons. Crucially, such claims can be both made and re-
buked using the same contested symbolic vocabulary. For instance, the
symbol of the red poppy can be used to attempt to signify moral equivalence between the dead of the First World War and those of a Loyalist paramilitary organization and at the same time—and conversely—an
unbridgeable moral gulf between the "heroes" of the Western Front
and the "terrorists" of the more recent conflict in (and about) Northern
Ireland. This latter mode of assertive signification is suggestive of an
underlying dominant, official, or otherwise hegemonic memorial narrative (Nora 1989; Papadakis 1993) that seeks to authoritatively establish
one conflict as just and another as wrongful: one worthy of active and
ongoing memorialization and the other fit, ultimately, for nothing other
than puposeful forgetting, "obliteration" (Scheper-Hughes and Bourgois
2004, 9) or "oblivion" (Augé 2004).

As argued by John McGarry and Brendan O'Leary (1995, 844), at
the heart of many explanations of the violence of the Troubles is the
more or less explicit claim that "the Northern Irish . . . [like] to indulge
in 'ancient hatreds', as if they are incapable of putting the past behind
them." Across the overlapping realms of academic, policy, and public discourse there is an almost uncontested acceptance that "the past" is perhaps *the* problem to be dealt with in the pursuit of lasting peace in
Northern Ireland. The expression "dealing with the past" has become a
catchall for almost all ongoing peace-building work: everything from
the issue of residential segregation of Protestants and Catholics to "in-
tegrating" education seems to fall under its rubric. For instance, in a
video on commemorations recorded for Finish the Job, the CRC's 2014

policy conference, Maureen Hetherington, director of the Junction,[6] argued:

> We can't really finish the job of community relations . . . unless we deal with the past. And commemorations can play a very important role in that. [But we] have to recognise and realise [that] the violence of a decade 1912 to 1922 had a lasting legacy on this island, and helped to create the conditions for our latest convulsion which we know as the Troubles. . . . Unfortunately we still have some areas that memorialise sites of memory. And that's against the idea that we build shared space. It creates contested space. It creates hurt. And it can re-traumatize and create ill-feeling. And I think that has to be challenged, and there has to be policy put in place. There is memorialisation, and sites of memory that aren't *officially* sanctioned, but nothing's done about them. Memorialisation of sites of memory: that has to be visited if we are thinking about the common and greater good. (CRC 2014; emphasis added)

Hetherington's call for the sanctioning of commemoration is part of a dominant narrative, or public transcript (Scott 1990), that maintains that the existence of unofficial or sectional (Ashplant, Dawson, and Roper 2000, 18–20) memorial forms is a (if not the) major risk to Northern Ireland's fragile peace but that also insists on the potential power of official forms of memorialization to help solve the vexed problem of "the past." This narrative is reflected in the proliferation in recent years of policies that have sought not only to limit the potential harm of commemoration, but to repurpose it for a peace-building agenda defined by a perceived need to promote good relations between Northern Ireland's two ethno-religious communities (see Burgess 2002; McVeigh 2002; Bryan 2006).

This community relations agenda is characterized by a duality of apparently contradictory approaches to the "problem" of the past, viewing it as both a cause of and a potential solution to conflict. These bifurcated readings of the problem are equally emphatic, however, on the central value of a revisionist historiography (and what Benjamin [1968] criticized as historicism) in seeking to solve it. Drawing on policy documents, participation in peace-building and community relations projects, observation of official commemorative ceremonies, and interviews with representatives of Northern Ireland's community relations sector, in this chapter I seek to demonstrate how commemoration, as a site of conflict, has been reconfigured during the present Decade of Centenaries as a site on which to build a "shared future." I suggest that in claiming to de-politicize the past through recovering the "fact" of history's "shared-ness", those involved in defining the policy of the Decade of Centenaries are instead engaged in an anti-politics (Ferguson 1990), which seeks to preclude or limit particular commemorative narratives and practices and thereby delegitimize particular, contestational political forms. The aim is to protect what Conor McCabe (2013; see also Baker 2014) has termed Northern Ireland's double transition—the simultaneous pursuit of reconciliation and finance-led economic growth, predicated on the profoundly ideological and essentially contestable assertion that they are (a) equally beneficial and (b) mutually reinforcing.

COMMEMORATING THE ORANGE STATE

"Not content merely to remind us of ancient quarrels," Ian McBride (2001, 4) has suggested, "Irish anniversaries have an uncanny way of making history themselves" (see also Leersen 2001). Haunting Maureen Hetherington's video testimony cited above are the ghosts of a pervasive argument popularized by the prominent Irish politician and academic Conor Cruise O'Brien. In his 1972 polemic, *States of Ireland*, O'Brien no-toriously asserted that commemoration is a—if not the—primary cause of conflict in (Northern) Ireland (see also Daly and O'Callaghan 2007). Specifically, O'Brien argued that the commemorations in 1966 of the Golden Jubilees of 1916's Easter Rising and the Battle of the Somme had provided the catalyst for the violence of the early years of the Troubles, the late 1960s and early 1970s.

According to O'Brien, events to commemorate the fiftieth anniversary of the Rising had, in equal measure, been reinvigorating for a mori-bund "physical force" Republican movement and unsettling for Ulster Unionists. Unionists had looked on aghast at commemorative events in the South, and their fury at the state's unwillingness to prevent similar events from going ahead in the North had manifested in increased support for the firebrand preacher Reverend Ian Paisley and his brand of hard-line, recalcitrant Unionism (see O'Donnell 2007). Then, in July 2016, Northern Irish Prime Minister Terence O'Neill was forced to return early from a commemorative pilgrimage to France to condemn a series of murders by a group calling itself the Ulster Volunteer Force. These violent acts by a group of "heavily armed Protestants dedicated to [their] cause" (Mulvenna 2016, 34) provided early warnings of a political crisis that would culminate in 1969 with British troops being called in to restore order to the streets of Derry and Belfast. "Just as the 1966 commemorations in Dublin favoured a recrudescence of the IRA," lamented O'Brien (1972, 150), "so the Northern commemorations, clashing with those of the South, favoured the recrudescence of armed Protestant extremism."

In ways discussed further below, this was a gross overattribution of blame for the spiraling sectarian violence of the Troubles to commemoration per se. But O'Brien was right to suggest that Somme commemorations, including during the Golden Jubilee, provided an important means by which the patterns of inclusion and exclusion that defined the Northern Irish polity—and that were at the heart of the burgeoning conflict—were mirrored, mediated, and replicated. The newly (re) formed UVF's adoption of the symbolism and nomenclature of the 36th (Ulster) Division in the mid-1960s built on the Somme's broader and divisive deployment in the exclusionary projects of state and nation building in the Orange State (Farrell 1980; McGaughey 2012). In particular, since the founding of Northern Ireland, Somme commemorations had become an increasingly dominant feature of the commemorative calendar of one of the central pillars of this project: the Orange Order (see Bryan 2000).[7]

Beginning in 1919, a state commemoration, hosted initially by the Belfast Corporation and then by the Belfast City Council—which with the suspension of the Northern Ireland Parliament and the introduction of direct rule in 1972 became the most powerful and symbolically significant of Northern Ireland's domestic political institutions—was held annually on 1 July at the cenotaph at Belfast City Hall and continued uninterrupted during the Troubles. This ceremony included representatives of the Unionist political parties, the Orange Order, the police and security forces, and the central British state. The British state's

ceremonial duties at the cenotaph on 1 July were fulfilled by the gover-
nor of Northern Ireland until the position was abolished in 1973, where-
upon they were taken up by the newly created office of secretary of state.
A resolution, which from 1919 was passed almost unchanged every year
at a special session of the Belfast City Council on 1 July, read:

> That we, the Lord Mayor and Citizens of the City of Belfast, on the
> *nth* Anniversary of the Battle of the Somme, desire again to record
> our feelings of gratitude to the brave men of the 36th (Ulster) Divi-
> sion who, by their glorious conduct in that Battle, made an imper-
> ishable name for themselves and their Province and whose heroism
> will never be forgotten so long as the British Commonwealth lasts.
> (Leonard 2003, 5)

The fiftieth anniversary of the Somme in 1966, in particular, was a grand
state occasion of definitively British disposition. In addition to Terence
O'Neill's "pilgrimage" to the Ulster Tower, the Somme's Golden Jubilee
was marked with great pomp and circumstance during a ceremony on
the Balmoral showgrounds, in which Queen Elizabeth II herself per-
formed a review of Northern Irish Somme veterans.

Further to these specific forms of Somme commemoration, the
reinstatement and redesignation of Armistice Day as Remembrance
Sunday following the Second World War and the expansion of its commemorative activities to incorporate the memory of members of the
British armed forces killed in more recent conflicts—including, from the
late 1960s, the Troubles themselves—were all broader British trends
reproduced in Northern Ireland. In this way, war commemoration in
general and of the First World War and the Battle of the Somme in particular has traditionally been of central importance in representing,
maintaining, and asserting Northern Ireland's Britishness and its place
within the Union. This, for example, helps to explain the IRA's choice of
a Remembrance Sunday service in Enniskillen in 1987 as a "legitimate
target" (see McDaniel 1997; Robinson 2010).

Commemoration (or a lack thereof) of the First World War in the
Irish Free State and, later, the Republic of Ireland, as well as by Nationalists in the North, is conventionally described in terms of what Martin
(1967) called the "great oblivion." The suggestion is that Irish partici-

pation in the Great War was largely forgotten precisely because of its associations with Britishness. Commemoration of the war jarred with the Republican and Nationalist politics of Irish state building, which took the Easter Rising as its foundational episode. Higgins (2012, 91), for instance, has identified a prevalent trope in discourses about Irish history and politics whereby it is commonly asserted that "remembering the Rising was not simply an assertion of the politics of independence, [but] a rejection of the founding myth of the [Northern Irish] state. For many . . . it was axiomatic that to glorify the events of Easter Week 1916 was to desecrate the memory of the First World War dead: in order to remember the Rising it was necessary to forget the Somme."

The Enniskillen Remembrance Day bombing in 1987, it is argued, was a watershed moment in Irish cultural memory of the First World War (see, e.g., Myers 2013). Such was the outrage at the killing of eleven people (one more person would later die of his wounds) and the injuring of sixty-three others as they participated in the Remembrance Sunday service at Enniskillen's war memorial that the bombing was condemned even by Sinn Féin in their weekly newspaper, *An Phoblacht*. In the years following Enniskillen, Irish participation in Remembrance services increased. Street sales of the British Legion's red poppy in the Republic of Ireland had been abandoned altogether in 1971, before which approximately 25,000 had been sold annually. In 1988, sale of the poppy resumed, and 45,000 were sold (Jeffrey 2015). In the wake of the "peace process" in the early 1990s, the paramilitary cease-fires in 1994, and the Good Friday Agreement in 1998, Irish Nationalist reengagement with the First World War accelerated North and South of the border. In post-Agreement Northern Ireland, its commemoration would come to play a prominent role in the symbolic dismantling of the Orange State and the ushering in of a new politics based on "parity of esteem" between the two "traditions" of Unionism and Nationalism.

COMMEMORATING THE "NEW" NORTHERN IRELAND

On 11 November 1998, just months after the signing of the Good Friday Agreement, Queen Elizabeth II and Irish president Mary McAleese stood side by side on the outskirts of the Belgian village of Messines to inaugurate the new Island of Ireland Peace Park. The opening of the park—built near the site where the 36th (Ulster) and 16th (Irish) Divisions had faced the Germans side by side during 1917's Battle of Messines—represented the culmination of a project begun by the Journey of Reconciliation Trust in 1996. It had been the brainchild of Glenn Barr, a Loyalist from Derry and onetime brigadier of the North West Brigade of the UDA, and Paddy Harte, a Fine Gael TD for Donegal. According to a representative of the Trust's successor, the International School for Peace Studies (ISPS), which has its headquarters in Derry, the Peace Park was conceived in part as a response to the perceived discrepancy between sites of memory for Unionists and those for Nationalists who had fought in the Great War. While the 36th (Ulster) Division was commemorated with the suitably "splendid" Ulster Tower, only a neglected and unkempt cross outside a church in the village of Guillemont stood in testament to the 16th (Irish) Division's wartime "sacrifices" (ISPS representative, interview with author, 2015).

Dismayed at the way in which Irishmen of different political and religious persuasions were thus "divided in death," Barr and Harte undertook to build something "noncontentious and nonpolitical" that would serve as a fitting tribute to all of Ireland's war dead and unite their descendants in the memory of their shared sacrifice. They sought funding for their project from the International Fund for Ireland (IFI), an independent fund established in 1986 by the British and Irish governments with financial contributions from the governments of the United States, Canada, Australia, and New Zealand. The park is laden with symbolism. Modeled on a design from the eighth century, the round tower is an allusion to a time "long before there was political strife" in Ireland. It was built by young people from across the island of Ireland, using stone from an old workhouse in Mullingar, Co. Westmeath, avowedly symbolizing the poverty of the majority of those Irishmen who had fought and died on the Western Front. It is thirty-two meters high, one meter for each of the counties in Ireland. Four plots of Irish yew trees represent the four provinces. Three name stones represent the three divisions raised in Ireland between 1914 and 1918: the 10th and 16th (Irish) Divisions and the 36th (Ulster) Division (ISPS representative, interview with author,

2015; see also ISPS 2007b). At the heart of the park, a stone bears an inscription of the Peace Pledge:

> From the crest of this ridge, which was the scene of terrific carnage in the First World War on which we have built a peace park and Round Tower to commemorate the thousands of young men from all parts of Ireland who fought a common enemy, defended democracy and the rights of all nations, whose graves are in shockingly uncountable numbers and those who have no graves, we condemn war and the futility of war. We repudiate and denounce violence, aggression, intimidation, threats and unfriendly behaviour.
>
> As Protestants and Catholics, we apologise for the terrible deeds we have done to each other and ask forgiveness. From this sacred shrine of remembrance, where soldiers of all nationalities, creeds and political allegiances were united in death, we appeal to all people in Ireland to help build a peaceful and tolerant society. Let us remember the solidarity and trust that developed between Protestant and Catholic soldiers when they served together in these trenches.
>
> As we jointly thank the armistice of 11 November 1918—when the guns fell silent along this western front—we affirm that a fitting tribute to the principles for which men and women from the Island of Ireland died in both World Wars would be permanent peace.

The opening of the Peace Park in 1998 by the two heads of state was "as symbolic a gesture, as symbolic of the landscape of the time as the 16th and 36th going off to fight the war had been at that time" (ISPS representative, interview with author, 2015). The Peace Park would come to occupy a central place in a number of peace-building projects, including the International School for Peace Studies' own Fellowship program (ISPS 2007a). Building on their initial meeting in Belgium, subsequent joint commemorative ceremonies were attended by Queen Elizabeth and President McAleese at the National Garden of Remembrance and at the Irish National War Memorial Gardens during the queen's state visit to Ireland in 2011. In 2014 a new Commonwealth War Graves Cross of Sacrifice was inaugurated at Glasnevin Cemetery by President Michael D. Higgins, and a representative of the Irish government participated in the Remembrance Sunday service at the cenotaph in Whitehall for the first time. These events and developments have all been widely lauded as symbolizing a new, more reconciled and "mature" relationship between the Republic of Ireland and the United Kingdom (see, e.g., Madigan 2011).

Mirroring this symbolic representation of a new political accommodation within and between Ireland and the United Kingdom, state rituals of remembrance have also been used in attempts to reinforce and lend legitimacy to new political arrangements in post-Agreement Northern Ireland itself. What were once uncomplicatedly Unionist rituals have been purposefully and deliberately reoriented to make them more cross-communal and inclusive of both traditions on the island of Ireland. For example, in 2014, at the Remembrance Sunday ceremony at the Belfast cenotaph, alongside the poppy wreaths laid by Peter Robinson, then leader of the Democratic Unionist Party and Northern Ireland's first minister; Theresa Villiers, secretary of state for Northern Ireland; and representatives of the Unionist political parties and the British Army, Navy, and Air Force was one laid by Lord Mayor Nichola Mallon, a Nationalist of the Social Democratic and Labour Party (SDLP).[8] For the third year running, a laurel wreath was also laid on behalf of the Irish government by then minister for foreign affairs, Charlie Flanagan.[9]

Since 2012, a representative of the Irish government has also participated in the 1 July Somme commemoration at the cenotaph. In 2010, the wording of the Somme resolution passed by Belfast City Council on 1 July was changed to incorporate the 16th (Irish) Division, and references to the Province and the British Commonwealth were removed. The new wording, which has been used every year since 2010, reads:

> That we, the Lord Mayor and Citizens of the City of Belfast, on the *nth* Anniversary of the Battle of the Somme, desire again to record our feelings of gratitude to the brave men of the 36th (Ulster) Division, the 16th (Irish) Division and other forces who, by their glorious conduct in that battle, made an imperishable name for themselves and their people and whose heroism will never be forgotten.

While at the time of writing a Sinn Féin representative has yet to participate in the official ceremony at the cenotaph, subsequent Sinn Féin

Lord Mayors of Belfast have continued to lay a wreath on the morning of 1 July during a smaller, low-key ceremony inaugurated by Alex Maskey during his term as mayor in 2002.

Although he did not attend the Remembrance Sunday ceremony in 2013, then Lord Mayor Máirtín Ó Muilleoir did accept the British Legion's invitation to attend that year's Armistice Day service at the cenotaph on 11 November. Building on the new tradition established by Maskey in 2002, Ó Muilleoir set another new precedent in 2013, which, in turn, was followed by the next Sinn Féin Lord Mayor, Arder Carson, in 2015. In a video interview with *An Phoblacht* following the Armistice Day ceremony, Ó Muilleoir said:

> What I did today was really reaching out to the Unionist, Protestant community of Belfast, for whom Remembrance is a major, major event each year, and in doing so I hope to build the peace. [It was] the right place to be if we want to build the peace, and build a better Belfast. Remember also the fact that many of those who died, many of the Irishmen who died, had joined the British Army to fight for the freedom of Belgium and the freedom of small nations: many for independence and Home Rule as well, and we need to make sure that they are written into the story. (*An Phoblacht* 2013)

In Britain, commemoration of the "Glorious Dead" of the First World War has long hinged on the veneration of an Unknown Soldier, sanctified as embodying, without equal, all that is noble and virtuous in the character of the (national) community (see Anderson 2006 [1983]). In Northern Ireland during the Decade of Centenaries, this trope appears—at least on the surface—to have become increasingly cross-communal.[10]

As noted by Keith Jeffrey (2013, 123), "Much of this enhanced First World War commemoration draws on a belief that shared military experience and the shared human costs of that experience might transcend local Irish political sectarian differences. . . . [A]nd [it] has indeed helped undermine the barriers of mutual communal ignorance that sustain much of the social antagonism on [the island of Ireland]." The ritual reorientation of First World War social memory in Northern Ireland has been both the cause and the consequence of profound social and political transformation—including, notably, within the politics of Irish Nationalism (see Grayson 2010). Nationalists' and Republicans' rediscovery of their First World War heritage, which has in large part been led from the grassroots by groups such as the 6th Connaught Rangers Research Project (CRRP 2011) has, for some, been of great personal significance. For example, Brenda Winter-Palmer, a native of Nationalist West Belfast, has described her 2014 play, *Medal in the Drawer*, which recounts the wartime experiences of her uncle William Kerr—a Roman Catholic from Belfast's Springfield Road who served with the 36th (Ulster) Division—as the "reclamation of a family history which has never been properly commemorated" (*News Letter* 2016a).

The new commemorative dispensation that prevails in Northern Ireland has also helped to facilitate innovative forms of reconciliatory dialogue and the building of new relationships between Nationalists and Unionists. Alex Maskey (interview with author, 2015) and Máirtín Ó Muilleoir (email correspondence, 1 December 2014) have both attested to the positive reception of their commemorative initiatives by groups that include the British Legion and the Somme Association, as well as by Unionists more generally. In their *Decade of Anniversaries Toolkit*, the CRC and HLF (2013) identify twenty-four projects in which critical exploration of the conflicted history of the period 1912–23 has been an effective tool for building new and better relationships within and across Northern Ireland's divided communities. For example, they cite the work of the Fellowship of Messines Association, a group founded in 2002 by the first graduates of the ISPS's Fellowship program that brings together former political prisoners—both Loyalist and Republican—and trade unionists to pursue joint peace-building initiatives focusing on the examination and discussion of history, identity, and politics (see also Grayson 2010).

FROM PAST CONFLICT TO SHARED FUTURE?

According to Elisabetta Viggiani (2013, 18), "The lack of an obvious political elite as a result of an unstable governmental settlement for over thirty years has brought about a state of affairs where the local government [in Northern Ireland] has carefully selected its involvement in commemorative practices, thus, in part, abdicating its right to manufacture memory and the role of nation building that comes with it" (see also McDowell and Braniff 2014, 43). Viggiani finds that there is no dominant, official, or otherwise culturally hegemonic approach to commemoration in post-Agreement Northern Ireland,[11] as neither the state nor, in its absence, any other political organization or paramilitary grouping has been able to capture the public space—either discursive or physical—in order to populate it with their particular, unitary narrative on the past.

While it is perhaps more contested than in less ethnonationally divided polities (its reconciliatory consequences notwithstanding), I contend that there *is* an identifiably hegemonic discourse on memory, commemoration, and the past in Northern Ireland during the Decade of Centenaries. At the very least, there is a clearly discernible public transcript on who or what may legitimately be commemorated, how, by whom, and for what reasons (Hocking 2015). This transcript emphasizes "cross-communal" unity and a "shared future" over the political division of the past. It belongs definitively to what McLaughlin and Baker (2010, 11) have termed the propaganda of peace, which is "the work of a variety of social forces through a range of media and cultural forms, and its purpose is to bring society, culture or nation behind a core idea or principle, in this case, the promise of peace and its economic dividends after decades of conflict." While it is produced and promoted by the state, this propaganda of peace in Northern Ireland also has deep roots in civil society.

> While institutions of the state play a key role in the propaganda of peace, they act in concert with other hegemonic social forces such as local businesses and political elites, trade unions, the voluntary and community sector, academia and the media. Persuading for peace is not less propaganda because of its association with civil society and its apparently benign intentions, for it displays a coherent set of ideas and values that seek to mobilise people to act and behave in the interests of power. (McLaughlin and Baker 2010, 11)

A number of different actors are involved in the (re)production of the propaganda of peace and its public transcript on commemoration during the Decade of Centenaries, among them, the civil service and local government good relations departments, funding bodies, arm's-length agencies and quangos, and a number of nongovernmental organizations. Combined, these groups and institutions constitute Northern Ireland's peace-building or community relations "sector." They are supported in their work by members of the business community; a number of high-profile academics, particularly professional historians; and the "commentariat" (Hobsbawm and Lloyd 2008) in Northern Ireland, the Republic of Ireland, and, to a lesser extent, Great Britain.

The concept of a Decade of Centenaries is itself in large part a product of the propaganda of peace and its public transcript on commemoration: a construct of peace-building and community relations policy (see Heartfield and Rooney 2015). This policy is the product of and functions at every level of politics as it pertains to Northern Ireland, including that of international diplomacy between the United Kingdom and Ireland. Following Queen Elizabeth II's state visit to the Republic of Ireland in 2011, on 12 March 2012, Prime Minister David Cameron and Taoiseach Enda Kenny issued a joint statement, "looking ahead to the next 10 years" of Anglo-Irish relations (Department of the Taoiseach 2012). The statement, which was made following a series of talks between the two heads of government, noted that "2012 . . . marks the beginning of a decade of centenary commemorations of events that helped shape our political destinies," and continued, "This series of commemorations offers us an opportunity to explore and reflect on key episodes of our past. We will do so in a spirit of historical accuracy, mutual respect, inclusiveness and reconciliation. But we want to ensure that this is a decade not only of remembering but also of looking forward; a decade of renewed and strengthened co-operation between our two countries." It stressed the primarily economic nature of this cooperation, including in terms of the role of both governments in promoting and guaranteeing the peace process in Northern Ireland:

> The UK and Ireland both have open and globalised economies and we share a commitment to boosting growth as the cornerstone of economic recovery and job creation. . . . Above all, we stand together with the people of Northern Ireland and its Executive in our determination to make sure that society there is never again blighted by violent conflict. But our aim, along with the Executive, is more than that: it is a society that is not only peaceful, but stable, prosper-

ous, and based on a genuinely shared future for all. . . . We support the Northern Ireland Executive in its objective of rebalancing the economy, and we have asked our embassies in emerging markets to support its efforts in promoting jobs, growth and investment in Northern Ireland. (Department of the Taoiseach 2012)

Three days later, on 13 March 2012, the onus on reconciliation, sharedness, and, crucially, economic investment and growth in the Joint Statement was mirrored in a statement on the Decade of Centenaries from the Northern Ireland Executive, according to which the Executive

> unanimously agreed that the Minister for Enterprise, Trade and In-vestment and the Minister for Culture, Arts and Leisure will jointly bring forward a programme for a decade which will offer a real op-portunity for our society to benefit economically and continue its transformation into a vibrant, diverse and enriched place to visit.
>
> Many of the commemorative anniversaries throughout the de-cade have international as well as local significance and will inevi-tably attract higher numbers of visitors to the region.
>
> These significant events will be organised under the principles of; educational focus, reflection, inclusivity, tolerance, respect, re-sponsibility and interdependence. (NIE 2012)

In 2013 the Executive published its comprehensive good relations strategy, *Together: Building a United Community* (*T:BUC*), a follow-up to 2005's *A Shared Future*, which had been produced under direct rule, prior to the restoration of devolution under the terms of the 2007 St. Andrews Agreement (see Hughes 2009). Under section 5, "Cultural Ex-pression and Diversity," of *T:BUC*, paragraphs 5.29–5.44 deal with the Decade of Centenaries, explicitly reaffirming the principles of the 2012 Executive statement and the "intent to mark significant anniversaries throughout the decade in an inclusive way and in a manner that will . . . help our society to benefit economically and continue its transformation into a vibrant, diverse and enriching place to visit" (OFMDFM 2013, 96). It stresses:

> Our most recent past is only one aspect of an intricate and complex history that has shaped the identity of many within our community

today. . . . The decade of commemorations presents an opportunity to celebrate our shared differences in a way which will position Northern Ireland as powerful example in conflict resolution and transformation on the world stage. The legacy of the ensuing 10 years should be such that we attract even greater positive worldwide interest, increased visitors and further stimulate the economy. . . . [W]e believe that exploring our past can be enormously helpful in building a better future. (93–94)

Of course, policy, as Bolton and Jeffrey (2008, 604) suggest, "is what policy does, in addition to what it claims to be" (see also Shore and Wright 1997; Cramer and Goodhand 2014). While the Executive Statement on the Decade of Centenaries and policy commitments under the terms of *T:BUC* were initially welcomed by senior civil servants, veteran community relations professionals and others involved in project delivery during the Decade of Centenaries, some have identified what they view as the Northern Ireland Executive's subsequent lack of leadership on the issue of commemoration. For instance, one such professional suggested in a 2014 interview:

Where we are weak is in the absence of *follow-through* from the Executive and the inability of DCAL [Department for Culture, Arts and Leisure] and DETI [Department for Enterprise, Trade and Investment] to take a lead on the Decade. I think they made great progress in putting out the statement and I was able to say to people, you know, "You have a fair wind in dealing with this: the Executive is encouraging you, they have tasked DETI and DCAL to take this forward, and they got that out and got that done." [But] they have not been able to follow it up, obviously because the politics of it is very difficult for them . . . they weren't able to hold that ground! (Good Relations professional, interview with author, 2014)

The devolved government's production of policy on the centenaries has been awkward, as exemplified in *T:BUC*'s oxymoronic allusions to "shared differences," and its implementation has been haphazard at best.[12] Nonetheless, this policy both reflects and has contributed to creating a political environment in which certain commemorative discourses and practices are promoted over others.

Vehement disagreement persists between Northern Ireland's political parties on the issue of "the past" (which, as examined in more depth below, is often a euphemism for specific debates about the causes, violence, and legacy of the Troubles). However, as identified by Julia Andrade-Rocha (2015), drawing on Bourdieu's (1989) concept of structuralist constructivism—the dialectical relationship between structures (which constrain behavior) and individual and collective agency (which transforms or preserves structures)—these and other ideological conflicts between political parties are ultimately subordinated to the interests and structural power of the (neoliberal) peace-building state. These interests are guaranteed and protected by institutions such as the Northern Ireland Equality Commission and the Parades Commission; human rights legislation; the joint involvement of the British, Irish, and other governments (including, significantly, that of the United States); and, crucially, international capital. The marginalization of politics and of political contestation in Northern Irish policy making, as identified by Andrade-Rocha, mirrors what James Ferguson (1990) called "techno-politics" in the "anti-politics machine" of the developmental state in Lesotho. Politics is depoliticized, reduced to a series of avowedly technical problems that require technical solutions. The dominance of "experts"— a position occupied during the Decade of Centenaries by academic historians—in providing these solutions represents attempts to circumvent contestational (party) politics and to strengthen the bureaucratic power of the state.

The techno-politics of commemoration in Northern Ireland during the Decade of Centenaries finds its ultimate expression in the Community Relations Council and Heritage Lottery Fund's "Principles for Commemoration" (table 3.1). These principles were developed in conversations between the two organizations, as well as in roundtable discussions with professional historians, media commentators, and representatives of community organizations, charities, and local government between 2010 and 2011 (CRC representative, interview with author, 2014). The principles underpin a series of guidance notes for funding bodies (CRC and HLF 2011), which in turn have influenced the way that funding is allocated for commemorative activity, including by the HLF and, to a lesser extent, the CRC. At the time of writing, since 2013 the HLF has allocated in excess of £331,000 to forty-one projects in Northern Ireland in the form of small grants of between £3,000 and £10,000 through its First World War: Then and Now grant program (HLF 2016). A number of larger grants and capital funding have also been awarded; among these, Derry's cross-community Diamond War Memorial project, received an award of £49,800 (see Hocking 2011, 2015; Myers 2013). In 2015, the Nerve Centre–led Creative Centenaries project received a grant of £182,800 from the HLF. The refurbishment of the HMS *Caroline* in Belfast in time for the centenary of 1916's Battle of Jutland was funded by the HLF to the tune of £12 million, the largest such grant ever given by the organization (BBC News 2014b).

Table 3.1. Principles for Commemoration

---

1. Start from the historical **facts**;
2. Recognise the **implications** and **consequences** of what happened;
3. Understand that different **perceptions** and **interpretations** exist; and
4. Show how events and activities can deepen **understanding** of the period.
All to be seen in the context of an '**inclusive and accepting society**'.

Source: CRC and HLF 2013

Other funders and organizers of commemorative activity, including Belfast City Council, have attested to the importance of the CRC and HLF principles in determining whether and how to finance, host, or otherwise facilitate commemorative programs during the Decade of Centenaries (BCC Good Relations Unit representative, interview with author, 2014). In sum, and as suggested by a respondent at the CRC:

> People *have* been using the principles: funders in local authorities; Good Relations programmes who've been major funders of activity; the Heritage Lottery Fund, who've been major funders; and ourselves. [We] ask people how they *specifically* address the principles. Now there are a few aspects to that: (a) are you actually giving people *solid* information?; (b) where is your attempt at showing different perspectives?; (c) how are you doing that in a way that is "accepting and inclusive" . . . are you trying to have *some* dialogue? And I think that has *really* influenced the programming that people have done. (CRC representative, interview with author, 2014)

Central to much of this programming has been an implicit assertion that the (alleged) fact of the First World War's "shared sacrifice" lends its violence a certain legitimacy, which that of the more recent conflict in Northern Ireland conspicuously lacks (Jeffrey 2013, 2015).

"SHARED DIFFERENCES" OR "GULF BETWEEN NEIGHBOURS"?

As Edna Longley (2001, 230) has suggested, in (Northern) Ireland "commemoration now functions as a contradictory site of conflict and conflict resolution." At the root of this contradiction is a latent and often unacknowledged conflict between two divergent and distinctly political ways of conceiving the meaning of violence in "the past" and its (potential) relationship to peace-building. This conflict is demonstrated, for example, in contradictions between approaches in two 2013 good relations policy documents: *T:BUC* and the draft "Agreement among the Parties of the Northern Ireland Executive on Parades, Select Commemorations and Related Protests; Flags and Emblems; and Contending with the Past."

In 2013, under the terms of *Together: Building a United Community*, a panel composed of representatives of the five parties in the Northern Ireland Executive was established to address a number of unresolved and intractable issues in Northern Ireland's peace process, namely, parades, select commemorations, and related protests; flags and emblems; and contending with the past. The panel was cochaired by the American diplomat Richard Haass and Meghan O'Sullivan, a Harvard professor. By the end of its negotiations in December 2013, it had failed to reach agreement. However, a draft version was published unilaterally by the cochairs on 31 December 2013 and its enduring influence is clearly evident in both 2014's Stormont House Agreement and 2015's "A Fresh Start: The Stormont Agreement and Implementation Plan."[13] Under the heading "Contending with the Past," the draft agreement makes this bleak observation:

> Despite the desire of most citizens to look ahead and move forward, Northern Ireland remains constrained by its past. . . . The past continues to permeate our government, institutions, and people. It

creates mistrust among leaders at all levels of society who wish to continue tackling problems of the modern world. It maintains the gulf between neighbours who pass each other in the street or in the shops. Without facing this issue, Northern Ireland and its people will find it challenging to achieve the future its people desire and deserve. (Panel of Parties in the NI Executive 2013, 19)

Notably absent in this formulation of the "problem" of the past is the assertion in the parent *T:BUC* document that "exploring our past can be enormously helpful in building a better future" (OFMDFM 2013, 94). Likewise, the *exclusive* onus on the violence of the thirty-year period between 1969 and 1998 in the section "Contending with the Past" in the Haass-O'Sullivan document is in stark contrast to *T:BUC*'s suggestion that "our most recent past is only *one* aspect of an intricate and complex history" (OFMDFM 2013, 93; emphasis added). In Haass-O'Sullivan, as is often the case in broader political discourses in Northern Ireland, "the past" is a euphemism for "the Troubles" (which is itself a euphemism).

This suggests that the past per se is not as important in defining Northern Ireland's present as it is often assumed or argued to be. As O'Leary and McGarry have suggested:

The salience of [the Troubles'] 'historical causes' can be grossly exaggerated. The present conflict is not an exotic rave from the grave of Europe's past, a 'replay' of twelfth-century feudal wars of conquest, or a 'repeat' for modern television audiences of seventeenth-century wars of religion. . . . There are 'historical' dimensions to the conflict, but many of its key characteristics and causes are modern rather than archaic, and can be seen as part of the processes of 'modernization' which have not stopped in the wider world—despite fashionable assertions to the contrary. (1996, 55)

In other words, "the past" is not the cause or source of the conflict in and about Northern Ireland. Rather, it is this conflict that conditions how and why the past is received and enacted in the present (cf. Jarman 1997). Specifically, narratives on violence in the past are tied to particular ideas about politics in the present. And within the realm of policy as it pertains to the Decade of Centenaries, not all violence is created equal.

Just three months after David Cameron had revealed his plans for a national commemoration that would "ensure that the sacrifice and service of one hundred years ago is still remembered in a hundred years' time" (*Guardian* 2012), his secretary of state for Northern Ireland, Theresa Villiers, was interviewed by the BBC at the height of the flag protests. Condemning the violence of the rioters as reminiscent of that of the Troubles, she insisted, "Northern Ireland is in a global race for investment and jobs and we need to be projecting the reality of a forward-looking, modern Northern Ireland, not one which is tied up in the kind of conflict which is associated with its past rather than its present" (BBC News 2013b). As part of the same political project in Northern Ireland—itself a reflection of the broader national(ist) projects of subsequent Conservative governments in the United Kingdom and Fine Gael–led government in Ireland (Mycock 2014a, 2014b)—one conflict in Northern Ireland's past is earmarked for active and ongoing commemoration and another for deliberate and purposeful forgetting.

At the heart of this Janus-faced approach to the the past in Northern Ireland is a unifying philosophy, a "reductive fallacy," which is that "the 'wrong' historiography *causes* political instability" (Regan 2013, 23; emphasis added), and conversely, therefore, that the "correct" historiography can help to promote and protect the prevailing political and economic institutions in postconflict Northern Ireland. This claim and associated espousals as to the importance of historical fact in depoliticizing the past is reflected in current policy. Fact, and its accumulation, is seen to hold the key to reconciliation. Haass-O'Sullivan, for instance, claims that "creating opportunities to retrieve as much information as possible is essential to assisting victims and their families and to contending with the past. Only through gaining the fullest possible picture of what happened during the conflict and why can Northern Ireland begin to constructively confront its past" (Panel of Parties in the NI Executive 2013, 30). The attendant proposal for an Independent Commission for Information Retrieval (ICIR), under the directorship of an Implementation and Reconciliation Group (IRG), in Haass-O'Sullivan has echoes of the South African postapartheid process of Truth and Reconciliation (Posel 2008), guaranteeing a limited form of legal amnesty for those who come forward to provide the requested information.[14] Among the draft agreement's proposed instruments for contending with the past is an "internal unit to analyse patterns or themes" emerging from the evidence garnered through the ICIR as well as from other relevant documentation, including public records and evidence from legacy cases examined by a new and independent Historical Investigations Unit (HIU). Crucially, "as themes are agreed or identified, the themes unit will analyse them rigorously, on the strict basis of the evidence in front of them, and without political influence from within or outside the unit." In addition, a proposed Historical Timeline Group composed of independent academic historians would work to produce a definitive "factual chronology of the conflict," a "factual resource for the work of other projects relating to the past" (Panel of Parties in the NI Executive 2013, 32–38).

The proposals in both Haass-O'Sullivan and Stormont House on the issue of the past have undertones of those made during the talks process by Arkiv, a group of professional historians formed during (and in response to) the talks process in 2013. In their submission to the Panel of Parties chaired by Haass and O'Sullivan, Arkiv (2013) called for a "commission of historical clarification," to be "appointed by both governments and consisting of British and Irish historians under the chairmanship of an independent and internationally recognised historian and provided with access to British, Northern Irish and Irish archives." The group warned, in particular, against processes for dealing the past that are "heavily biased towards state violations and crime." "These are legitimate areas of inquiry," they continued, "but they are dwarfed in historic significance, morally and politically, by the actions of paramilitaries." They concluded their submission with the assertion that "the current impasse and focus on an overarching approach facilitates the multiplication of lies about the past and, in so doing, contributes to the validation of political movements in the present. . . . [A] commission of historical clarification can work to circumscribe the past and fence-in historical narratives thereby helping to remove them from the political frontline" (Arkiv 2013). The depoliticization of the past through the rigorously historicist process of clarification will finally "liberate us all from [it]" (Arkiv 2014). In other words, fact, liberated from its historical and political context, has the potential in turn to liberate Northern Ireland from the politico-historical conditions under which that fact was produced. "The truth," it is argued, will set Northern Ireland free.

However, in his study of the South African Truth and Reconciliation Commission (TRC) on which the Haass-O'Sullivan proposals are modeled, Richard Wilson (2001) has demonstrated the limited transformative power of the truth per se, arguing that the revelation of truths about past violence divorced from a wider and deeper analysis of the social, economic, and cultural conditions under which that violence took place—and in which those truths were produced—is ultimately psychologically and emotionally unsatisfactory, for victims and perpetrators alike (see also Schinkel 2010). Identifying what actually happened, in and of itself, does not address the need—expressed by Arkiv and the other architects of Haass-O'Sullivan and Stormont House—to understand *why* it happened.[15] Furthermore, Arkiv's espoused commitment to objectivism belies the fact that theirs is, however ethically valid and morally justifiable, nonetheless an intrinsically political position, one that implies a particular, subjective (and disparaging) view of the forms of political violence that prevailed in Northern Ireland between 1969 and 1998 and on contemporary forms of party politics and political identification that continue to be shaped through reference to that violence (McGarry and O'Leary 1995; Little 2006, 2008; Rolston 2010).

In the final analysis, Arkiv's proposal amounts to an expression of, and acts to reinforce, a core revisionist argument—that extrastate violence, and the form of political conflict in and about Northern Ireland since 1969, was, and remains, illegitimate—which, despite the group's protestations to the contrary, has become dominant and even hegemonic in politics and policy making as it pertains to Northern Ireland (see Perry 2010; Rolston 2010; cf. Gkotzaridis 2001). Indeed, the prevailing, euphemistic referral to the conflict in and about Northern Ireland in terms of "the past" or "the Troubles" rather than of "war" is itself an indication of the preeminence of this argument in official political discourses in Britain and Ireland, and a demonstration that these discourses remain "profoundly uncomfortable, not just with the existence of an odious little war on [their] doorstep, but with small-scale war more generally" (Smith 1999, 91; see also Cramer 2006, 63). Rooted in a revisionist historiography that is founded on the dismissal of what Edwards and McGrattan (2011) have termed "terroristic narratives,"[16] the aim of the propaganda of peace and of its public transcript on commemoration during the Decade of Centenaries is ultimately to deny validation to or justification for the conflict in and about Northern Ireland since 1969, and the violence of its nonstate actors in particular.[17] As a consequence, and as Jeffrey (2013, 123) notes, "one thing largely absent (to our great cost) from what we might call the 'civil war' of the Troubles is any sustained sense that shared military experience on each side of the conflict might have any sort of reconciling potential."

By contrast, properly understood, and given appropriate custodianship, the violence of the period 1912–22/23—and particularly that of the 1914–18 Great War—is lauded in the Decade of Centenaries' public transcript as instructive and as holding precisely the reconciliatory potential that the violence of the Troubles is perceived as so notably lacking. In an op-ed in the *Belfast Telegraph* in 2011, Duncan Morrow, then CRC chief executive, and Paul Mullan, head of the HLF in Northern Ireland contended:

> In Northern Ireland, political anniversaries are usually associated with moments of contention. Remembering is something we do apart; a competition for dominance, not a chance to re-examine evidence. Every event is a matter of partisan celebration or a deliberate avoidance, with a risk that every commemoration is a re-run of the division of the past. . . . In Northern Ireland, we have sometimes been better at myth making than history. . . . [But] with so many events in the next Decade, we have a real opportunity to turn Northern Ireland into a centre of tolerance, pluralism and robust learning rather than the usual inter-community ding-dong where nobody learns much but we restate our old positions and make some new wounds. (Morrow and Mullan 2011, 6)

With a view to maximizing and seizing upon the reconciliatory potential of the Decade, the CRC and HLF convened a one-day conference—titled "Remembering the Future"—at Belfast City Hall in March 2011. In his introductory speech at this conference, the historian Éamon Phoenix (2011, 15) affirmed that "as a fundamental principle it is essential that any [commemorative] programmes dealing with 1912–1922 should reflect the historical facts, seek to explode myths and propagandistic distortions and place events in their broadest historical perspective." The central claim that marries the argument put forward by Morrow and Mullan in their *Belfast Telegraph* editorial with the exhortation in Phoenix's speech is that, properly understood, history can pre-vent or provide a remedy to the types of conflict in Northern Ireland that have been caused by memory. This, in turn, is reflected in the CRC and HLF's "Principles for Commemoration," the foremost of which is to start from the historical facts. As my respondent at the CRC argued, "This history *matters* and we need to think about it and to see it, and it matters just because in some ways it put us onto separate train tracks. But the issue around that is that, well, history doesn't actually *work* like that, you know, that's not actually what the historical record will say and that's not actually how people lived it at the time" (interview with author, 2014).

The (peace-building) project of correcting the avowed aberrations in the historical record that have rendered it divided rather than shared is thus presented as an exercise in empiricist objectivity: in starting from the historical facts. In practice, however, this project actually requires that certain facts—in particular, the names and number of Irish National-ists who fought in the British Army between 1914 and 1918—are tacitly or even actively privileged not only as more reconciliatory but also, therefore, truer than others. This privileging is couched in the language of "recovery," based on the (contestable) premise that, in what Phoenix might term a propagandistic distortion of the historical record, British military service by Irish Nationalists during the First World War was airbrushed out of official history on both sides of the Irish border. An emerging orthodoxy in mainstream Irish memorial and historical narrativization—that is, that which was forgotten is now, at long last, remembered—is based on a (willfully) selective reading of the history of First World War commemoration in Ireland (see Jeffrey 2000; Johnson 2007; Yeates 2014; Hanley 2015). More fundamentally, this orthodoxy denies that the foundations of the twentieth-century Irish Republican project—the very roots of the Irish state itself—are to be found in a deliberate rejection of British imperialism in general and of Irish in-volvement in the First World War in particular. Irish Nationalism's rela-tionship with the Great War is marked less by the passivity of what F. X. Martin called collective amnesia and more by Guy Beiner's (2013) active process of social forgetting.

Carolyn Nordstrom and JoAnn Martin (1992, 14) assert that the only fact in war, the only biological reality, is that "wounds bleed and people die" (see also Eltringham 2003). Beyond this biological reality there is only debate and interpretation. Why were (or are) people prepared to kill or be killed? Were (or are) these reasons justified? What long-term or ongoing meaning does their violence possess? These questions belong definitively to the realm not of the empirical but of the ethical, the interpretive and the political. Different individuals or groups may reasonably hold differing or divergent views on these questions based on the same empirical evidence. As Brian Hanley (2015) has suggested, the differences of interpretation about the legitimacy (or otherwise) of forms of past violence that exist (and in large part define the opposition) between Unionists and Nationalists cannot simply be dismissed as an "inter-community ding-dong." Divergent answers to these questions speak to and are born of fundamental normative differences between opposing political positions, which render antagonistic debate not only understandable, but inevitable. These are the sorts of disagreements that are definitive of politics as such.

As William, a historian and playwright involved in a number of commemorative projects during the Decade of Centenaries, confided to me:

> So, for example, "They all went off to the war together: the 16th and the 36th Division, we all went off, and you know what, we put aside our terrible differences and fought the Germans." This is not true. For a start, it's not true that they loved each other in the trenches. They didn't. But you know, what it turns its back on is the reality that here, during the war, it's quite clear that there was a lot of heading off in different directions. The war polarized, very, very, very much polarized opinion. (Interview with author, 2014)

Nonetheless, where it can be demonstrated that Unionists and Nationalists fought and died together on the battlefields of France or Belgium, this is heralded not only as better for community relations in the present, but as *therefore* truer than accounts that see the war (or remembrance thereof) as a source or cause of political division. This construction of sharedness as truth is based on a particular reading of recent scholarship—including, notably, Richard Grayson's *Belfast Boys: How Unionists and Nationalists Fought and Died Together in the First World War* (2009)—which is more critical and nuanced than is suggested by such reductive interpretations of it. However, much of this scholarship is itself rooted in a particular moral and political paradigm through which its evidence is both produced and analyzed (Fitzpatrick 2011; Hanley 2015, 2016): one that seeks to locate the foundations for a shared future on the battlefields of the Western Front. In sum, the suggestion is that proof of their ancestors having fought side by side in the trenches could or should function to mitigate or render illegitimate political differences between Unionists and Nationalists in the "new" Northern Ireland.

While attempts to challenge the domination of the (Northern) Irish memorial zeitgeist by more partisan or exclusive Unionist commemorations of the First World War have created space for new and reconciliatory forms of dialogue, emergent narratives on a cross-communal or shared sacrifice for freedom have also resulted in somewhat of an ethical paradox. An imperial conflict that claimed the lives of some 18 million people (Faulkner 2013, 2016), and one of the bloodiest wars in human history, has come to be celebrated by the proponents and architects of the propaganda of peace, who have lauded it, at the most reductive, as a "war that stopped a war" between Unionists and Nationalists in Ireland (BBC 2014). This in turn both reflects and reinforces the assertions made by British nationalists and Conservative politicians, including former secretary of state for education, Michael Gove (2014), that, despite (leftist) deviations in its historiography, the First World War had been a good war. Any claim that the First World War was a virtuous struggle to, for example, guarantee the freedom of small nations is not an assertion of demonstrable fact. Refuted by historians including Cambridge professor Richard Evans (2014), this is an intrinsically ideological argument that is, at best, essentially contested.

Fundamentally, there is nothing intrinsically reconciliatory about raw historical fact—names, dates, and places—before intelligible narritivization. And narrative, as demonstrated in chapter 1, is as much (and perhaps more) an issue of ethical and political judgment as it is one of evidence. Ultimately, the project of starting from the historical facts is—however understandably or beneficially—more about controlling or disciplining the narrative than it is about the purely empirical.

> It's not about "the First World War started on the 4th August," and that's the end of it. It's not those types of *facts*. It's about historical

narratives. It's about books, it's about learned scholarship, it's absolutely not about, "Do you remember the *date* of the Battle of the Boyne, or of the Battle of Poitiers?" It's not about the military history either. I mean, I suppose, we're looking at these as *politically* significant things. (CRC representative, interview with author, 2014)

During the present decade, an increasingly dominant historiography has implicitly marked certain forms of political violence and, by extension, political identification as good, right, and legitimate and others as bad and wrong. One conflict is deemed worthy of particular forms of commemoration because of its avowed role in the construction of a shared future, the other marked, in the final analysis, for purposeful forgetting.

Building a shared future is surely a laudable aim, but it nonetheless requires the delegitimization or even negation of counternarratives or interventions that challenge the particular regimes of knowledge and power inherent in the propaganda of peace's construction(s) of the past. As such, Keith Jeffrey has identified

an implicit political agenda and a clear anxiety to pre-empt any overtly . . . political commemoration and in effect fill the Irish 'commemorative space' with officially approved activities, lest something more unsuitable occur. . . . While this all provides work for historians, there is a danger that, despite the explicit obeisance to 'the historical facts' and 'high-level' scholarship, they may be drawn into officially sanctioned activities with an officially sanctioned agenda which prioritises a separate and distinct public good of inclusivity, understanding and mutual respect. (2015, 182)

In sum, the Decade of Centenaries is "epitomized by a boom in memory-making dominated by the narrative that 'we're all in this together' thus telescoping a view of history that denie[s] agency and structure of violence" (McDowell and Braniff 2014, 42). This amounts, in the final analysis, to a form of ritual and epistemological santization of the commemorative space and an exercise, therefore, in political power. Crucially, by many Loyalists, the extent of the "inclusivity, understanding and mutual respect" and the peace dividend that underpin the propaganda of peace and its new commemorative orthodoxy is passionately contested, recognized as belonging to what they have termed a culture war.

CHAPTER FOUR

Peace as Defeat

Loyalism and the Culture War in the "New" Northern Ireland

On the site of what was once one of the world's largest and busiest ship-yards stands Titanic Belfast, the impressive centerpiece in metal and glass of urban redevelopment in Belfast's Titanic Quarter (see Neill 2006; Etchart 2008; Neill, Murray, and Grist 2014). The main attraction at Titanic Belfast is its interactive "Titanic Experience" exhibit, and it has also become a popular venue for conferences, weddings, and corporate events. At a total cost of more than £100 million—including £60 million in public money—it is the most expensive tourism project ever completed in Northern Ireland. It opened its doors in March 2012, and by October 2015 it was celebrating almost two million visitors and an estimated cumulative net contribution of £105 million to the Northern Irish economy (Deloitte 2015). Titanic Belfast provides a user-friendly and entertaining point of access to Belfast's "heritage"; the "Titanic Experience" exhibit charts an evolutionary narrative from the preindustrial period to the boom years of the late nineteenth and early twentieth century, largely bypassing Belfast's blighted history of ethnonational and sectarian conflict and culminating with the city's ongoing postindustrial renaissance as a center of information technology and finance. The companies making use of Titanic Belfast's conference facilities are often multinational giants in communications or consultancy: when I sat with my mum in the café following our tour of the exhibit in 2015, we were surrounded by the internationally accented, jargon-laden chatter and coffee-cup clinking of suited executives attending a conference on "big data."

About a mile away, as the crow flies, on "Protestant" East Belfast's Newtownards Road, in the shadow of Harland and Wolff's iconic yellow cranes—Samson and Goliath—there is what at first sight appears to be a well-stocked, brightly lit, and cheerfully independent record store. Closer inspection, however, reveals that is no such thing. The storefront is false: a large sticker plastered over the window of what is an otherwise vacant commercial property (fig. 4.1). Walking down the Newtownards Road after the Orange Order's 1 July East Belfast Somme Parade in 2014, I passed several such fake storefronts: a shoemaker's, a greengrocer's, and Mahood's Bicycle Store. Counterintuitively, they only served to heighten the palpable lack of economic vitality in Inner East Belfast. Still faintly visible on parts of the road were the traces of paint bombs that I had seen being thrown at armored police Land Rovers by young, masked men during a night of rioting almost exactly one year before. Mingling with the sounds of drums and flutes that drifted from farther down the road were those in my memory of smashing glass and fireworks.

Figure 4.1. Fake shop fronts on Newtownards Road, 1 July 2014.

On 12 July 2013, a decision by the Parades Commission to prohibit the return leg of an Orange Order Twelfth of July procession along a stretch of North Belfast's Crumlin Road precipitated several nights of rioting across the city, including the one I witnessed on the Newtownards Road. These riots followed several weeks of protest and a number of violent incidents that had occurred earlier in the year, following the decision taken in late 2012 by the Belfast City Council to restrict the flying of the Union flag over Belfast City Hall to no more than eighteen designated days per year. They also preceded clashes between police and Loyalists protesting against a Republican "anti-internment" march in Belfast City Centre on the evening of 9 August, in which more than fifty police officers were injured. These violent incidents were all read by my Loyalist interlocutors as the result of, or as expressions of what they view as, the same overarching culture war that is currently being waged against Loyalism in the "new" Northern Ireland.

The East Belfast mural shown in figure 4.2 displays a litany of Loyalist grievances (couched in the language of demands) plotted against perceived Republican political and economic gains. Murals often come and go in Belfast's constantly shifting symbolic landscape (see McCormick and Jarman 2005),[1] but the sentiments expressed here have continued to fester in the Loyalist political-cultural zeitgeist. As Paul, a young activist with the Loyalist Progressive Unionist Party, put it to me in quite stark terms:

> We would think that, or there's a perception that, we're suffering at the hands of a culture war. . . . We've agreed to peace, we fought hard for peace. And yet, none of our communities are experiencing the peace dividend that we were promised. We're seeing that our cultural traditions are being blocked, inhibited. Our communities are suffering high unemployment, anti-social behaviour, drugs, [and] there's no inward investment. (Interview with author, 2015)

As was rendered readily apparent by the flag protests, a substantive section of the so-called Loyalist community perceive the peace afforded by the Good Friday Agreement as a form of defeat. A survey conducted for the BBC in 2013 found that a majority—some 53 percent—of

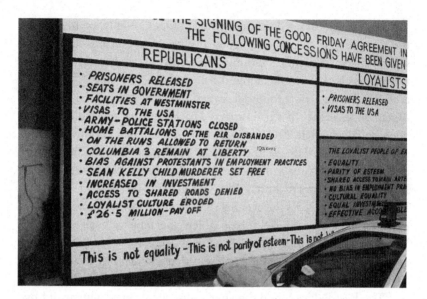

Figure 4.2. "Concessions Given" mural, Vicarage Street, Belfast.

"working-class" Unionists believed that the current political system actively favors Nationalism over Unionism (see Ipsos MORI 2013).[2] More
meaningfully, narratives of loss and decline prevail in everyday conversations, both on- and off-line, with and between Loyalists. In a report on
the flag protests published by Queen's University Belfast, one interviewee, asked whether she would describe the environment in which she
had grown up as "Peace time," responded, "Peace? I haven't grown up in
Peace. You can't live in a peaceful society when your national territory is
constantly under threat. When your identity is constantly under threat
and when your life is subsequently under threat" (quoted in Nolan et al.
2014, 97). Peace-building has served to turn on its head the Unionist hegemony that was the foundation of the Northern Irish polity. Whether
or not the Orange State (Farrell 1980; See also Buckland 2001) ever actually provided Loyalists with either material or psychological security,
(See Finlayson 2001; Mulvenna 2015), its erosion and transformation has
nonetheless resulted in an ontological crisis for Loyalism. Peace is perceived as threatening. This threat has physical manifestations, but it is
more profoundly existential: it is an issue of identity or of being.

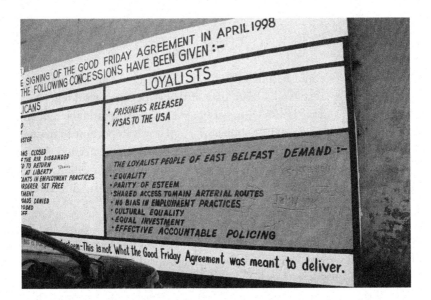

In this chapter, I examine the nexus between socioeconomics, identity politics, and culture in "postconflict" Northern Ireland as it is understood, experienced, and negotiated by Loyalists. First, I explore further the meanings and experiences of Loyalism and its foundational claim of loyalty, arguing that the intersection of social memory and political economy is central to it. I then assess how this claim of loyalty functions under conditions of postindustrialism and consociational politics, predicated on institutions and norms such as parity of esteem and equality. Finally, I examine how and why, viewed through the Loyalist lens, political, social, and economic transformation in postconflict Northern Ireland is understood as a culture war. I suggest that this is representative, ultimately, of the fear at the center of Loyalist "knowledge" about "Republican hatred." This knowledge is the means by which Loyalists are able to make sense of and confront the complex and myriad sociocultural, political, and economic trends that define the new Northern Ireland. This discussion of the culture war provides the necessary precursor to my examination in chapter 5 of why and how Loyalist commemoration functions as a site of ideological rededication, identity reinforcement, and political contestation in a context defined for Loyalists by socioeconomic insecurity, cultural dislocation, and alienation.

"LOYALTY" AND THE POLITICS OF FEAR

Loyalism is contested: definitions . . . , what it's about, what it's for,
what it's against. And a large part of that is between working-class
Loyalists and big house Unionists, between Loyalists and the media,
between Loyalists and Republicans. . . . [I]t was important to maintain solidarity and a united front against Republicanism, and I think
that has had the impact of stunting, to a degree, our thinking, our
development, our ideas, our ideology, our politics. (Paul, interview
with author, 2015)

As I suggested in chapter 2, "Loyalism" is a term imbued with multiple
layers of political and sociological meaning. It can be portrayed simply
as a form of hard-line Unionism or as a militant expression of sectarian
and political Protestantism (Bruce 1994). It has perhaps most commonly
been associated with the violent and (often seemingly pathological)
paramilitarism of the UVF and the UDA or the "triumphalism" and ethnic chauvinism of Loyal Order parades (Bruce 1992, 1994; Bryan 2000;
Taylor 2000; McAuley 2010, 2016; Smithey 2011). Perhaps the defining
image of the Loyalist in the popular imagination is that of the tattooed
and bald weightlifter: an image that has been greatly influenced by the
ultraviolent, hypermasculine, far Right politics and gangsterism of
Johnny Adair's UDA C Company (cf. Baker 2015; Wood 2006). Violence,
sectarianism, and bigotry are undoubtedly among Loyalism's defining
features, but it defies such neat categorization.

The chief factor that distinguishes Loyalism from wider Unionism
is class. As identified by numerous scholars of Loyalism (see, e.g., Bell
1990; McAuley 2010, 2016; Ramsey 2011; Reed 2015) and usually affirmed by Loyalists themselves, very generally, "the term Loyalist places
someone as working class, while the Unionist label positions someone as
upper class" (Gallaher 2007, 31). In this postulation, "class" is both a
socioeconomic—in a straightforwardly materialist sense—and a cultural
label, representing an interaction between materiality, discourse, and
practice. It is a term imbued with what Bourdieu (1984) identified as
both implicit and explicit judgments on particular tastes and aesthetic
forms. In his polemic *Chavs* (2011), Owen Jones argues that the working

class is demonized in contemporary political and public discourses in the United Kingdom, the very term "working class" itself used to signify particular forms of deviance and violence in a way that marginalizes or justifies the vulnerability, alienation, and economic precariousness of those to whom the label is ascribed. In Northern Ireland, where the lived reality of being working class is also defined by particular forms of sectarian habitus (Bell 1990), "Loyalist" has been employed as a term of derision, including by the social media satirists Loyalists Against Democracy (LAD) during and since the flag protests of late 2012 and early 2013 (see Nolan et al. 2014). Bill, a senior member of the PUP in East Belfast, argued:

> I think it's a perjorative term. For me, the label "Loyalism" is a classist term. It's Unionists who are prepared to be violent. You know, and it makes clear water from the nice constitutional Unionists, the nice constitutional Unionist who won't make any waves and the ones who have guns! But Sinn Féin usually have it about right: they talk about *Unionist* paramilitaries. And they're probably more accurate than the term "Loyalist." (Interview with author, 2014)

For Bill, "Loyalist" had become an intrinsically classist and derogatory label and as such should be abandoned. Others insisted that the term ought to be reappropriated and rehabilitated. "Loyalism" is therefore a term fraught with contestation even among those who define themselves as Loyalist.

McGovern and Shirlow appositely observed:

> The 'Loyalty' that is so substantial in the construction of the Collective [Loyalist] Self can be given to institutions or groups such as [political parties], the British state or paramilitary organisations, ideals or principles or to a range of communal and inter-personal relationships (neighbours, family, fellow-workers). What is important too is that through the enunciation of allegiance these miscellaneous loci of self-identity can be fused: loyalty to the state, to the Union, to the local community and the family blend to mean one and the same thing, the 'British/Protestant way of life'. (1997, 179)

Thus, "I am loyal" can come to serve as a sufficient or self-referential in-
dicator of identity—collapsing multiple markers into a single claim or
affirmation—with little perceptible need to define precisely to whom or
to what (cf. Finlayson 1997). However, despite this process of fusion,
what McGovern and Shirlow describe as "miscellaneous loci of self-
identity" can and often do exist in a fractious and hierarchical relationship with one another. Each of my interlocutors identified a different
one of these "loci" as the primary object of their loyalty. This helps to
explain the contested and ambiguous nature of what Miller (1978) identified as Ulster Loyalism's conditionality (see also Ruane and Todd 1996).
The irony of avowedly loyal protesters engaging in street battles with
the "forces of the crown" during the riot I witnessed on the Newtownards Road would seem to confirm the conditional nature of loyalty to
the state in particular.

The label "conditional" implies that in the final analysis loyalty is
contractual: an issue of agency. But this does not fully capture its structural complexities. If loyalty were (wholly) conditional, then ultimately
Loyalists could presumably decide, either individually or en masse, to
revoke it completely. The advocacy of varying versions of independence
for Ulster by some Loyalists is indicative of the potential for this even-
tuality, but the option of independence was not favored by any of my
Loyalist interlocutors. Historically, it has not had a particularly wide or
popular following beyond sections of the UDA and other fringe and ad
hoc political organizations (Wood 2006; McAuley 2010). Loyalty is generally described as something, like family, that one does not simply
choose. Bill compared the relationship between Loyalists and the British
state to that between Frankenstein and his monster and a child and its
abusive parent.

> Basically, the Northern Protestants have always been an embarrass-
> ment to the [British] establishment, and to whatever government's
> in power. It's almost like Ireland is England's Frankenstein, you
> know, turned on her and haunting her! So they have a moral obliga-
> tion, and I think that is all that they have, and also the consequences
> in Ireland of what might happen if they withdraw without a final
> settlement. And that's the only thing . . . I mean, [former Secretary
> of State for Northern Ireland Patrick] Mayhew said that Britain has

no selfish or strategic interest in Northern Ireland. And I believe he's right! And they never had for a long, long time. . . . Northern Ireland has been an embarrassment: the Ulster Protestants are an unwanted child, really, that won't go away, that hangs on tight to its abusive mother's apron strings. (Interview with author, 2014)

Both similes imply a particular lack of agency on the part of Loyalists in their relationship with the object of their loyalty: variously creator, master, or parent. Bill also hints at the perceived neglect at the heart of this one-way relationship. Trying to grapple with what "loyalty" could possibly mean under such ambiguous and apparently unrequited terms as these, I quite exasperatedly inquired of Gary, a PUP member and member of the Territorial Army living in the Village area of South Belfast, "So according to [everything you've just told me], the British state apparently has never done a fucking thing for you, so why maintain . . . "

G: It's not about the British state. The British state has done fuck all for someone living on some shit-hole street in London. But there's a difference between identity and government. And actually, the reason I describe myself as a Loyalist . . . I don't describe myself as loyal to the political establishment, I'm loyal to the idea of the United Kingdom, but—

JE: But what is that if it isn't an affinity with a particular state? Because the United Kingdom is a nation-state. The "state" bit is important, surely? And if we both agree that that state has no intrinsic interest in protecting the poor and the vulnerable *anywhere* in the UK, least of all in Northern Ireland . . .

G: [Interrupting] There's a difference between loyalty to the nation or the state and loyalty to an idea. My Britishness is not based on who is in power. It's not based on the Conservatives being in government or Labour being in government, or the Green Party, or whoever. It's deeper and more fundamental than that. And what's more, I don't believe they have a right to determine my identity either. I suppose it's the old UVF mentality coming to the fore: "Fuck you. You're not going to tell me I'm not British!" That's essentially what they did. They were basically telling the British government, "You will not tell us whether we're British or not."

JE: But there's such . . .

G: Irony? I know, it's a great irony, I love it.

JE: But it's *so* incongruous! "You, Britain, the British government cannot force us *not* to be British!" It's *such* a weird argument!

G: It's great, isn't it!

JE: It's bizarre! It doesn't make sense . . .

G: [Pauses] It is not for the state, or for Labour, or the Conservatives to tell us who or what we are.

JE: But it *is*! If they want rid, they'll get rid!

G: That's separate. The border could go tomorrow. It's not gonna change who I *am*.

For Gary, the loyalty at the core of his identity was seemingly, and contradictorily, defined by its opposition to the British state or "establishment," and potentially even the democratic will of the United Kingdom's wider citizenry. The idea that their identity is embattled—beset by the belligerence of Irish Republicanism on the one hand and the ambivalence of middle-class Unionists, the British state, and the wider British national community on the other—is central to Loyalists' self-identification as members of a "a beleaguered frontier group ultimately dependent on its own sources for its security" (Bell 1987, 165). As it was put by Mike, "In this community, in Northern Ireland, the predicament that we have here is that we're constantly striving to be British, to prove our Britishness. It's something that, if you were born in . . . Ilford, say, you take for granted." "Or even where I come from?," I asked. "Yeah, *you* take for granted that you're British. *My* Britishness is fought for here."

That this made their "Britishness" more "dearly held" and (thereby) authentic than its mainland varieties—including that at the root of my lived identity—is another core tenet of Loyalism. The suggestion is that where their ongoing fight to maintain their Britishness has contributed to Loyalists' remembering what it really means to be British, the lack of a comparable struggle in the rest of the United Kingdom has contributed to a cultural laziness that caused mainlanders to forget. I return to this relationship between conflict, memory, and the construction of an "authentic" identity in subsequent chapters. For now it is sufficient to

say that many Loyalists see themselves as the last defenders of an authentically British identity and morality that has been willfully neglected
or abandoned elsewhere in the United Kingdom.

Perhaps paradoxically, and in ways that are discussed below, it is
their loyalty that determines Loyalists' key distinction and thereby
alienation from mainland Britain and mainstream British culture(s).
This, in part, determines their vulnerability in relation to the state.
Some argue explicitly that it makes them a soft target for draconian policies that have served to criminalize their loyalty and, thereby, their very
identity. When, following the flag protests of 2012 and 2013, some three
hundred Loyalists were convicted for offenses that included rioting, obstructing traffic, disorderly behavior, taking part in unsanctioned processions, and assaulting police officers (Nolan et al. 2014, 122), "their
only crime was loyalty" emerged as a common refrain among their
friends and supporters on social media platforms. Likewise, *My Only
Crime Was Loyalty* was the title given by Jamie Bryson, one of the flag
movement's most prominent (and self-styled) leaders, to his self-
published account of the protests and his subsequent arrest and trial.
Joshua, a UVF former prisoner from East Belfast, explained to me how
the flag protests in particular had brought to a head his long-running
internal grappling with loyalty, what it means and whether it is even possible in such a nonreciprocal relationship as that between Loyalists and
the state to which they proffer their loyalty:

> The British government'll sell you out tomorrow if they get a
> chance. And always will and always have, y'know? And people can't
> see it! What is this loyalty about? I can't grasp it. At one time I
> could. But now, when you really sit down to look at it . . . [Pause]
> You know, the government would sell us out tomorrow. And [loy-
> alty] is just a form of insecurity. (Interview with author, 2014)

The connection between loyalty and insecurity suggested by Joshua
is reflected in numerous studies of Ulster Loyalism since the late 1980s.
Scholars of Loyalism have identified what is commonly referred to as a
transition in its defining political psychology during the twentieth and
early twenty-first century from one of (sectarian) triumphalism to one
of defeatism (see, e.g., Finlay 2001; Spencer 2008; McAuley 2010). As

though to demonstrate the role of academics in the coproduction of the social reality they study, many Loyalists I spoke with cited this body of scholarship as evidence to validate their experience of the period of "peace" since the Good Friday Agreement of 1998 as one of defeat(ism). While this arguably represents somewhat of a transformation in Loyalist cultural-political consciousness since the advent of the peace process (Beiner 2007a), it is also arguable that both supremacism and defeatism are at work in the construction of postconflict Ulster Loyalist identity. Rather than one having superseded the other, they are better thought of as two sides of the same coin. The relationship between them is defined by fluctuation, even in the course of one conversation, but ultimately they are best characterized as mutually constitutive.

Take, for instance, the maxim No Surrender, which is omnipresent in contemporary forms of Loyalist cultural production: it appeared on numerous banners during the flag protests and in speeches at the Civil Rights Camp at Twaddell Avenue,[3] and one of my interlocutors even used the abbreviation "NS" to sign off text messages to me. The slogan has its roots in Ulster Protestant social memory of the late seventeenth-century Siege of Derry (see McBride 1997). It is celebratory, lauding the tenacity of the Protestant community and their triumph over a treacherous (Catholic) Other. But it is simultaneously an expression of a perceived weakness in the face of an ongoing existential threat. As Cohen (2007, 957) suggests, "At its heart, the basic structure is the story of withstanding a surrounding enemy. It blends a mix of heroism, sacrifice and critically, a sense of victimisation at the hands of a morally (religiously) inferior and debased opponent." Intrinsic to Loyalist identity is this memorial dialectic between triumph and trauma, strength and vulnerability, exhibited in a narrative that traces from the "massacres" of Protestants in 1641 and 1798 through the Siege of Derry, the Battle of the Boyne, and the Battle of the Somme to events of the more recent conflict, including the IRA bombing of Enniskillen on Remembrance Sunday 1987 and the Shankill Bomb of 1993 (McBride 2001; Beiner 2007a; Robinson 2010).

As indicated in chapter 1, this is not to suggest that these events or "the past" itself provide a sufficient explanation for the psychosocial, political, or economic trajectory that Loyalism has taken. Rather, their social memory—their ghosts—provide a framework through which Loyalists are able to understand and explain their situation in a present defined by particular political, socioeconomic, and cultural processes and the relations that sustain them. These processes and Loyalists' interpretations of them are rooted in notions such as community or identity, but these also exist in a symbiotic relationship with the more brute matter of political economy. Quite explicitly, when I asked Gary about whether he would ever accept and feel accepted in a United Ireland, he responded, "I suppose all this shit about which nation-state I belong to has less to do with my identity than . . . it's all class stuff. It's about poverty, it's about deprivation. I mean, I'd probably get about the same in the Republic of Ireland, but my identity would be targeted *as well*. I suppose it's the lesser of two evils for me." Our conversation continued.

JE: A lot of the complaints you're making, a lot of them are about class issues: about deprivation, education, and then you're also saying that the institutions of the state in Northern Ireland, and the wider United Kingdom, are all geared towards trying to strip away your sense of Britishness?

G: But there is a belief that within the state that I belong to, should it get sufficiently far enough, I can politically challenge that.

JE: Which you couldn't do in a United Ireland?

G: Well, I suppose I could, but the agenda that would be forced upon me. . . . I understand what you're saying, but there's a difference for me between what the UK, as a nation-state is doing, and what Republicans are doing. The state isn't actively bothered about my identity. It doesn't give two shits about it. It's more to do with realpolitik, with the politics of capitalism. Whereas Republicans' attacks are against my cultural identity, against *me* as a human being. The British government don't give two shits if I bang a drum and play a flute, as long as I do it with a minimum of fuss. As long as they don't have to waste any money on me, they'll be quite happy with that. As long as I conform, to a degree. You know, we can all have our surface cultural identities, as long as underneath it we are conformists.

Conversations in which I participated at the Orange Hall or band hall following any given commemorative parade were often, perhaps usually, not straightforwardly concerned with the question of Northern Ireland's constitutional future per se. Rather, they were commonly rooted in and related to more material concerns—finding and keeping a job, low wages, unfair and zero hours contracts, the experience of being on "the bru,"[4] and the difficulties associated with these economic realities. Rob, for instance, complained that his low wage meant that he couldn't afford to buy or maintain a car, forcing him to walk the several miles to and from his job in a warehouse each day. This work was irregular and informal, and on any given day he might arrive at the warehouse to find that he was not needed for that shift. Rob ascribed his experience of precariousness (see Standing 2011) in the labor market to the preferential treatment afforded to Catholics, and he couched this in the terms of a particular symbolic conflict (see Harrison 1995). Rob complained about what he called the banning—more through convention and "peer pressure" than formal policy—of wearing the poppy in his workplace as demonstrative of a system of political correctness, which meant that Catholics constituted a majority of the workers at his warehouse. For Rob, this represented the discrimination he felt he had encountered in the world of work and led to his lived experience of peace as defeat.

DEINDUSTRIALIZATION AND DISLOCATION

Capitalism doesn't care if you're loyal to it. (IRSP activist, conversation with author, 2013)

There was, I thought, often a disconnection or inconsistency between economic reality and some Loyalists' (self-)perception of it. For example, Donald would often insist on the superior work ethic of working-class Unionists in contrast to the idleness of Nationalist "scroungers." He was the first indignantly to suggest to me that Catholics are "perfectly accepting" of the queen when it is her head on the money they claim from the bru. Ironically, however, Donald himself was unemployed and on long-term state support. This idea was often repeated, and often by people who, like Donald, were themselves claiming unemployment benefits or Disability Living Allowance (DLA). The overwhelming impression was one of cognitive dissonance, of a story acknowledging its lack of foundation in its very articulation. The dichotomy between Protestant "'workers" and Catholic "shirkers" is patently false, in a way in which many Loyalists, including those who continue to propound the myth, are all too aware. Again, it reflects the dualism inherent in the story Loyalism tells itself about itself. On the one hand, Protestants are superior to Catholics because of their superior work ethic. On the other hand, they are economically vulnerable because their jobs have been usurped by those very same Catholics. In either case, the Catholic Other is described in terms of the threat it represents and signifies Loyalists' insecurity about material processes over which they have little influence.

As Finlay (2001, 16) intimates, "Protestant supremacism, whether or not it originated in the seventeenth century settler *ideologies*, had a *material* basis in the uneven development of capitalism in Ireland and articulated ideas about modernity and progress that had currency beyond Northern Ireland. By the same token, protestant defeatism, in some degree, expresses a loss of confidence in the modernist project" (emphasis added). This uneven development has been marked by Ulster's rise and fall as the British Empire's industrial heartland. Throughout the nineteenth century, heavy industry, notably shipbuilding, rope making, and textiles, came to play an increasingly dominant role in the economy of the northeastern corner of Ireland. By 1900, "the area around Belfast had . . . become one of the most industrialized places in the world, and one of the most prosperous regions of the United Kingdom" (Rowthorn and Wayne 1988, 22). In 1911, over half of the industrial jobs in Ireland were located in Ulster, and the overwhelming majority of them were held by Protestant men (Rowthorn and Wayne 1988, 22). In the years following the establishment of the Northern Irish state, a particular accommodation between capital and labor[5] was reached through preferential treatment for Protestant workers in the job market, exclusion of Catholics from the industrial workplace, and membership of politicians, public servants, industrialists, and workers alike in the fraternal Loyal Orders and Protestant churches (Farrell 1980; Bryan 2000; Ó Murchú 2005; Kaufmann 2007).

Sugden (1996, cited in Bairner 1999, 128) has indicated the historic prevalence of a culture of "hard men" in Northern Ireland, which was central to the construction of Protestant identity before the Troubles: "Hard men" were "those who worked in shipyards, mills and factories, inhabiting a proud physically tough and exclusively male occupational culture which cast a long shadow over popular recreation outside the workplace" (see also Feldman 1991). The "cult of the hard man" was multisited, straddling the workplace, the home, and public spaces, including pubs, Orange Halls, and boxing clubs. According to Bairner (1999), the Protestant worker's existential understanding of his position in the world was located in a Calvinist reading of the dignity inherent in hard manual labor and in his being in the vanguard of the imperial economy (see also Spencer 2008).

Perhaps more accurately, *ex post*, the Protestant worker's sense of purpose is seen by Loyalists as conspicuously lacking in the present rather than having been consciously experienced in the past. In fact, while the position of the Protestant hard man was one of relative material and symbolic power, many Loyalists insist that it was never experienced as such. Severe food poverty in Belfast resulted in rioting by both Protestants and Catholics in the early 1930s (McAuley 2016), and the terminal decline of the industry on which Northern Irish relations of production hinged was apparent to bosses and workers alike as early as the late 1950s (Ó Murchú 2005). Many older Loyalists stressed to me that the poverty was equally as intense and the quality of the "two up, two down" housing on the Shankill as poor as that on the Falls in the 1960s and early 1970s; or they described the chronic sense of insecurity they felt in the face of first the Civil Rights Movement and then the IRA's bombing campaign. Mulvenna (2015) has questioned whether the Protestant working class ever constituted a "labour aristocracy" in Northern Ireland at all. During our interview, Benjamin, a youth and community worker based in the Donegall Pass area of South Belfast, insisted:

> One thing that does stick out is my parents always telling me about inequality and saying, well, there was Catholics living at the bottom end of our street, in the same type of houses as we did. So how was there an inequality there? Their house was the exact same as our

house. It was at the opposite end of the street! You know, obviously there wasn't peace walls then. (Interview with author, 2015)

Despite the important questions this raises about the extent of the Northern Irish state's historic "Orangeness," there can be little doubt that it guaranteed the material advantage and symbolic power of Protestants over Catholics, however marginally (see Whyte 1983; Buckland 2001). Arguably, however, this institutionalization of Protestant privilege was itself a manifestation of the insecurity at the heart of Unionism. By their very nature, positions of power such as that of the Protestant hard man are intrinsically imbued with a latent and constant mimetic threat from a hostile Other. The (masculine) power of hard men is "terrifyingly fragile because it does not really exist in the sense we are led to think it exists" (Kaufman 2001, 7). As Girard (1996) argues, mimetic rivalry and fear of the Other are perhaps the defining experience of those in such positions of (relative) power who must, of necessity, construct that Other over which to exercise it.

Challenges to the status quo, to established political settlements and socioeconomic arrangements, are threats to the established patterns of power that are born of them and that provide the context in which identities—a sense of belonging and a (gendered) existential understanding of one's position in the world—are constructed. Change therefore becomes synonymous with threat. According to Frankie, a seasoned community development professional and lifelong resident of the Shankill, "The seminal hymn of Unionism, 'Abide with Me,' has a line in it: 'Change and decay and all around I see/O Thou who changest not, Abide with me.' The significance of that in my head is that change and decay are linked. Change is linked with decay. [It's] not linked with dynamism and energy that keeps the world . . . ticking over" (interview with author, 2015). Paradoxically, the greater the power that accrues to the dominant individual or group, the greater the perceived risk of its usurpation and thereby the sense and experience of powerlessness. In extremis, this powerlessness manifests as what Hannah Arendt (2005 [1954], 337) termed the "will to dominate": "Out of the conviction of one's own impotence and the fear of the power of . . . others comes the will to dominate, which is the will of the tyrant." Thus understood, the supremacism of which Loyalism is accused is not only the counterpart to, but is born of a chronic sense of insecurity and powerlessness.

As McGovern and Shirlow suggest:

> A loss of socio-economic status, which is the outcome of deindustri-
> alisation and the onset of post-industrialism, is 'recognised' as an-
> other example of Catholic besiegement aided and abetted by the
> folly of a British state which fails to come to the 'assuagement' of the
> assaulted people and discharge the obligations owed to the Loyal. As
> a result, the 'Loyal People' must defend themselves. 'Defence' thus
> emerges as the primary discourse defining and mediating practice
> between the Self and Other. (1997, 179)

In line with broader trends across the United Kingdom, Northern Ireland's decline as a space of industry and empire since the Second World
War has been sharp and profound. Since the 1950s, the Northern Irish
economy has experienced an ongoing process of deindustrialization. By
the mid-1980s, employment in manufacturing in Northern Ireland was
a little over 50 percent of what it had been in 1955, with almost fifty
thousand jobs lost in the sector between 1955 and 1985 (Rowthorn and
Wayne 1988, 81). Around three quarters of these jobs had been held by
Protestant men (McGovern and Shirlow 1997, 195). The decline of employment in manufacturing has been accompanied by a concurrent rise
in employment in services and a shift in the sectoral balance of the labor
market. In Belfast, between 1961 and 1991, while employment in manufacturing declined by over 70 percent, jobs in private services increased
by 54 percent, and public sector employment increased by over 150 percent (McGovern and Shirlow 1997, 195). By the third quarter of 2015, of
729,740 "employee jobs" in Northern Ireland, 597,630 (82 percent)
were in services, compared to just 80,460 (11 percent) in manufacturing
(NISRA 2015, 7).

Owing in part to antidiscrimination legislation introduced in Northern Ireland since the advent of direct rule in the 1970s, including the Fair
Employment Acts of 1976 and 1989 and, most recently, the 1998 Northern Ireland Act,[6] increasingly, a greater share of total jobs, and particularly those in services and in the public sector, have gone to Catholics
than had been allowed under the sectarianized, industrial labor regime

of the first half of the twentieth century. While by 2013 aggregate unemployment remained higher among Catholics than Protestants, the
overall trend—particularly since the early 1990s—has been one of con-
vergence. In 1992, the unemployment rate among Catholics stood at
18 percent, 9 percentage points higher than for Protestants. By 2013, it
had halved to 9 percent, 3 percentage points higher than the 6 percent
rate among Protestants. Between 1992 and 2013, the lowest unemployment rates for both Protestants and Catholics—3 percent and 5 percent,
respectively—were recorded in 2008. However, with the onset of the
recession that followed the international financial crisis of 2008, unemployment climbed sharply for both groups (OFMDFM 2014).

According to the Northern Ireland Equality Commission's twenty-
fifth *Fair Employment Monitoring Report* (2014), while Protestants made
up the majority of the workforce in 2014, they also made up a greater
proportion of those leaving it. By contrast, since 2008, Catholics have
consistently constituted a narrow majority of job applicants (52.3 percent in 2014) and, since 2006, of appointees (51.8 percent in 2014). Protestant workers in both the public and private sectors tend to be older
than Catholics, and trends would suggest that both decreasing Protestant and increasing Catholic representation in the workforce are set to
continue in the long term. The aggregate unemployment data masks a
problem of youth unemployment for both Catholics and Protestants,
but this problem seems particularly acute for Protestants aged sixteen to
twenty-four, of whom 24 percent were unemployed in 2012, as compared to 17 percent of Catholics (Nolan 2014, 87).

Benjamin and I discussed these trends.

B: I hear young men on a constant basis saying that they don't want
to live in these communities anymore. It saddens me. But I hear it,
and I have to admit to hearing it.

JE: What reasons do they give?

B: Just that they're shit holes, they're run by paramilitaries: paramilitaries tell them what they can do and what they can't do. And the
way out is through the British Army! You know, their first calling
point is the army. . . . I suppose deprivation is still a big thing. These
areas are still suffering high deprivation levels.

JE: And have seen very little in terms of benefit from the "peace dividend"?

B: It's right on our doorstep too, you know? You know, the Gasworks, there's not too many people even from [this part of South Belfast] who's working currently in the Gasworks, literally on the doorstep . . .

JE: Oh! 'Cause presumably a lot of people from [this area] would have originally worked . . .

B: Originally worked in the Gasworks! That's where the employment of people would have been!

JE: So it's like a smack in the face . . .

B: Even in the different areas, on the Shankill, you'd the likes of Mackie's,[7] where people were going straight into . . . or in East Belfast, the shipyard. Again, people talk about equality and stuff, but yet I see every high-power position being filled by people from a Nationalist background, who aren't young! They're in their sixties. I'm not saying there wasn't inequalities, there *was* certain inequalities. But I believe that people within working-class Protestant areas are also suffering from it.

The problems identified by Benjamin are compounded by what amounts to a crisis—recognized at least as early as 2004 (see Purvis et al. 2011; PUP 2015)—in education for Protestants in general and poor or working-class Protestant boys in particular. According to data in the third *Northern Ireland Peace Monitoring Report*, authored by Paul Nolan and published by the CRC in 2014, a mere 19.7 percent of Protestant boys receiving free school meals achieve at least 5 GCSEs grade A*–C,[8] placing them a full 57 percentage points behind Northern Ireland's highest-achieving group: Catholic girls not receiving free school meals (Nolan 2014, 97). In fact, it marks them as the third lowest achieving group in terms of educational attainment across the whole of the United Kingdom, ahead only of Roma children and the children of Irish Travellers. Nolan (2014, 98) also found that while over half (52.8 percent) of Catholic girls go on to higher education, the figure is less than a third (32.4 percent) for Protestant boys.

In his seminal study, *Learning to Labour* (1977), Paul Willis revealed how an acculturated opposition to education on the part of working-class "lads" in the north of England contributed to the (re)production of their class position. Their negative and combative attitude to learning both mirrored and reproduced a broader culture of anti-intellectualism and antipathy to education on the part of white, working-class men in particular. This was a reflection, in large part, of the perceived inevitability of their finding "jobs for life" in the industrial labor force in the years following their formal education, which they therefore came to view essentially as a waste of time. Suggested by Benjamin in the exchange quoted above and elaborated by Purvis and colleagues (2011, 11) is a similar trend in which "generations of working class Protestants were heavily involved in manufacturing industry and viewed getting a trade as the main form of educational requirement. . . . Given the historic predominance of trades and apprenticeships, educational attainment via schools, colleges and universities had not been prioritised among this section of Northern Ireland's working class." Under conditions of postindustrialism,

> the collapse in this labour market and the movement towards a consumerist, service driven economy has, to a degree, left elements of the Protestant working class stranded with redundant skill-sets and abilities [and thereby an inability to] respond to new 'flexible', less regulated labour markets driven by educational qualifications and skills tied to computerisation and portable learning. The collapse of established, long-term inter-generational labour markets [has] led to some aiming for new skills but [has left] many merely feeling 'out of sync' with contemporary requirements. For the latter group, the traditional labour market was replaced by social fatalism, low wage employment, insecure casualised work, feminised labour and benefit dependency. (Purvis et al. 2011, 11)

Nonetheless, "within that group, education remains both under-valued and under-appreciated" (11).

In the wake of the protracted ethnosectarian violence, rapid deindustrialization and attendant processes of socioeconomic and cultural transformation that have characterized Northern Ireland since the mid-twentieth century, "the Protestant working class has been demor-alised on two fronts simultaneously. The Troubles—which forced Prot-estants into cultural and political 'retreat'—coincided with the massive erosion of the industrial base which had provided them with their eco-nomic security" (Hall 1994, 14–15). Processes of socioeconomic and cul-tural change are read through the memorial lens by which Loyalism and its politics of identity, defined by an ethnonational, zero-sum mimetic rivalry, are constructed. Loyalists assert that the supposed material and symbolic ascendancy of Protestants in Northern Ireland's Orange State (Farrell 1980) was never experienced by working-class Unionists as such (see also Hall 1994, 2015a; McAuley 2010, 2016; Mulvenna 2015), and on-going "transformation in the regime of accumulation which [has given] rise to the post-industrial mode of social regulation, [is understood as] the latest onslaught to hit the besieged garrison" (McGovern and Shirlow 1997, 179). Mirroring the Foucauldian notion that "politics is the continuation of war by other means" (Foucault 2004, 15), the po-litical settlement reached through the Belfast Agreement is read as a continuation of this onslaught.

Loyalists tend to a sense of fatalism. They are able to externalize their problems, attributing them to forces beyond their control or struc-tures in which they perceive themselves as having no agency. This is ex-emplary of what Bauman (2006, 2) defines as fear: "'Fear' is the name we give to our *uncertainty*: to our *ignorance* of the threat and what is to be done—what can and can't be—to stop it in its tracks—or to fight it back if stopping it is beyond our power." This central place of fear in the Loy-alist experience mirrors its role in the construction of what the anthro-pologist Stef Jansen termed the Serbian "knowledge" of his respondent, Matija—an "ultranationalist" Bosnian Serb—about "Muslim hatred." Matija's narration of himself as representing a "nationalised history of victimisation" was "inextricably related to fear: it was *knowledge through fear* and *fear through knowledge*" (Jansen 2003, 219; cf. Petersen 2002). Throughout the late twentieth and early twenty-first century, and par-ticularly in the years since the Agreement, the fear that is definitive of the Loyalist ontology has become increasingly liquid and finds its ex-pression in the so-called culture war and the "knowledge" of Republican "hatred" that has characterized postconflict Loyalist politics in North-ern Ireland.

"PARITY OF ESTEEM" OR "CULTURE WAR"?

The persecution of a majority is not easily achieved, however it can be done by layering lye upon lye, the aim is creating guilt for actions ancestors did not carry out. . . . Firstly you tell your story of social deprivation, poor housing, lack of education, voting rights, low rates of pay, etc. If your timeframe is within the Industrial Revolution you will be giving a fair representation of your people's past. However when you frame that conversation in such a way you put your ethnic identity into every part of the story, you claim those conditions for your group alone. . . . Once you have turned the target group into villains . . . you then produce laws to redress the imbalance. However it is not possible to create laws that bar you from being a Protestant, Catholic, Black, Gypsy, etc. These laws will target the activities the group carry out. These laws will also aim to affect the behaviour and look of the group. Look at the Flags and Emblems act, a case of scorched earth with Sinn Féin wanting the removal of everything rather than look at the emblems we hold dear. (Northern Ireland PUL Community Info, Politics and Debates 2015)

Speaking from the platform at the field in Derry's Wilton Park during the Orange Order's flagship demonstration on the Twelfth of July in 2013, Grand Master Edward Stevenson lamented, "Republicans are engaging in a cultural war to erode all symbols of Britishness [in Northern Ireland]. The shameful decision to strip down the union flag from Belfast City Hall, following on from the outrageous naming of a children's play park in Newry after an IRA terrorist,[9] are just some examples of the so-called 'shared future' envisaged by Sinn Féin" (BBC News 2013a). Conflict over flags, parades, and commemorative rituals and symbols in the north of Ireland is not new. The functioning of Loyal Order parades as sites of violent confrontation, and attendant concerns about their impact on law and order, predate the founding of the Northern Irish state by several decades (Jarman 1997; Bryan 2000; Nolan et al. 2014). Of course, the catalyst for the Troubles themselves was provided by one such confrontation in Derry in 1969. However, the notion of all-out culture war as characterizing contemporary politics is a particular and defining feature of post-Agreement Loyalist discourse.

Its roots are located in the Drumcree dispute of the mid- to late 1990s. Between 1995 and 2000, the annual three-way confrontation in Portadown between Orange brethren and their supporters, Garvaghy Road residents, and the police and security forces over a contested parade route attracted international media attention. The scenes of violent clashes between police and protesters I watched as a child on the 6 o'clock news provided my earliest frame of reference for the so-called marching season. For Gregory, a Loyalist originally from the Shankill Road but now living and working in East Belfast, a veteran of the Drumcree conflict, this "stand-off" and the extremes of violence that accompanied it were the deliberate contrivance of Republicans in the mid-1990s where previously no such cultural conflict had existed.[10] Evidencing this claim, Gregory alluded to a statement made at a party conference by Sinn Féin president Gerry Adams in 1997:

> Ask any activist in the north, 'did Drumcree happen by accident?', and he will tell you, 'no'. Three years of work on the lower Ormeau Road, Portadown and parts of Fermanagh and Newry, Armagh and in Bellaghy and up in Derry. Three years of work went into creating that situation and fair play to those people who put the work in. They are the type of scene changes that we have to focus on and develop and exploit. (*News Letter* 2014)

According to Gregory, the "banning" of the parade's return leg along the Garvaghy Road in July 1998 represented state acquiescence to a deliberate attempt to stir tensions on the part of Sinn Féin: a strategy of appeasement or even the active promotion of a Republican agenda in an effort to keep Republicans "onside" during the peace process. This, he suggested, has provided a model for the "creation" of similar disputes at other locations throughout Northern Ireland, including most recently at the junction of Twaddell Avenue and the Crumlin Road: the so-called Ardoyne shop-fronts (interview with author, 2014).

Gregory's assertions were mirrored by Benjamin, who argued that Republicans are

> creating issues: the flag; Donegall Street, throughout the whole Troubles was not a contentious parading area, all of a sudden, it be-

comes *the* contentious area.[11] You know, so there's a continuation, a chipping away and chipping away at British identity there as well. It's a deliberate strategy from Sinn Féin, which they've made quite clear over this last couple of weeks with Mr Adams and his Trojan Horse! (Interview with author, 2014)

Here Benjamin is referring to another comment made by Gerry Adams at a public meeting in Fermanagh in 2014. Responding to a question from the audience about the "bigotry" of the DUP—Sinn Féin's partner in the Northern Ireland Executive—Adams said:

The point is to actually break these bastards—that's the point. And what's going to break them is equality. That's what's going to break them—equality. Who could be afraid of equality? Who could be afraid of treating somebody the way you want to be treated. That's what we need to keep the focus on—that's the Trojan Horse of the entire Republican strategy—is to reach out to people on the basis of equality. (*Impartial Reporter* 2014)

Adams's comments were widely understood by Loyalists as referring not only to the DUP but also to the wider PUL community. Since the 1990s, Loyalist concerns (and, for that matter, Adams's claims) about Sinn Féin strategy have become more total. The language of "tradition" that Bryan (2000) identified as central to Loyalist political discourses in the 1990s has been replaced in the mid-2010s with the more all-encompassing signifiers "culture" and "identity." The street-level organization and agitation used by Republicans to block "traditional" parade routes on the Lower Ormeau Road and at Drumcree in the 1990s had by the mid-2010s evolved into the entire (duplicitous) policy agenda of a party with its hands on the levers of state power. Thus, the culture war taking place on several fronts simultaneously has become a state-directed assault on Loyalism as a way of life or state of being, hidden behind the language of equality and masquerading as the pursuit of parity of esteem.

Central to Loyalism's culture war is the claim that having failed to bomb Northern Ireland out of the United Kingdom during more than thirty years of armed struggle, Republicans in general and Sinn Féin in particular are instead using their political power deliberately to "strip

the Britishness out of Northern Ireland" (Gregory, interview with author, 2014). For some, this represents the next phase in their strategy to
pave the way to a United Ireland. Others, like Sarah, a young Loyalist
and PUP activist, view it slightly differently:

> The more I look at it, as a kind of *compensatory* mechanism, they're
> trying to "Green" Northern Ireland. Right? So if you can't have a
> United Ireland, you'll have an Irish Northern Ireland. And also, let's
> just poke the Unionist bear. And it's always the same stuff. And then
> afterwards they'll say, "Where's the leadership? Look at the state of
> Unionism: rudderless! Abject, violent, we always knew it!" And they
> are then, just by default, one up in being kind of statesmen; peace-
> makers. (Interview with author, 2015)

Mirroring subtle disagreements about its end goal, the specific ways
in which the culture war operates, how Republicans are able so effectively to "create issues" or dictate events in the ways that Gregory, Benjamin, and Sarah suggest, are also unclear. Often, the perpetrators are
mired in mystery or conspiracy, and with even seemingly innocuous or
trivial changes representing further proof of their strategic gain. As argued, for example, by Tim:

> I was talking to a fella this week, a good friend of mine, he's an ex-
> lifer, and he was telling me he was talking to a couple of Provos and
> I don't, I just, I didn't accept what he'd said. The Provos were telling
> him that they're as far away from a United Ireland today as they
> were when they started their struggle. So, I'm thinking to me-self,
> but if you look at the news at night on the TV, it's all about the flag
> being took down, and the flag has been took down—the Union
> Jack—long before City Hall—because they started it in all the Pri-
> mary schools. And then this wee green flag went up.[12] Nobody seen
> it, but that's what they were doing. . . . The Protestants today—this
> is just the way I see it—we're losing it bit, by bit, by bit. Even, see
> that wee village on the border down South? That guy there got
> killed on a farm?[13] I don't give two shits about him! But they're
> bringing the news from down South into Northern Ireland. And

that's another bit in my head. You know? That's the way I see it. (Focus group conducted by author, 2015)

Central to the process of "stripping" Northern Ireland of its British-ness is the alleged rewriting of history: an attempt to cast Loyalists as the villains, or even to write them out altogether. So all-encompassing is "Republican hatred" that even the decisions of Hollywood movie direc-tors provide evidence of it. Daniel, a senior Orangeman originally from East Antrim, argued:

> I've said in the context of the 1914 [UVF] gun-running, for example, that it's the greatest movie that was never made! It's got all the drama and the tension, and all the storylines that you would want in a big-screen film, but we're not a PC community, so nobody's going to do that for us! We don't have too many friends in Hollywood who want to make a screen-play or a film about us . . . you know, there's *The Wind that Shakes the Barley*, there's *Michael Collins*, there's all these films . . . but we're not PC [in Hollywood].

While they underestimate their own political agency, Loyalists tend to overascribe it to Republicans and, in particular, exaggerate Sinn Féin's capacity to dictate events in and beyond Northern Ireland. While they demonstrate a degree of strategizing on the part of Sinn Féin (see Bean 2007), Gerry Adams's comments cited above are perhaps less candid ad-missions than attempts to stake a claim to processes and events that were not exclusively of his party's making (Bryan, Fraser, and Dunn 1995; Jar-man 2003) in order to generate political capital by creating an impres-sion of greater control, or by appearing more decisive than is necessarily the case. Further, rather than open hostility, for the most part, the defin-ing attitude I encountered among Republicans in general, and members of Sinn Féin in particular, to Loyalism, its cultural practices and forms of cultural production, was ambivalence. When I asked Lughaidh, a Sinn Féin member from West Belfast, whether he felt Republicans would seek restrictions on Loyalists' commemoration of the centenary of the Battle of the Somme in Belfast in 2016, he responded, "No, I don't foresee any clash. Because we have no interest in obstructing their commemorations, or we have no interest in condemning or running them down or whatever. We just wanna let them get on with it, in the hope that they will let us get on with what we want to do" (interview with author, 2015).

While there has nonetheless been some political tension between Unionists and Nationalists over the routes and nature of commemorative parades to mark the "Unionist" centenaries since 2012, by and large these have proceeded as planned and without hindrance. Indeed, the vast majority of the Unionist parades in Northern Ireland each year (92 percent in 2012–13) proceed unrestricted, and their number each year is growing. In 2013, there were 2,687 parades associated with the Protestant/Unionist/Loyalist tradition, of which only 388 were deemed to be contentious (Nolan 2014, 160–62). The 'shameful decision' to limit the flying of the Union flag above Belfast City Hall to designated days—which has become emblematic of the culture war—actually represents a significant change in policy for Sinn Féin, which had traditionally opposed its flying altogether.

Ultimately, while it is rooted in Loyalist knowledge of Republican hatred, the culture war is actually as much a marker of Loyalism's disconnection with and fear of broader trends in British (and, indeed, Western) political economy and culture(s) in the postcolonial moment of deindustrialization, multiculturalism, and rights-based politics. Crucially, just as "the filling of the space of the 'Hater,'" as defined by Matija, "alternated effortlessly between 'Muslims' and 'the West'" (Jansen 2003, 221), so too is the antagonistic role of adversary in Loyalism's culture war readily filled by different agents at different times. Almost anything to which Loyalists are opposed becomes evidence of Republican hatred. This creates a discursive space in which Loyalists attempt to "appear likeable to [them]selves" (233). The "knowledge" that *everybody* hates us and the assertion that we don't care "paradoxically . . . allows [them] to exercise a certain degree of power and carve out a sense of worth for [their] existence in a situation of overwhelming powerlessness" (232).

The multiple battlefronts of the culture war include issues such as marriage equality (Northern Ireland is the only part of the British Isles in which gay marriage is not permissible under law), abortion (which remains illegal in Northern Ireland), and questions of religious and cultural diversity, integration, and inclusion. Islamophobia, in particular, has been a notable and upsetting feature of my encounter with Loyalism: exemplified not only by Pastor James McConnell's widely publicized labeling of Islam as a "doctrine spawned in hell" in 2014 (see BBC News 2014d) but also by the support he received from Loyalists at public rallies and on social media. It also found visceral expression in the campaign organized by some Loyalists against the accommodation of Syrian refugees in Northern Ireland (see McDonald 2015). Also in 2014, the so-called Gay Cake Row sparked by Asher's Bakery's decision to refuse an order for a cake decorated with a slogan promoting marriage equality (see BBC News 2015) prompted the following exchange between Benjamin and me.

> B: You know the cake one, the recent big sort of case with the Equality Commission is whether or not the cake company should be brought to court? I don't believe they should be. That's inequality, because they have a Christian belief, so they should be entitled to have their belief. They shouldn't have to make the cake.
>
> JE: Uh huh. I, um, have a different view, but . . .
>
> B: Oh, right?
>
> JE: I don't want to get into it necessarily . . . my problem is, OK, the DUP's response to this is to say that this is an issue of conscience, and . . . there should be legislation that says, "if this goes against my religious principles, then I shouldn't have to do it." One problem is how far do you take that . . . I think that that company was chosen deliberately because they knew they had a Christian ethos. I can see why. I can see the point that the [LGBTQ rights] campaigners were trying to make, but I can see why you would think it's a questionable tactic. So, maybe let's park the cake?
>
> B: I suppose that's where you need to be careful with how far you go with it . . . the only reason I had mentioned the cake, is that they are getting themselves involved in cases like that. They don't get themselves involved in cases that are continually going year in, year out. You know, if they're going to spend money looking into cases like that, why not look into something that actually affects large amounts of *ordinary* people?

It is important to stress that Benjamin is not, by my reckoning, homophobic. Our discussion was introspective, thoughtful, and good-
humored. But his comments are indicative of a social world in which, of
necessity, the promotion of greater equality for some—in this case, those
who identify as lesbian or gay and who wish to marry—must by its very
nature represent unequal treatment for "ordinary" Loyalists (despite the
fact, of course, that there are Loyalists who also define as lesbian, gay,
bisexual, transgendered, queer, or intersex). This demonstrates Loyalism's idea of itself as embattled "ordinariness"; its authenticity or "de-
cency" is beset by a sense of existential threat from what it perceives as
perverse trends in the mainstream, many of which are at work reorienting Britishness in the moment of multiculturalism. Indeed, Loyalism
and the particular "ethnic" form of Britishness it espouses are archetypal
of the postcolonial melancholy (Gilroy 2005) against which the champi-
ons of multicultural Britishness actively construct their project.[14]

As noted by one Republican participant in a Farset Community
Think Tank focus group in 2015:

> In many ways I feel that the Unionists here are out of step with
> what's happening in Britain. In terms of multiculturalism and inclu-
> siveness, politicians in Britain wouldn't get away with what politi-
> cians here get away with. Peter Robinson's comment that he would
> be happy to send a Muslim to the shops for him[15] would have been
> a resignation issue if he had been a British prime minister—that
> comment wouldn't have been allowed to stand. Or the attitude here
> to gay people . . . would not be tolerated in mainstream British poli-
> tics. So, in many ways, although Unionists always claim it is all
> about their 'Britishness', they are becoming further removed from
> what Britishness stands for in its modern-day context, and, ironi-
> cally, republicanism is probably more in line with that modern out-
> look, in terms of rights-based issues and cultural inclusiveness. (Hall
> 2015b, 23)

"Republican hatred" is a cypher for the vast array of social, economic and cultural processes that Loyalists perceive as being ranged
against them. The culture war therefore represents a liquid fear about

the pace and nature of social, cultural, and economic change in Northern Ireland, the wider United Kingdom, and further afield—only some of which is the explicit purview of Republicanism per se and much of which is indicative of wider and even global political and economic trends—and the role of globalization in eroding ethnic dominance in the nation-state (Wright 2004; Kaufmann 2004). It is a demonstration of Loyalists' sense of their own inability—despite their protestations—to influence, stop, or reverse these trends. Some have suggested that Loyalism may itself have come to represent a minority group deserving special rights (Long 2015). Paradoxically, according to such a view, Loyalists are ultimately marked as a group deserving of special rights by their very opposition to the idea of special group rights, which they identify as a wide-reaching conspiracy to eradicate their way of life.

Crucially, as both cause and consequence of the culture war, Loyalist ontology has been disrupted to such an extent that Loyalists feel this conspiracy amounts to attempts to alter even history itself. It is against this backdrop that commemoration during the Decade of Centenaries takes place. This view is summarized in an exchange between Ryan and Jeremy, UVF former prisoners, during a focus group.

> R: I feel that our identity [is] under attack. But our identity was firmly made clear by the sacrifice of what basically was our grandfathers and great-uncles—our flesh and blood—and it can't be tarnished, it can't be rolled away. I would need to go back to the whole idea of narrative, and I certainly feel there's a narrative out there at the minute that we Loyalist, Protestant Ulstermen are the baddies and [therefore], "we have to take away their flags and all the symbolism." I'm OK for living in a shared society but there is pride in what has went before: not the ugly stuff, but there was good stuff so why should we lose that? Because we're not asking the Irish Republic to withdraw their tricolour.
>
> J: I think that's really important, that historical thing of the term "Loyalism," the term "Loyalist" is kind of steroid-filled, porn mags in the jails, ignorant: that's the stereotype. That wasn't the reality, and I think that people, when their identity is being challenged that way, they're then going back and showing, historically, what we've got to be proud of.

It is this reassertion of a confident Loyalism, or "showing historically what we've got to be proud of," that provides the basis for Loyalist commemorative discourse and practice during the Decade of Centenaries. Commemoration has become a—if not the—chief means by which Loyalists' assert the moral validity of their worldview or identity in the face of the culture war.

CHAPTER FIVE

"Our culture is their bravery"

Commemoration and the Culture War

JE: So what does it actually feel like for you when you're walking the streets on a commemorative parade?

M: Pride. Pride. Pride that we've got so many people out. Pride that there's so many people making such an effort. It's such an effort to put that on. I think this last ten years has seen a massive increase in—what would you call it—a sense of wanting to believe in something? I think the last ten years, people are learning more and more and more. It's all about knowledge. It's about getting more and more people to wise up, to learn what they're about.

JE: It's about belief you said. What do you mean by that?

M: *Belonging*: "this is why I'm British." This is the sacrifice that gives me the right to say, "I'm British." . . . That's my belief. Unfortunately Republicans didn't think that, because they've been trying to take it away from us for forty years. I'd like to think that what we do in the Somme Associations is continue to strive to push our Britishness forward. To let everyone see. To let government see. Let our own Unionist parties see. That if *they* wanna be lackeys, well, we *won't*. *I* am not prepared. I don't accept it. (Mike, interview with author, 2015)

On a bright and blustery Saturday afternoon in February 2015, the 1st Shankill Somme Association held its annual parade and service of remembrance. The parade began with a wreath-laying ceremony at the European War Memorial in Woodvale Park, accompanied by a haunting lament on bagpipes. Sponsored by the Shankill Road–based City of Belfast Army Benevolent Fund (ABF) and inaugurated in 2014, the memorial is designed to resemble one of the Giant's Causeway's six-sided pillars. The polished granite memorial commemorates not only—as is conventional—British First World War dead but also the "lost generations" of Belgium, France, and Germany (fig. 5.1). The chair of the City of Belfast ABF, Bobby Foster, told the *Belfast Telegraph*'s Nevin Farrell (2014), "We are well pleased with how [the European War Memorial] was received in the community. . . . We decided that in this decade of centenaries we would come up with something completely different and it needed to include Ireland and the UK and other combatants. . . . This is a totally inclusive war memorial, there is nothing like it anywhere." Following the laying of a wreath at the memorial by a representative of the 1st Shankill Somme Association, the parade, including three ranks of men in period UVF costume, were led out of the park by the Ulster Volunteer Force Regimental Flute Band. After marching down the Shankill Road to the car park of the Shankill Leisure Centre on Northumberland Street, where it was met by the representatives of other Somme Associations from across Belfast and beyond, the parade returned to the 1st Shankill Somme Association's own memorial garden, beside the Mountainview Bar (in which the group holds its monthly meetings), for the service of Remembrance (fig. 5.2).

The service followed what had become a familiar pattern. Following his opening oration, the master of ceremonies handed over to Reverend Edith Quirey, who began her address by noting, "For me, personally, I had six great uncles, all in the one regiment, all brothers, all at the Somme. So many of us have been touched by all of those things that happened one hundred years ago." "Sadly," she lamented, "still today our world is tearing itself apart with hatred, violence and murder." Where I was standing on the pavement outside the Garden of Remembrance, I was aware of the slightly hushed chatter of the small group of women standing next to me—and the tuts and steely glances it evoked from the rows of suited men inside—during the lament on the bagpipes and the one-minute silence that followed the playing of the Last Post by a lone bugler. The service was brought to a close with the playing of "God Save the Queen" by the Regimental Band.

Figure 5.1. European War Memorial, Woodvale Park, Belfast.

Figure 5.2. 1st Shankill Somme Association Garden of Reflection, Belfast.

The 1st Shankill Somme Association's is one of a growing number of parades, services of remembrance, and other such events organized each year by an expanding number of Somme associations and societies to commemorate the sacrifice of Ulstermen during the First World War in general and the 36th (Ulster) Division at the Battle of the Somme in particular. The 36th (Ulster) Division Memorial Association was formally established as an umbrella organization for these groups in 2006, the year of the Battle of the Somme's ninetieth anniversary. According to a representative of the association, at its founding in 2006 there were about seven or eight affiliated groups. By 2014, there were an estimated fifty-plus such groups (Sammy, interview with author, 2014). The majority are based in Northern Ireland, but an increasing number are also found on the British mainland, including in Glasgow, Liverpool, and Corby. In 2006, the cumulative total of applications to the Northern Ireland Parades Commission with Somme Association, Somme Society, Friends of the Somme, or 36th (Ulster) Division Memorial Association in the title was two. In 2015, this total had increased more than sixfold, to thirteen.

The day after the 1st Shankill Somme Association's parade, a video of the event appeared on the Facebook page *PUL Media* (2015), with accompanying text that is worth quoting here in full.

> Where & What is your culture is a question Republicans like to ask PUL People.
> The simple answer to this question is this.
> Your/my Culture is Remembering the Sacrifice of those who died to keep us living within the country we do today.
> Our Culture lies with our Brave Dead on the Battlefields of Ireland, within Derry's Walls and along the River Boyne. It lies on the Battlefields of France & Belgium. In fact, Our Culture lies on every piece of land, be it WWII, Falklands, Northern Ireland, Iraq, Afghanistan, or any other War & Conflict within any other country that British Soldiers Fought & Died on in the past, & every Battlefield they will Fight & Die on in the future.
> No other country & its people in the world would be asked to deny their Brave Soldiers in Death & The History around their deaths, so why are the people of Northern Ireland being asked to? SF IRA Gangs did not stop us Celebrating and Remembering Our Dead & Our History. Those who enforce the Republican Appeasement Policy on PUL People, with Police Brutality & Corrupt Courts will not stop us from Celebrating Our Dead and Our History & nor will the Republican Hoods that Fire Shots, Throw Bombs and Attack PUL People with Knives.
> Our Culture is Their Bravery
> Stop the Republican Appeasement Policy
> Sticks & Stones Will Break Your Bones But Flutes Will Never Harm You
> Let Them Home.[1]

In a cultural-political context defined by the culture war, commemoration has become a primary site for the reassertion of Loyalist identity and a—if not the—predominant form of Loyalist cultural production and transmission. Indeed, according to *PUL Media*, commemoration represents the zenith and even the totality of Loyalist cultural expression. Quite explicitly, commemoration is therefore about more than simply remembering. It is the chief means by which the politics of the "new" Northern Ireland—what *PUL Media* terms the "Republican Appeasement Policy"—is confronted and contested. As such, it is central to the construction of Loyalist identity as authentic and Loyalist knowledge as truthful in a hostile and malignant social world corrupted by hatred and lies. In ways I elaborate below, the 1st Shankill Somme Association's wreath laying at the European War Memorial was a ritual claim of inclusivity on Loyalism's terms, terms that both deliberately eschew "parity of esteem" and reassert the moral validity and authenticity of Loyalist social memory.

In this chapter, I demonstrate that commemoration, memorialization, and especially the (semi-ritualized) practice of genealogy are central to the construction of the Loyalist self, its affinities and experiences of kinship. Genealogy, and its role in this process of self-identification, forms a vital but sometimes ambiguous part of commemoration's function in Loyalists' locating themselves as members of a particular politico-historical community and in determining its symbolic construction (Cohen 1989), the maintenance of its boundaries, and its relationship with both the Other and the state. Since the late 1990s these relations have come to be defined by the culture war. While the Somme, its genealogy and representation through commemorative tradition, is often assumed or argued "always" to have been central to the construction of Loyalist identity over time, I argue that the contemporary cult of the Somme is a phenomenon peculiar to and at work in redefining Loyalism in the new Northern Ireland. Crucially, it demonstrates Loyalists' attempts to resist the terms of the peace process and claim about parity of esteem and to counter what they have termed the rewriting of history that underpins it.

GENEALOGIES OF THE SOMME

For almost all of the Loyalist commemorators I interviewed, the answer to my questions "Why commemorate?" and "What, to you, is the personal significance of First World War commemoration?" referenced at least one ancestor who had fought at the Somme. Indeed, when I opened my interview with a senior East Belfast Orangeman about his role in

Somme commemorations by asking first about "the relationship between the Orange Order and the Somme" before his own "personal relationship with, or personal thoughts about the significance of the Battle
of the Somme, and commemorating the Battle of the Somme," he was
quick to suggest that I had asked those questions in the wrong order, as
it is the latter that, in his view, is key to explaining the former. Jamie, a
former member of an East Belfast Loyalist flute band, suggested that
during his time in the band its involvement in First World War commemoration had been driven primarily by a handful of senior bandsmen
who had family connections to the war. I wanted to know more about
the direction of causality.

> JE: And in terms of the guys in the band that do have this family
> connection to the Somme, would you say that their family connec-
> tion drove their interest in the war, or was it the other way round?
> Were they driven to find that family connection because they al-
> ready had an interest in the war?
>
> J: Good question. [Pauses] I believe, anyway, sort of 90 percent of
> the interest in the war does come from a personal interest. . . .
> I think for most people it's the starting point: it's the grandmother
> telling you a story about the great-uncle that you never knew, or the
> photograph on the wall, or it's the death penny.[2] [For] [m]ost people
> that clicks, or it begins the process. (Interview with author, 2014)

The connection that many Loyalists feel to the Somme is described
in terms of blood and is one of deep emotional significance. For instance, Laura, a member of a Somme society based in South Belfast, described how her first visit to her great-uncle's grave affected her.

> I remember the first time I went to his grave I walked over and I had
> my black sunglasses on, and I just walked over and I said, "This is it."
> And Sammy put his arms round me and I felt myself filling up, cry-
> ing. He says, "You're alright," he says, "it's natural for to feel that
> way." That's my blood lying in there. Now that's *my blood*, and I'm
> the next generation now to follow him, to pay my respects to him,
> to make sure his name lives forever more, y'know, for what he done,
> for King and Country. (Interview with author, 2014)

During my visit to the battlefields of France and Belgium with the International School for Peace Studies in November 2014, I was surprised at the level of emotion I experienced as I watched a fellow participant become the first member of her family to visit the grave of her great-uncle. It was deeply moving and intimate in a way I had not anticipated, and I felt like a voyeur. "He was only nineteen," she kept repeating tearfully. "Only nineteen, and all the way out here, all on his own." Many Loyalists told me that they felt they had "lost" family members at the Somme despite never having known them personally, given that their deaths had occurred long before these interlocutors were born. This is perhaps the ultimate expression of the emotion of commemoration and of locating "family" at the Somme.

As Lawler (2008, 38–39) suggests, "Blood *symbolises* connection[;] it is not itself connection. . . . Kin relations are, *by definition*, cultural. Kin are quite simply those persons we *recognise* as kin." Anne-Marie Kramer (2011a, 381) describes genealogy as an "*imaginative* memory practice which produces kinship, auto/biographical selves and interiorities, making visible the simultaneous process of self-making and the embedding of the self in kinship networks" (emphasis added; see also Nash 2008). In personalizing the past, it "accounts for the self in the present, signifies existence and provides meaning," allowing for a construction of the self that is able to connect "beyond and of itself" (Kramer 2011a, 380). The practice of tracing family members to the Somme is therefore a creative one, an "imaginative and performative memory act" (Kramer 2011b, 429) by which Loyalists draw on the idea of blood to construct their heritage or origins. For many of my interlocutors, this practice often culminated with a highly symbolic visit to a relative's grave or memorial to lay a wreath or poppy cross, such that this process also involved a ritualized placing of this heritage in space as well as time (cf. Basu 2005; Switzer 2013). This kind of genealogical practice is often presented in terms of (re)discovering a fundamental (and theretofore "lost") relationship on the part of the practitioner and of restoring to the "lost" family member the relationship that had been denied him by his death and location in a foreign field, beyond the borders of the places of home and family. During our interview, Laura talked of her plans to revisit her great-uncle's grave:

I'm going over to France on Sunday, and I know it sounds stupid, but I have stones just sitting over there, pebbles. I went and picked them up off his mum and dad's grave, his sister's grave, and my nanny's [grandmother's] grave, to put on his grave. And then I'll bring stuff home to put on their graves. . . . I'm taking orange lily bulbs out with me this year as well. I'll put the lilies in the grave. I did the same at my nanny's grave, and his mummy's grave, putting orange lilies down. But that was something I done when my nanny was alive. Every 1 July I bought her orange lilies and her sweet william. Because all my nanny's ones, all her brothers and all, they were all in the Orange Lodges you see. It's the way we were all brought up! So it's something I still do even though they're dead. I still take the lilies, but I wanna put a couple of wee bulbs in to see if they'll grow, just so to have that wee connection with back home, to his mummy and stuff. (Interview with author, 2014)

Loyalist genealogy of the Somme not only serves to mediate and cement relationships with ancestors but also provides for exploration and creative expression of relationships with family members who are living or are within living memory. It was not unusual over the course of my fieldwork to hear stories about reconnections between estranged cousins or the reconciliation of fraught father-son relationships through a joint interest in the familial heritage of the First World War. For Laura, personal interest in the First World War was rooted in and became a (material) expression of her relationships with her grandmother and uncle.

JE: You said you were interested in the First World War since you were a child?

L: Yeah. My nanny had, from a wee girl my nanny always had a picture of a soldier in her living room and I used to, I always remember, as a wee girl: "Nanny, who is that? Who is that?" "That's your great-uncle." "Alright. Where is he?" "He's dead!" "Well, why is he dead, Nanny?" I always remember as a child asking these questions and then when I was nine years of age, I'll never forget it, I was in my uncle's house—my mummy's brother's house—and I seen a book in his cabinet. And there was soldiers on it and I says, "Can I read that book?" And he laughed at me, says, "You'll not be able to read it." And I said, "I wanna read it!" He says, "You'll not understand it!" "I wanna read the book!" And I took the book and I read it. And from then, when I was eleven he started work for Farset.[3] He actually lived in Thiepval Tower for three years. This is when they were getting the Tower refurbished, and sorting out the battlefields and still doing a lot of work over at it. So, 'cause I'd read the book he, uh, he brought me home bullets, and he brought me home a bayonet, and barbed wire. So he brought me all this home. It's actually, it's still in my mummy's house. It was in like a Quality Street jar— y'know the ones you get at Christmas? It was all put into that. Some of it's starting to crumble now. I've a broken bayonet, it's all corroded and rusted . . .

Then the Somme Heritage Centre used to bring out a book called *Somme News*, and he used to write articles and stuff in it. And I used to be all biz taking it into school saying, "My uncle wrote that, look, that's my great-uncle, he's buried in France! Look, my other uncle done this, my other uncle . . . " 'Cause there was five members of the family went out, and four of them come back. So that's how I got an interest in it.

While Laura spoke fondly of the role of genealogical practice and the collection of artifacts in her relationships with her living relatives, over the course of my research it was perhaps equally common for it to be a source or expression of intrafamilial conflict. I heard numerous stories of family members who had fallen out because of disagreements about who may rightfully lay claim to a given heirloom: a set of medals, a photograph, or a death penny.

Bearing some similarity to the impact of reunion of adopted children with their birth parents, as examined by Janet Carsten (2000, 2004), for many Loyalists, the process of reconnection and creation of kinship at the Somme has become an important part of what Carsten might call the completion of otherwise incomplete or partial personal biographies. When I interviewed Mike—a Somme Society member in his early fifties—at his office in an East Belfast community center, he told me:

My great-grandfather was killed on 1st July [1916], at the Battle of the Somme . . . he was twenty-three years of age. Left three children behind, one of whom was my grandfather. My grandfather never met his father, not that he can remember. You know what I mean? He was three when his father died, so he doesn't remember him at all. My own father knew very, very little about his grandfather, who'd been killed at the Battle of the Somme. And I'm pleased to say that I was able to take my father out to where he was killed. . . . I wanted my father to see it. I wanted my father to see where his granda was. (Interview with author, 2015)

On the wall above the desk in Mike's office was a photograph of three men—Mike's great-grandfather and two great-uncles—in British Army khaki. I asked him about the photograph.

M: In fact, in that photograph, we don't know who's who. We don't know which one's which.

JE: And there's no one left alive that can . . .

M: No one can tell me. My grandfather couldn't even have told me. Because on the back of the original photograph it says, "my father and his two brothers." There's no indication of who's who. I can take a wild guess that the smallest one at the front is my great-grandfather, because he looks like my granda did. My grandfather's dead now, but he looks like him. Wee small man. That's just what he looks like. That's what my granda was like, like a jockey! The two others are a lot bigger, and if you look at the likes of me, my father, my uncle, my cousins, we're all big! Funny, I've one male cousin and he's a wee small man and he's like my great-granda, who I think that is!

According to Wallis (2015), ultimately it is the location and definition of *self* that forms the "primary act of family history, because it fosters distinguishable individual and family identities expressible through historical evidence." First World War family research is a subjective practice of "self-making" (Wallis 2015; see also Saar 2002). It is a "tool by which to locate the specificity of an individual's life experiences in relation to the historical life experience of family members" (Kramer

2011a, 385). Mike's attempt to identify the men in the photograph based on their physical characteristics mirrors the trend identified by Wallis (2015) whereby family history researchers looking at their First World War heritage come to highly value information found on "enlistment attestation forms, such as a man's height, build and eye colour[,] . . . because they can draw perceived links between generations." For Mike, genealogy plays a central role in the completion not only of his father's biography but also of his own. The perceived links between generations of which the photograph provides evidence are not only physical, but cultural and, crucially, ideological.

During my interview with Mike, our conversation about inheritance moved uninterruptedly from physiognomy to politics.

> M: I've found out quite a bit about my great-grandfather, you know, and his father before him. Going right back to the 1890s or something, without even trying hard.
>
> JE: Did they sign the Covenant?
>
> M: All of them. Well, most of them. I actually have their signatures. My great-grandfather did. His father did. His mother did: she signed the Declaration. Uh, I think at least one of the brothers signed it. I'd like to find out more about them. It's finding the time . . . I might never have liked them! [Laughter] But I mean, that's neither here nor there! I'd love if you could get a parallel world where you could speak to them and say you know . . . but then isn't life always like that? People always wish they'd have done things, and wish they were able to do things.
>
> JE: What would you talk about?
>
> M: Hm . . . it's a pretty hypothetical question. I would ask them straight out: obviously they believed, if . . . my great-grandfather signed the Covenant, he obviously felt strongly about opposing Home Rule. He was obviously a Loyalist, if you wanna define him in those terms that we have nowadays. I'd like to think that he would be disappointed in the political situation in Northern Ireland now. I know I am. So, I daresay he would probably be of that ilk. Just guessing by, you know, him signing the Covenant.

JE: Why do you say you're disappointed?

M: I think it's been an absolute sellout here. I think the British government are absolutely scandalous. They have ditched the people of
Northern Ireland, pushed a government onto us, consisting of Sinn
Féin, who, like, shouldn't, just shouldn't be . . . and our own Unionist politicians are a disgrace. An absolute disgrace. Everything that
has been thrown at them, they've just sat back and taken. The lies
and the deceit from the British government regarding Sinn Féin:
the On the Runs, the letters, guns under the table, you name it.[4]
Everything that has ever raised its head here since they've struck up
this quasi-government. . . . I think the Loyalist people have been
abandoned. We have no voice. I have no political voice. I'm extremely disenfranchised. I don't trust the Unionist parties. I think
they're all about themselves.

For Laura, the role of communal identification in the formation of
kinship ties was already implicit in the symbolism of the floral
arrangements—orange lilies and sweet william—she gave to her grandmother each 1 July. She described the explicitly political nature and significance of her affinity with her ancestors at the Somme and its
manifestation in her relationships with living relatives in the present as
a chief factor in translating her interest in genealogy into active participation in public acts of commemoration, including reenactments and
parades.

JE: So, what, I'm really intrigued, what's it like, or what's *actually*
going through your head when you're walking in a commemorative
parade? Say it's the Covenant parade or . . .

L: Probably proudness. Proudness more than anything . . . when we
done the parade [marking the centenary of the formation of the
UVF] to Craigavon House, my great-aunty come down—she's
eighty-seven—and she stood at the Holywood Arches, and I seen
her and I started crying. Here's me, "My God! My aunty's here to
see me!" I was just like, just so proud that she had come out to see
me parade that day. And it was just like . . . it's like following in your
family's footsteps, y'know, you sort of think to yourself they're looking down on you. These are the steps they took so many years ago.
And now I'm doing the same thing.

JE: Do you mean physically the same steps, as in your walking on the same streets that they walked, or is it more . . . ?

L: No, I think it's more in terms of going back to them, going back to being, like, a staunch Unionist. That's what it's going back to. . . . I was quite emotional the first year I done the Ulster Hall event,[5] because I know the likes of my nanny and her brothers and sisters, if they'd have been there they'd have been so proud of me. Because my great-grandmother, she actually sung hymns in the Willowfield Unionist Hall, she actually sung for the boys before they went out to France. That's what she done, she sung hymns, and then it was her husband, her two brothers and two brothers-in-law all joined the 8th Battalion [Royal Irish Rifles].

Laura's idea of herself and her role within the kinship structures that her genealogical practice has helped to define are borne out through commemorative practice. This practice also served to locate this idea and these relationships within wider political and ideological frameworks. It provided proof and a means of articulating that she had inherited her forefathers' (and foremothers') "staunch" Unionism. As I discuss in more detail in chapter 6, commemoration also served to mediate her gendered position in her community.

Ultimately, and despite Jamie's claims cited above, for most of the Loyalist commemorators I interviewed, I found that was it their membership of the Unionist community—and the will to validate their claim to membership of it—that determined their interest in family history of the First World War rather than the converse. For most of the Loyalist commemorators I interviewed, political conviction and ideological affinity with their ancestors not only motivated their involvement in commemorative practice, but had provided the impetus for the very genealogical research by which that affinity was constructed. Mike, for instance, told me that his interest in the First World War in general and the Somme in particular had preceded any knowledge of a family connection.

I never knew [about my great-grandfather] 'til nine years ago, and a chance conversation with my grandmother. In saying that, we had formed our Somme Association round about that time, with the specific aim of going over to . . . we just missed the ninetieth anniversary when we decided. There was a lot of talk, and in the pub that I drink in, there's a lot of guys would've been, would think the same way I do. I would have said, you know, that, um, look, the ninetieth anniversary was coming up, it was all on the news, everyone was talking about it, Somme Associations were being formed, more so. If you go back twenty years, there was maybe three Somme Associations, if that. Now there's hundreds!

People wanna reach out and get [a] connection. They wanna think that the Battle of the Somme and the First World War wasn't just about people they'd never heard of. This was their relatives. Like when I took my father to the Somme to visit his granda's grave, he was quite taken aback by it: to see the amount of headstones, to see the, the magnitude of, you know, graveyards everywhere. So look, you know, it's—when we started our Somme Association, I knew about the Battle of the Somme, don't get me wrong, 'cause, like I say, I do have a knowledge of the First World War. And then when I found out that I had an actual great-granda who had been killed! For use of a better word, it was the icing on the cake! That was the Holy Grail for me then. [And I wanted] to go and find out more. If I had an affinity with it before, this just made it stronger. (Interview with author, 2015)

If, as Wallis (2015) suggests, genealogy and the practice of First World War family history research are about "construct[ing] a tangible legacy that extends beyond the lifetime of the researcher, and through this process . . . construct[ing] an ontologically secure and recognizable identity," then for Loyalists this process is intimately bound up with the perceived cultural, political, or spiritual needs of their community and, particularly in the context of the culture war, a specific set of ontological concerns and insecurities against which this identity is constructed. For some Loyalists, it takes place without and beyond there being any (known or researched) family connection to the Somme at all. When, for instance, I asked Sammy—an officeholder in another East Belfast Somme Society—about the personal significance of the Somme, he replied, "That's a difficult one! I don't have an answer!"

JE: Oh, really? So, OK, then there's no point in time you can kind of pinpoint that you became so interested or . . . ?

S: No, it was always something just that, sort of, fascinated me, if that's the right word? It intrigued me, and I got a phone call one Friday night saying, you know, "D'you wanna go to the Somme? There's places available." So I thought, "Well, why not?" Mind you, I'd a few drinks on me that Friday night! I suppose I was inclined to say yes! But I've no real personal interest in it, as such, you know? Let me put it like this, I've never done any family research into it whatsoever. I don't have time to sit and do family research. It would be great if somebody did it for me! But I suspect that there may not be any family connection, although there could be a great-uncle or something. I honestly don't know. I've never, like . . . I know my granny and my grandas, and that's it. You know, I haven't gone past that.

JE: Aha, so it's not the kind of, um, "who do you think you are" kind of interest that some people have?

S: You know, I just don't know what my *family* history entails. There's no military history in the family at all. It's just as you're growing up, you wondered why Orange Lodges had, you know, the Battle of the Somme on the front [of their banners] and that image that everybody sees of them going over the top on 1 July [1916]. You're told about this great sacrifice, but it was an opportunity to *see* that sacrifice I think. I'll always remember seeing my first poppies, you know. And the tears welled up in me . . . I just got very emotional. And you could see the big Thiepval Tower through the trees. So, sort of all that mix, all coming together. . . . So, really, that was sort of my introduction to the Somme. You know, there was no looking back from that point!

We went on to discuss how Sammy's involvement in his Somme Society had been motivated by this emotional experience and his affective attachment to the Somme beyond any blood ties to its battlefields. For Sammy (and indeed, for Laura and Mike), this involvement was self-evidently motivated by more than the will to remember, the role of family history in the construction of the self, or even its role in the articulation or legitimation of membership in a particular community. Ultimately it is about the (perpetual) (re)construction of that community, of educating that community in a story about itself.

JE: OK, so, for you, the main, if I'm right, the main role [of your Somme Society] is kind of facilitating people to go and see the battlefields themselves? That's sort of the main purpose of the group?

S: Well, no, it's a couple of things. But it's education first and foremost: educating the groups. They know about the Somme, but they don't *really* know an awful lot about it, if you know what I mean. So, if the idea is that, you know, we educate people, we assist people in getting there and all that sort of thing, but it's to hold events to . . . the purpose of holding events is to educate. So you're holding events to remember, also hoping that people take something away from those events as well.

JE: That education is about what?

S: It's just about learning [about] the sacrifice of your forefathers, you know? And what they did for us, that we may be free, as the Americans would say! And until you go and visit these places you'll never, ever, I believe, know deep in your heart the sacrifice that these fellas made. They did it for different reasons, so many different reasons: some did it for King and Empire, some did it just to go with their mates, some did it to go to foreign lands, and some did it for money! But at the end of the day, they never returned home.

So, it's our duty. . . . It's a requirement to remember, but it's trying to get people to realise that. And that's a big ask. You know, it's easy to say to me, "It's a requirement," because it is a requirement to me, because I'm sympathetic. But other people who are more concerned about cutting grass and . . . You know, you have, what I call [pause] B&Q people, Homebase people,[6] who, and it's not a criticism of them, but they're happier walking around B&Q on a Sunday, or Homebase on a Sunday, you know, looking at different wee plants and paint: garden center Unionism, there you go, garden-center Unionists. You know, there's nothing wrong with that. But at the end of the day, the only reason they're able to walk around the garden center is because of . . . [Pauses]

JE: That sacrifice you were talking about?

S: Yeah. So, it's a big job. You're never gonna get it anyway. [But] it's my job, this is the way I see myself, as an evangelist, for want of a better term. Obviously I can't do very much because I'm working and I've family and all the rest of it. But it's my job . . . that's the wrong word, it's my vocation, whatever you want to call it, to try and convince people.

In the final analysis, the fact of their ancestors having fought at the Somme does not sufficiently explain why and how Loyalists commemorate it. Indeed, the very fact of their ancestors having fought at the Somme is itself constructed through genealogical and other commemorative practices, and for some, blood connection is of no consequence in determining the will to remember the Somme's sacrifice at all. Furthermore, the imperative simply to remember this sacrifice says nothing about why it is or should be a collective and performative, let alone redemptive, experience. The ritual act of collective remembrance, and the narratives that it both reflects and constructs, contributes something to Loyalism and the Loyalist experience that is far more complex or significant than mere remembering. Crucially, this act does not proceed inexorably from the historical moment of the Somme itself but instead has been (re)invented over time to meet particular emotional, cultural, and political needs.

THE CULT OF THE SOMME: (RE)INVENTING A TRADITION

I was born in 1964, so I can remember the very early days of the Troubles. I can remember the fear, when your dad was out on duty with the UDR, waiting for him at four o'clock in the morning and hearing the front door opening and him coming home. But you see, to be honest, until I went to prison, I didn't really understand the history going back even forty years or fifty years to the . . . you know, talking about the Somme there. The Somme only became prevalent to me when I reached prison. See, to me, my history is . . . and I'll be bluntly honest about this, if somebody asked me, why are you a Loyalist? Well, just the history of the IRA from 1970 onwards, when they started bombing us and blowing us up. And that's if I wanna be brutally honest. It's only as I became older that I started to look into my past and realised the sacrifice at the Somme, for instance. (Stevie, interview with author, 2015)

The ubiquity of representations of the UVF, the 36th (Ulster) Division, and the Somme on Orange Order banners, on wall murals, and in other forms of Loyalist cultural production is echoed in the suggestion that remembrance of the sacrifice of the Somme has been a dominant feature of Loyalist discourse and practice almost from the moment the 36th (Ulster) Division began their advance into no-man's land on 1 July 1916. Guy Beiner (2007a) has suggested that the Somme was even subject to a particular form of Loyalist "pre-memory," fitting neatly into and gelling instantly with a set of memorial tropes and narratives that were already definitive of Unionist social memory and, thereby, broader political culture in 1916 (see also Officer 2001). It is commonly claimed by Orange brethren, particularly those in the Ballymacarrett District Loyal Orange Lodge (LOL) No. 6, that the district's East Belfast Somme memorial parade has been held annually since the battle's first anniversary, 1 July 1917 (see e.g., DUP 2015). In his interview with Peter Taylor for the latter's *Loyalists* (2000, 24), Augustus "Gusty" Spence, who at its (re)formation in 1965 became the UVF's first chief of staff, claimed that "he took in the history of loyalism 'with his mother's milk. . . . We were born and reared with the sacrifice of the Somme.'"

The argument, made explicit by O'Brien (1972; see also O'Donnell 2007; Switzer 2013) and at least tacitly accepted in many accounts of Loyalist violence during the Troubles—including Taylor's (1997, 2000) and, significantly, those of former Loyalist combatants themselves—is that just as Republicans were inspired or emboldened by the pageantry and militarism of the fiftieth anniversary of the Easter Rising, Loyalists were motivated to follow the example of their forebears and take up arms by Unionist memory of the Ulster Covenant and the original Ulster Volunteers and their sacrifice as the 36th (Ulster) Division, particularly during the Golden Jubilee of the Battle of the Somme in 1966. It is certainly no coincidence that in seeking legitimacy and popular support, the paramilitary organization formed in 1965 deliberately drew on the nomenclature, heraldry, and symbolism of its namesake. However, the attendant claim about the central role of Unionist memory in general and of the Somme in particular in catalyzing, justifying, or even causing Loyalist violence is more ambiguous, as evidenced in my interview with Joshua, a UVF former prisoner from East Belfast, who talked about his first confrontation with Gusty Spence when he entered the prison camp at Long Kesh.

> J: [It] was nearly one of the first questions. Davey Ervine always told that story, and Gusty did it with everybody: "Why are you in here?"
>
> JE: What did you say?
>
> J: Well, you had the script "there's a war on," yeah, and "our community needs to defend itself, so . . ." There was that script. But, at the same time, as far as Irish history goes, we were totally ignorant. We knew about the Battle of the Boyne, but we knew just that the Protestants beat the Catholics! [Laughs] That was the height of it. And then the Battle of the Somme, naturally, with me being in the UVF, you'd have knew all about the Somme.
>
> JE: Oh, so did you attach importance to the Battle of the Somme and the symbol of the Battle of the Somme before becoming involved?
>
> J: No! As a result of becoming involved, because you didn't know your history, y'know, you were ignorant about it. It was a community mythology. You knew it.
>
> JE: But did that play a big role in your life and in the decisions that you took?
>
> J: [Pauses] No, not really, no. No it wouldn't have done Jonathan, to be honest. Yes, y'know, you were aware of it. But for me it would all have started in '69. Whenever . . . whenever the shit hit the fan, you know? It would've been, that's you suddenly, "What is going on here?"

It is more likely that the agents of Loyalist violence during the Troubles were motivated by the immediate fact of IRA bombings and shootings, concerns about personal safety, the security of their families and communities, and (resultant or exacerbated) raw sectarianism rather than by more abstract considerations about heritage. Some UVF former prisoners—including Jeremy, a community worker I interviewed at his office in Ballymena—have suggested that the perceived elite status of the UVF over the UDA contributed to their decision to join the former rather than the latter. But for Jeremy, this elite status was only tangentially related to the organization's inherited symbolic pedigree as such, having more to do instead with its greater mystique and "professionalism," more selective recruitment strategy, and more overtly offensive (rather than defensive) military tactics (interview with author, 2015; see also *Balaclava Street* 2014a, 2014b). Generally, which of the two paramilitary groups individuals chose to join arguably had more to do with which group controlled the area they lived in, which one their friends or family had opted to join, or which one had co-opted members of the Tartan gang of which they were already a part (Mulvenna 2016) than with considerations about the importance of a given group's connection to the original UVF, the 36th (Ulster) Division, or the Somme.

For many in the UVF—including Stevie, Joshua, and Jeremy—the Somme story gained significance as a means of explaining and situating their violent deeds as members of the organization *after the fact*. In *Northern Ireland's Lost Opportunity* (2013), Tony Novosel details how education in history and politics was a pillar of the "Spence University," part of the regime developed and maintained by Gusty Spence for UVF and Red Hand Commando (RHC)[7] prisoners in Long Kesh prison in the 1970s. One of the outcomes of this educational program—much of it led by Spence himself—was the prominent role that the Somme came to play for prisoners in answering the question Spence posed to them when they first arrived in Long Kesh: "Why are you here?" (see Taylor 2000; Garland 2001; Sinnerton 2002). Its symbolism also became central to the UVF's and PUP's developing political project, particularly from the late 1970s on (Novosel 2013).[8] The enduring legacy of the Spence University's emphasis on the Somme story is evident in the formation of the first Somme associations by UVF prisoners in the late 1990s and early 2000s as part of their demobilization strategy (Orr 2014), as well as in the Shankill Road's wall murals, many of which are essentially direct copies of murals painted inside the huts of the prison camp (Hinson 2015). As such, Ulster Loyalism's Somme culture is perhaps rooted more in the cages of Long Kesh than in the trenches of the Western Front.

The claim that commemoration of the Somme has always featured prominently in the Loyalist commemorative calendar and been of central significance to broader Unionist culture is further troubled if one examines the history of the East Belfast Somme Memorial Parade. Its evolution is more complicated and contested than Orangemen's claims (see Hume 2005; *In Thiepval Wood* 2006) about the seamless and almost instantaneous adoption of the Somme's anniversary onto the marching season's calendar would necessarily suggest. While church services and local commemorative ceremonies were held throughout Ulster to mark the first anniversary of the Battle of the Somme (see Officer 2001; Switzer 2007, 2013), research in the archives of Ballymacarrett Orange Hall revealed no mention of an Orange parade in East Belfast on 1 July 1917. The first mention of any such parade appeared in the minute book of Albertbridge Church Total Abstinence LOL No. 987 in the entry for June 1918, in the form of a discussion about whether the lodge should meet at the Worshipful Master's house at seven or eight o'clock on the evening of 1 July.

The parade does not appear to have become an event of district-level significance until at least the early 1920s, and there is evidence that even then its significance was not unanimously agreed upon. In the early 1920s, some lodges debated whether they should take part in another major parade in such close proximity to the Twelfth of July. In June 1924 the secretary of Beersbridge Road Bible and Crown Defenders LOL No. 891 recorded, "Providing the District does not turn out we go out on our own and take the following route: meeting at the W. M.'s (Worshipful Master's) house 7:30 Clara Street, Beersbridge Road, Templemore Avenue, Newtownards Road, Bloomfield Avenue, Beersbridge Road, Clara Street and back to W. M. house." This proposed route is much shorter than the current six-mile circuit, and unlike the current route, it would not have taken the parade past the Nationalist enclave in the Short Strand. In email correspondence on 29 April 2015, one East Belfast Orangeman suggested that the route of the parade had originally been devised to take it past the homes that had been built for former servicemen on streets named for First World War battles off East Belfast's

Cregagh Road. In email correspondence with another senior Orange-man on 25 February 2016, he suggested that in his view, based on a re-view of district minute books, it was not until after the Second World War that the parade permanently adopted its present route, began to attain its current status, and became a prominent fixture on the district's commemorative calendar.

What some have termed Ulster Loyalism's cult of the Somme was not an inevitable consequence of the 36th (Ulster) Division's engage-ment with the enemy on 1 July 1916. Like other "invented traditions," its evolution over time has been defined as much by rupture and change as by continuity (see Bloch 1986; Bryan 2000). Crucially, despite the com-monplace assertion that the "cult of 1st July 1916 has never faltered" (Fitzpatrick 2016, 85), there is some suggestion that, beyond the com-pounds of Long Kesh, by the last half of the twentieth century it had begun to do just that. According to Frankie, a seasoned community worker and lifelong resident of the Shankill:

> In my upbringing here in Woodvale and the Shankill, the Somme was never a thing that was in my consciousness, you know, as a young lad growing up before the Troubles. And it never was a big, big thing during the Troubles, in my memory. . . . I would have been aware of the Battle of the Somme, but it would not have been some-thing that entered into my consciousness.
>
> When I got married I was living in the Lower Shankill and there was people two doors below us that always had a flag out on 1 July. But there was a lot of flags that went out then, which I always saw as bundled up into the Twelfth [of July], but theirs was quite specific and it was always put out on 1 July. And their family; their brother or father—I can't remember who it was—had been killed at the Battle of the Somme. And they always hung this out. I remember that, but that was it to me, in my twenties, and that was because they had a connection to the local church and I knew them [through it]. So it personalized the thing a bit. (Interview with author, 2015)

Philip Orr, historian and author of *The Road to the Somme* (2008), has spoken of how the idea for the book and the will to capture the oral his-tories of the few remaining survivors of the battle had been prompted by what he perceived in the mid-1980s as waning public interest in the Somme story. Nothing of any "real significance" on the subject, Orr (2012) notes, had been published for some sixty-five years, and the relevant records in libraries and military museums "lay under dust." Describing his first visit to the Ulster Tower at Thiepval on a detour when returning from Paris with a group of young people in 1983, Jackie Hewitt, manager of the Belfast-based Farset Youth & Community Development Group and cofounder of the Somme Association, recalled:

> My father had made mention of an 'Ulster Tower' in France, but that was the limit of my knowledge. We parked at the nearby war cemetery and immediately our group of young people—who were from Dublin as well as Belfast—were soon engrossed walking round the headstones, identifying the different Irish regiments. They were so enthusiastic that we decided we would take them inside the tower itself. However, a notice on the door said that anyone seeking access had to see a Madame Van Suyt, who lived at Hamel. At the young people's insistence we went to see Madame Van Suyt, who duly opened up the Tower. The interior was full of spiders and cobwebs, dust was lying thick on the floor and dead flies were everywhere. (Hall 2007, 14)

Likewise, Orr (2012) describes the Ulster Tower as being in a state of semidereliction during his visit in the late 1980s: "I had to hunt down a key in a nearby French village. [The tower] was little visited and empty" (see also Switzer 2013).

Work to refurbish the tower, coordinated by the Farset Somme Project, began shortly thereafter, and the tower was rededicated in 1989. In 1994, the Farset Somme Project became the Somme Association, which took over responsibility for managing the tower and the new Somme Heritage Centre in the village of Conlig, Co. Down. Throughout the 1990s and early 2000s, the flow of visitors to the Ulster Tower increased steadily, and in 2011 it received some 75,000 visitors (Switzer 2013). As Switzer (2013) suggests, this figure is representative to some extent of a more general growth in First World War battlefield tourism in the United Kingdom and across Europe, determined in large part by the advent of low-cost, short-haul airfares (see also Iles 2008). In his analysis of Loyalists' relationship with the Somme, William—a playwright and facilitator of community history projects who has spent more than twenty years working with the Loyalist community in Belfast and beyond—suggested, "Somme culture would never have happened if you hadn't had EasyJet" (interview with author, 2014). It is not necessarily the case that all or even most of the visitors to the Ulster Tower in this recent influx were Ulster Loyalists. Nonetheless, in Northern Ireland a notable aspect of this boom period in First World War commemoration has been its quintessentially Loyalist character.

In contrast to the declining membership of the Orange Order (Kaufmann 2007), the number of Somme associations and societies has grown and drawn an increasing number of members from beyond the ranks of the UVF's former prisoners—particularly since the formalization of the 36th (Ulster) Division Memorial Association in 2006. As Dominic Bryan (2014) has noted, the once ubiquitous image of "King Billy" crossing the Boyne in Loyalist wall murals in Belfast has been almost totally usurped by that of the soldiers of the 36th (Ulster) Division at the Somme. Since the 1994 cease-fires, and particularly since the Somme's ninetieth anniversary in 2006, the aesthetic of loyal order parades has been increasingly dominated by representations of the First World War in the form of regimental flags, the symbol of the poppy on uniforms and drums, and, most conspicuously, period costume.[9] The number of Somme commemorations has increased, and entirely new traditions, including a parade organized by the West Belfast Athletic and Cultural Society (WBACS) from the Shankill Road to the Belfast cenotaph on 1 July[10]—which has been held since 2000 (Philip, member of the WBACS committee, interview with author, 2015)—have been invented.

As Orr (2008, 2013) intimates, like the growth in battlefield tourism, this contemporary renewal of the cult of the Somme in Northern Ireland has been facilitated in part by broader sociological and technological trends in First World War commemoration in the United Kingdom, including the digital revolution in genealogical research. It also reflects the broader and expressly political trends in First World War commemoration in Ireland, North and South, in the era of peacebuilding, as outlined in chapter 3. Support and, crucially, funding, has been granted to cross-community commemorative projects, including the Farset Somme Project and Glenn Barr and Paddy Harte's Journey of Reconciliation Trust. The project of reimaging has helped to facilitate the proliferation of First World War imagery in Loyalist wall murals (cf. Rolston 2010). As identified by Orr (2013), as well as in my interview with Frankie, combined, these factors have (or are perceived as having) contributed to creating a cultural climate convivial to Loyalists' reacquainting themselves with their First World War heritage.

However, this process of reacquaintance arguably, and perhaps paradoxically, also represents Loyalists' refutation—often quite explicitly—of the terms and institutions of the peace-building project, its cross-communal politics and "parity of esteem," that have created this climate. Commemoration has become the primary battlefront in Loyalism's culture war, and Somme parades have become a key site of confrontation between Loyalism and Republicanism and, perhaps more acutely, between Loyalists and the state. For example, in 2011, the annual Ballymacarrett 1 July Somme parade was followed by a night of violent clashes between Loyalists, Nationalist residents of the Short Strand, and the PSNI (McDonald 2011). Since 2013, temporary metal barriers have been erected along the interface between the Short Strand and the Albertbridge Road in order to separate residents from spectators and paraders.

In 2015—following disorder after the parade the previous year—when the Parades Commission determined to restrict a Somme commemoration in Coleraine organized by Killowen LOL No. 930, Russell Watton (quoted in *Purple Standard* 2015a, 19), PUP councilor on Causeway Coast and Glens Borough Council, lamented, "It's a sad day for our country when law abiding people are not permitted to pay homage to those who fell facing the enemy in defence of our freedom, in order to appease those who wish to diminish it." The report on Somme parades in the *Purple Standard* in which Councilor Watton's comments appeared continued:

> This magazine unreservedly condemns the Parades Commission for its continued capitulation to Republicans, and we echo what Russell Watton has *rightfully* said, 'The Loyalist community must come together and defeat this treacherous conspiracy.' What we must maintain though, even in the face of this extreme provocation, is our dignity! We *will* win the day, but like our forebears, we must stand tall as we do it! What unites us is the respectful, dignified and proud

Remembrance of those who Volunteered for King and Country, and sacrificed their lives that we might live, free from oppression, free from tyranny and safe in this land we call home.

The culture war and the cult of the Somme are inextricably linked. Mutually constitutive, they are the products of the same cultural and political moment. As such, like the culture war itself, the latest incarnation of Loyalism's Somme cult can be traced to Drumcree. During the parades disputes of the mid- to late 1990s, Portadown Orangemen's assertions of their right to march on the Garvaghy Road hinged in large part on the claim that the contentious parade was a "time-honored" Somme commemoration. This has been largely uncontested in ongoing discourses about the dispute and its legacy. However, and as noted by Bryan (2014, 305–6), before 1998 the Orange Order in Portadown had made no such claim. In fact, the order had previously and publicly dated the Drumcree parade to 1807, some 109 years before the Battle of the Somme. Until 1998, the Drumcree parade had commemorated the Boyne, not the Somme. During the dispute, and under the conditions of the subsequent culture war it has precipitated, the Somme has come to play an increasingly prominent symbolic and political role in promoting the righteousness of the Loyalist cause, thereby overtaking the Boyne as the primary site of Loyalist social memory.

"THEY NEED TO LEARN THEIR HISTORY"

Traditionally, and as suggested by William,

the key moment in British history that the Orange Order and Loyalism anchored itself around was the story of the Glorious Revolution, and its consequences in Ireland, with the famous battles, the Williamite battles . . . [but that's] kind of disappeared from people's thinking. . . . It's gotten further and further away—the Battle of the Boyne—you know, people with long hair on white horses: it's pageantry, it's fancy-dress. It's just *so* long ago! But also, look at it! The prancing horse with the conqueror on top is seen in just about every plaza in Europe. It's an emblem of Empire: striding the world with the hooves up, isn't it? So, you know, it's a long time ago [and] to try and infatuate young men with the memory of it; that's a challenge for Loyalism. And secondly, it also is redolent with imperial power and subjection. (Interview with author, 2014)

By contrast, the Somme allows Loyalism to

plug itself in first of all to the biggest, most comprehensive, solemn ceremonial event in the British Isles. From Shetland to Cornwall, everybody wears the poppy, everybody remembers and gathers at eleven o'clock on November 11. So it ties Loyalism in to a universal ceremony of remembrance that helps it to feel it's part of a bigger story, and it also brings it up to date . . . above all else, it's about ordinary guys from your street. So therefore, that's a bit more politically correct if nothing else, than the conqueror on the horse. (Interview with author, 2014)

Bryan (2014) suggests that, on one level, the rebranding of the Drumcree parade, and the growth of the cult of the Somme it has precipitated, represents Loyalists' attempt to make a claim about the solemnity, significance, and validity of their cultural traditions in terms comprehensible beyond Northern Ireland.

However, more fundamentally, it is also representative of a trend whereby Loyalist commemorators perceive and represent themselves as the sole custodians of a righteous and sacrificial history that—particularly in the moment of peace-building and the culture war—has been otherwise forgotten, not only on the British mainland, but also in Northern Ireland itself. Reflected in Sammy's comments about "garden center Unionism" is what has become the ubiquitous suggestion that people in Northern Ireland in general and in the PUL community in particular need to be taught *their* history. During our interview, Derek, an East Belfast community development worker and UDA former prisoner who has also been involved in organizing commemorative events, including with the Unionist Centenary Committee, insisted:

We haven't got an identity, a historical identity. You say to kids, "What's your identity?" "Ah, flute bands." Do you know what I mean? "King Billy". . . but what *is* it? Where does it go to? "Ah, Battle of the Boyne." When was it? "1690." "What was it about?" "Don't know." "Why do you burn bonfires?" "Don't know." They don't *know*. They identify with things, but you know, as far as framing an identity, they don't know a historical identity. If you're talking to somebody from the Republican community, they'll go right back to the Celts, and they'll know their history because they've been taught it in schools. They've been taught that line. And they'll identify a line, a historical context, a debating line. They've been taught a debating line, where we're invaders, we're planters, d'you know what I mean? And we came and took their land, whereas our kids have no historical context at all, d'you know what I mean? (Interview with author, 2014)

This claim mirrors the logic at the heart of the Spence University project—itself a reflection of broader and more widely accepted claims about the role of history in public life (see Bryan 2016)—that knowing one's history is fundamental to one's explaining one's (or even having an) identity. Drawing in part on the types of genealogical practice outlined above, for Loyalists, the process of identity formation is therefore couched in the language of teaching or learning "their" history, of recovering or restoring the truth of the Loyalist experience, and of protecting "real" history from attempts on the part of proponents of the peace process ("peace propagandists") to rewrite it. In the face of the revisionism that Loyalists perceive to be at the heart of claims of parity of esteem, commemoration during the Decade of the Centenaries provides an opportunity to (re)assert their place in history and, thereby, the validity and morality of their ontology in the present. This idea was reinforced in my interview with Laura.

L: Reading back on things, I mean, Thiepval Tower was given to the people of Ulster. Thiepval Tower was built for the 36th (Ulster) Division. Then when Farset come on board, I think it was the early eighties Farset come on board, mid-eighties they come on board. And they done then all the work to get Thiepval Tower back into the way it was, 'cause it'd been lying derelict for so long. And then they set up the Somme Heritage Centre, and it was set up as the 36th

(Ulster) Division Museum. But over the years it's changed to the Irishsoldier.org. . . . Look, there's too much bitterness about. There's far too much bitterness about. And I think it's an issue that should've been addressed a long, long time ago. And I think the only way to address it now, is by teaching people their history. And that's the truth. I think, I think the majority of Catholics need to know . . . they need to know the likes of this, they need to know that they fought alongside, or that the 16th and the 36th fought together. They need to know this sort of stuff. And I don't think the Somme Association's helping an awful lot in this situation.

JE: Because they're shying away from . . . ?

L: They're shying away from the 36th (Ulster) Division. And to me the reason they're doing it is for funding. To me the only reason they're doing the whole Irishsoldier.org is for funding. . . . Give me twenty kids for six weeks, I'll take them on a step by step, take them to Craigavon House, take them to Stormont, take them down to Helen's Tower, wee silly things like that there. Y'know, teach the kids that we're not, that Protestants *aren't* bad people.

There are parallels between Laura's argument and those I discussed in chapter 3 about a perceived need for the construction of a shared history during the Decade of Centenaries, for example, her suggestion that better history and a correction of the historical record is crucial to promoting better relationships between Unionists and Nationalists. To this end, Laura too is concerned with starting from "the facts" and with historical "truth." The paradigm (neither more nor less political) that shapes these claims, however, is clearly different from that which frames those of the CRC, HLF, academic historians, and other peace propagandists. Laura's are claims made on Loyalists' terms. Based on their analysis of the same evidence, Loyalists (often explicitly) contest the conclusions reached by proponents of the shared history thesis, refuting what they view as attempts to write them out of history. As suggested by Matthew, a senior East Belfast Orangeman:

It was a *British* war . . . people fought for different reasons. But at the end of the day, they fought for the United Kingdom. They fought for King and Empire. So you can't just for [the sake of] revisionism water that down. . . . I have a very good friend from the Republic who would carry a tricolour at commemorations of the Somme. Now, that would irk me. Because the tricolour was the flag that was used to murder British soldiers in 1916, and Commonwealth soldiers, you know, and [fellow] Irishmen! So I see no place for it there, I have to say. But I can understand that that's his flag now, but his tradition going back, is a British tradition. I understand why he does it, but it does irk me because it's a contradiction. (Interview with author, 2015)

Mike expressed similar views in our interview.

M: One of the things I do disagree with wholeheartedly is at any commemorative event [for the First World War in Ireland], that the Irish tricolour's at it. And that's not being . . . just, if they're gonna do it, do it right. There was no tricolour in 1916. I find that a wee bit . . .

JE: A bit jarring?

M: Yeah, and it's not because I have a dislike of anything Irish, I just think that it's . . . it's just one of my wee little dislikes, my little quirks. I just think it's a bit stupid when you see an Irish tricolour at it. 'Cause there was no Irish flag back then.

JE: Is it in some way because that flag is like a rejection of . . . it represents rejection . . .

M: Of Britishness. It's a rejection of Britishness. It's a flag that's been hijacked by Republicans; as in Sinn Féin/IRA.

The analysis at the heart of Loyalist commemoration explicitly repudiates a perceived artificial and symbolic balancing of Unionism and Nationalism in the pursuit of parity of esteem, which in Loyalists' view amounts to a distortion of reality. Some have referred to this balancing derogatorily as "the Greening of the Great War" (Burke 2016). Crucially, for Loyalists, to claim a symbolic and moral equivalence between Unionism and Nationalism as ideological or cultural-political projects is historically invalid. It is a category error.

Ritually exemplified in the 1st Shankill Somme Association's wreath laying at the European War Memorial, Loyalists also claim that theirs is a version of history and a commemorative tradition that is not only apolitical and truthful but also thereby inclusive and reconciliatory in a way that is broader and more authentic than "official" or "shared" commemoration. Vital to Loyalist commemorators' claims of inclusion is the acceptance, on the part of those being "included," that those who fought for Britain during the First World War did so for an unequivocally (and virtuous) British or Unionist cause.

> Let's not forget, you know, if we're looking for reconciliation: over a million Muslims were under the British Empire, fighting for the crown. Now there's a pretty good one to be throwing up nowadays! And other issues that are about the place, when people begin to get on their high horse about Muslims. . . . People forget that they fought for the Empire as well. Totally different religion, totally different reasons, maybe they were poor and joined up, all of those reasons. But they fought as part of the war against the Hun. And so they all equally deserve to be remembered, no matter what their religious affiliation. But they fought for the Union Jack! (Matthew, interview with author, 2015)

Drawing on his years of work with Loyalist groups—including marching bands, former prisoners' organizations, and local history societies—on a series of community, historical, and dramatic projects, William described what he had identified in this aspect of Somme culture as providing relief from "the burden of sectarian stigma." He continued:

> The way things are constructed in the contemporary world: the freedom fighter, though he may do wrong things, nonetheless, seems like a guy who's doing it for a purpose, right? A progressive purpose; if sometimes a deluded one. The guy who is just going out and cutting throats on the Shankill Road is a just a, well, a butcher. So you're living all the time with this stigma, and it's coming at you also from your own camp, from your own Unionist leadership as well. But you go [to France and Belgium] and you discover rituals of

sublimity; vast, towering monuments; a sense of being part of a bigger story. You know, Republicanism's got a bigger story that includes everything from Martin Luther King to Gandhi—with a few guns thrown in as well, and the odd car bomb taking out civilians, but, you know, "We did give a warning, and it wasn't passed on." So they've got all that. For Loyalists, this is a way of getting an "all that." You've got this bigger picture. And you know, these guys I think, this idea of sitting down in Ypres near the Cloth Hall and drinking a beer and looking around you: it's a good feeling. It's a good feeling, and gives you some kind of sense of dignity back. [So] that's very important, I think, that it's part of a bigger story. (Interview with author, 2014)

In 2005, before the current policing regimen for the 1 July East Belfast Somme Memorial Parade was instituted, a group of women walked at its head carrying two banners. The messages on the banners were directed at protesting Short Strand residents. The first proclaimed:

Our Flags are not those of murder gangs. . . . They are the flags of the men who died fighting for the freedom of the country in which you live.

And the second:

On the 1st July we remember all who never returned home from the Somme. In particular we remember the soldiers of Ireland who made the ultimate sacrifice for King & Country. 36th Ulster Division ~ 16th Irish Division.

As critically dissected by William, this particular claim to inclusivity in Loyalist commemorative discourse functions as follows:

When, [as a Loyalist, you visit] Theipval Wood, and look around that space, around Thiepval, you're able almost to map out where all the different battalions were. And you're kind of remapping out Ulster. But you're doing it in a place where the Nationalists don't *matter* anymore. Because they're down the road, in the army, down the road. They're with us. . . . They're in on *our* side. You're able to kid yourself that they would have come along, kid yourself that they . . . you know, you're able to do the equivalent and opposite of what Nationalists and Republicans do when they talk about "Catholic, Protestant, and Dissenter," when they say, "Well, the Prods [Protestants] are really gonna come in with us. They were in 1798, they'll come in with us again!" And you're able to do the equivalent and opposite of that on the Loyalist side and say, "Well, you know, they came, and they were in the army and they were down the road, at Grandcourt or Guillemont or wherever it was, fighting alongside us." You're able to dream a certain kind of event that didn't happen. (Interview with author, 2014)

I contend that it is this, above all, that explains the growth of Loyalism's contemporary Somme culture. Commemorating the sacrifice of the Somme is the process by which Loyalist knowledge is made truthful and "a certain kind of event that didn't happen" made real. In a present defined by the myriad crises of the culture war, it is the means by which the redemptive promise of an imagined past or Golden Age (Smith 1997) is invoked to remember a future in which those crises can be overcome. In the next chapter, I examine in greater depth the content of this eschatological or hauntological promise of the Somme and the intracommunal conflicts it both belies and seeks to elide.

CHAPTER SIX

The Ghost Dance

Memory Work and Loyalism's Conflicted Hauntology

S: You see we were [in Thiepval Wood for] 1 July [2006]: the corn's out, or the wheat's out, and you get the poppies, and it's just the most picturesque place you've ever seen! But you think to yourself, "Jesus, a hundred odd years ago it was a slaughter, people being killed here, and they're still buried out there." So you're going over ground knowing there could be people still buried beneath you. . . . What do you call her, used to play in the Regimental Band: Scotch girl? Well, she started to do a recital on the flute—was it Jenny? Anyway, halfway through it, you could hear it, something happened. And afterwards, I said to her, I said, "Jenny what happened there?" She said, "Simon, I'm not messing about," she says, "I was playing, and my collar was [turned] down, and it was as if somebody came along and fixed my tunic." And as soon as she said that there, the hairs on my arm just shot up.

JE: Goosebumps?

S: Ah, it was amazing!

JE: Like a kind of ghostly presence or something?

S: Yeah. And when she said that . . . There were about thirty of us there, but I could just imagine there was more. There was all the souls of . . . all of those souls were just there and they were with us, if you know what I mean? It's hard to explain, like. (Simon, interview with author, 2015)

9 May 2015. "Another day. Another parade," I thought sleepily, as I conceded that I didn't have time to press "snooze" again. Somewhat reluctantly I dragged myself out of bed. 8:15: a little later than I had intended. Many months in the planning, today thousands of Loyalists from across Northern Ireland would participate in the Unionist Centenary Committee and 36th (Ulster) Division Memorial Association's centennial commemoration and reenactment of the Ulster Division's Belfast City Hall march-past. In 1915, the march-past had been the Division's final parade in Ireland before they boarded the boats that would take them first to England and then, eventually, to France and the Somme.

I made my way first to the Shankill Road for a smaller feeder parade in advance of the main event. I arrived with just enough time to lock up my bike before noticing that the parade was on its way down the road. There were a handful of spectators on either side of the street, but the turnout seemed to be fairly low. In the real world, I reminded myself grumpily, it was 8:45 on a Saturday. However, as the parade passed I was roused from drowsiness. The vintage cars, the rows of reenactors marching smartly and in step, carrying handcrafted replica wooden rifles and in khaki uniforms, and the UVF Regimental Band playing immaculately—all made for an impressive display. The notably (and unusually, in my experience) high caliber of the band afforded some sense of the talent and vitality of the band scene so often vaunted by Loyalists (see Ramsey 2011; NIYF 2013).

As the parade passed and the reenactors boarded the buses that would take them to the starting point of the main parade in North Belfast, I spotted Jamie on the street corner and crossed the road to meet him, eagerly sharing my thoughts on the spectacle. He agreed to a point but was disquieted. This *should* be a day for solemn reflection. The bands and the pageantry all rendered it more celebratory than he felt appropriate. I was a little abashed and upon reassessment, found it hard not to agree. We were "remembering" a moment when thousands of young men had left Ireland's shores for the mud and barbarism of the Western Front, hundreds of them never to return. We agreed that today's parade—and indeed, commemorative parades generally—are more to do with the people parading than with those they claim to be remembering: "We were here," not "Lest We Forget."

At the city hall as we waited for the main parade, we bumped into Lawrence, who had word from stewards at the parade's starting point in North Belfast. "The UDA aren't walking," he told us ruefully. Something to do with an ongoing feud, apparently. At any rate, events commemorating the UVF and the 36th (Ulster) Division were politically difficult for them, so the feud was, he suspected, really a convenient excuse. Lawrence had also heard that there had been some tense and, as far as he knew, unresolved exchanges between the 36th (Ulster) Division Memorial Association and the UVF in North Belfast, about who would lead the parade. If Lawrence was right and there had been a confrontation at the parade's starting point, then its outcome became apparent as the parade emerged at the top of Royal Avenue.

Following the color party at the head of the parade there came several rows of men, some in period costume and others in black suits, flat caps, and 11th (South Antrim) Battalion Royal Irish Rifles or 15th (North Belfast) Battalion Royal Irish Rifles armbands. These men sported black UVF ties. The banner of the 36th (Ulster) Division Memorial Association and the members of its constituent Somme Associations followed after. Save for the occasional contingent of women in the costume of the UVF nursing corps (billowing white and light blue juxtaposed to the somber black) and the vibrant uniforms of the bands, much of the first half of the parade consisted of similar rows of men in black suits and armbands, some sporting flat caps in an attempt at period costume. As with the first group, for the most part, the armbands worn by the men in each bloc designated it as corresponding to a particular, historical detachment of Carson's Army: 9th (West Belfast) Battalion Royal Irish Rifles, 10th (South Belfast) Battalion Royal Irish Rifles, and so on. However, some were less discreet about the significance of these designations: "UVF East Belfast" proclaimed the armbands worn by the men in one particularly large phalanx. Each cohort of UVF men was accompanied by a regimental band, sporting the colors and standards of a given UVF brigade or battalion area.

Factional conflict and some confusion had also been evident in advance of the parade during a debate about its "official" end point. On 6 May, the Shankill Historical Society (2015) had posted a "Notice to anyone coming to Belfast for the parade this Saturday" on social media:[1]

The parade is finishing at Cambrai Street off the Shankill Road, it has been said that the parade is finishing at Dee Street in East Belfast, this is only the finishing point for the loyal orders attending on the day, the main body of the parade along with the 36th (Ulster) Division Memorial Assoc. and their bands WILL finish at Cambrai Street, Shankill Road. Shankill Band Shop (next to Subway) will be open Friday 10–5pm, Saturday 9–5pm and Sunday 9–5pm.

But this notice was refuted by the parade's organizational committee on its Facebook page: "No idea where this inaccurate information was obtained but it's wrong. The 36th (Ulster) Division Memorial Association finishes in Dee Street (in East Belfast) as previously stated" (Review of the 36th–Ulster Division–Belfast 2015).

As the tramp of marching feet—interrupted intermittently by the flutes and drums of the bands—began to recede, Jamie and I elected to follow the "official" notice from the parade organizers and head over to the Newtownards Road in East Belfast. However, in the event, both Facebook posts turned out to be correct, as one parade became two. In its coverage of the day's events, the UVF-affiliated magazine, the *Purple Standard*, reported:

The route of the parade saw its final stages pass Belfast City Hall, and make for the Old Town Hall, where there would be a 'General Salute'. Following this, the parade split, with the 2015/2016 Committee[2] veering left to St. Anne's Cathedral, where William ('Billy') Hutchinson laid a wreath of poppies at the tomb of Sir Edward Carson, before setting off for dismissal points on the Shankill Road.

The remainder of the parade, incorporating the Loyal Orders and the Somme Associations etc., made their way to be dismissed at Dee Street, just off the Newtownards Road. (2015b, 10)

The protracted disentangling of the two parades meant that Jamie and I had a lengthy wait at the bottom of the Newtownards Road before the head of the "official" parade appeared. Across the street, a police Land Rover sported in large letters the Parades Commission's determination: "ONLY HYMN TUNES SHALL BE PLAYED PAST THIS POINT." Another pronouncement in similar style beyond St. Matthew's

Catholic Church and the intersection with the Short Strand marked the end of this restriction. "They'd better not play hymns," muttered one older woman, ominously. When the parade eventually arrived, some of the bands did not disappoint her, playing loud renditions of what appeared to be prohibited tunes, including "The Sash My Father Wore." The many bands that did choose to play hymns—or, even worse, nothing at all—were loudly chastised. "Call yourselves Loyalists?!," the woman angrily demanded of one band. "Eyes front!," barked the band captain to his drummers, many of whom had clearly been startled or upset. Jamie, a former band captain, explained how this kind of behavior puts bands in a difficult situation. How should they respond to their audience? Is it the audience to whom they are ultimately loyal? Opinion in the parading fraternity on these and other questions is, he lamented, split.

On first reading of this (thick) description of one Loyalist commemorative parade, the minutiae—who walked, in what order, to where, watched by whom and how—may seem of little consequence. However, these minute details and the microconflicts they represent mirror, reproduce, and magnify the structural fault lines in the foundations of the PUL community's symbolic construction at a macro level. Commemoration allows the Unionist Centenary Committee (2015) to claim, "Another successful year for our community with the outstanding event being the parade through Belfast by our entire community on the 9th May 2015," while simultaneously replicating a series of conflicts that act to destabilize this very claim. Ritually, spatially, and discursively, commemoration seeks to elide conflict but in the very moment of its elision acts to reproduce it.

Drawing on the Derridean (2006 [1993]) concept of hauntology, in this chapter I seek to deconstruct Loyalism's contemporary commemoration of the Somme—its "ghost dance." I argue that to do so reveals the Somme's emancipatory or eschatological promise for Loyalism and the PUL community. The Somme represents an unfulfilled salvational promise for the soul of this community, and commemoration stresses its inherent unity. However, particularly in the moment of peace-building, this promise remains intrinsically unfulfillable and this community, un(re)constructable. First, I demonstrate that—although not conventionally understood as such—Loyalism, as a social and political movement, remains an incomplete project animated by and calling on the ghosts of its imagined past. I argue that this project is characterized by forms of resonance across time and space: a perpetual process of deconstruction and reconstruction. I demonstrate the particular promise of unity that is represented by the Somme, then explore further the intra-, inter-, and extracommunal conflicts that its commemoration claims to have overcome. In its attempt to construct and represent this unity, Loyalist commemoration instead betrays its impossibility, re-creating the very division it is intended to surmount. Finally, in the impossibility of the Somme's promise for Loyalism exists potential for personal and political transformation. This idea is explored further in chapter 7.

LOYALISM AND THE "NEVER-ENDING OUGHT TO BE"

> This is what the LORD says: "When seventy years are completed for Babylon, I will come to you and fulfil my good promise to bring you back to this place. . . . I will gather you from all the nations and places where I have banished you," declares the LORD, "and will bring you back to the place from which I carried you into exile." (Jeremiah 29:10–14)

In the process of writing my field notes following the 9 May reenactment, I received an email from William. One part of his email was especially arresting, as it spoke directly and eloquently to an idea that was starting to take shape in my own reflections on the nature of Loyalism and, in particular, its Somme culture. It read:

> I was thinking of the image of the children of Israel making their way to the 'promised land' and getting lost for forty years in the wilderness *en route*. . . . At least to get lost is a sign you are still trying to get there, travelling and searching still for the heroic promise: an apotheosis imagined, whether at Twaddell or the Menin Gate.
>
> A few years ago I was watching with a crowd on the Lisburn Road [on the Twelfth of July] for the first hint of a swirling banner and the marching (sword carrying) vanguard of men appearing around a bend on the highway and into view—and it felt like the

children of Israel had at last found their way out of the wilderness and were heading, freshly watered, booted and suited and assured of their route towards the Promised Land, the (Elysian) Field.

Until the next parade when they would have to do it all over again . . . and again . . . and again . . . because if they stopped parading (and stopped being stopped parading) the hope of being in the better place that they'd always been assured (or assured themselves) was theirs would finally die.

'Let them home' the cry goes up unto God. And the heavens are as brass, yea but our God can part the Red Sea and unto him yet again we cry.

In its 2008 treatise, *The Coming Insurrection*, which has gained notoriety and influence among those both actively involved in global(ized) social movements and in the study thereof (see Trott 2011), the Invisible Committee suggests:

> Revolutionary movements do not spread by contamination, but by *resonance*. . . . A body that resonates does so according to its own mode. An insurrection is not like a plague or a forest fire—a linear process which spreads place to place after an initial spark. It rather takes the shape of a music, whose focal points, though disbursed in time and space, succeed in imposing the rhythm of their own vibrations, always taking on more density. (2009, 6)

Thus defined, "resonance" across space and time is comparable to Jacques Derrida's (1976) concept of *différance*. Any act that produces forms of signification or meaning—for Derrida, principally through speech or in writing but also conceivably in forms of material production, or through performance (cf. Butler 1990), ritual practice, or other forms of what Bourdieu (1991, 130) termed the "labour of representation"—is comprehensible only in its relation to other or previous acts of signification. However, the reproduction or reiteration of comprehensible signs is not merely or principally an act of repetition, but of the production of new forms of meaning. The production of a given set of signs in one context can have a (potentially radically) different meaning in another. Meaning is consistently and endlessly deferred, and that of previous iterations is, ultimately, irrecoverable. A particular sign manifests (or resonates) in different ways at different times, both mirroring and serving to shape changes in the context in which it is (re)produced.

As activists and intellectuals on the radical Left, it is unlikely that either the Invisible Committee or Jacques Derrida would identify a movement on the Right as worthy of the label "revolutionary" or (perhaps) even of analysis as a movement per se. Indeed, as suggested in chapter 2, the right wing has not always been comfortable terrain for scholars of social movements in general. The term "social movement" is conventionally reserved for or seen as synonymous with those groups or communities on the (far) Left that claim a politics that is unequivocally antihegemonic in ways that Loyalism—by virtue of its claims to "prostatism" (cf. Bruce 1992), the complications of its actually existing relationship with the state, and the depth (not to mention violence and moral bankruptcy) of state collusion with Loyalist paramilitarism (see Sluka 2000; Cadwallader 2013; Urwin 2016)—cannot. This helps to explain why, in the Northern Irish context, the term "movement" and assertions about the kinds of revolutionary resonance identified by the Invisible Committee have generally been confined to examinations of the role of the Easter Rising in the Republican political tradition.

In his essay, "What Is Living and What Is Dead in the Ideal of 1916?," Arthur Aughey (1991, 83–84) argued, "Political life is always conditional and its achievements transient. The [Irish] Free State of 1921, is not the Free State of 1937, is not the Republic of 1991. None of them is the Republic of 1916. But to celebrate the fixed community envisaged by the Easter Rebellion is to celebrate a never-ending ought to be." This *incompleteness* that defines the Republican project is a well-recognized feature of the conflicted politics of Irish Nationalism. It is reflected and re-created in Republican commemorative discourse and practice (see Browne 2016). While different political groupings, organizations, and interests in Ireland, North and South, have attempted to use commemoration of the Easter Rising as "a means of containment" for their particular programs, this has consistently "resist[ed] its own aim: rather than marking the borders of identity by incorporating the past, it sends 'Irishness' into the future as something on the way to being formed" (Greenlaw 2004, 3; see also Graff-McRae 2010; Higgins 2012, 2016; Bean 2016).

During my interview with Seosamh, a Sinn Féin activist and member of the National Graves Association based in North Belfast,[3] he illustrated what in his view is a key distinction between Republican and Loyalist commemoration.

> The Proclamation is a living document. The Proclamation isn't something that we have reached, or isn't even something that we have said we can't reach. It's a living document, it's what people like me say we subscribe to. It's what we say motivates us. . . . Don't underestimate the fear that actually is something in Unionism. And when people are frightened they close ranks. They circle the wagons. They do all of that, you know? The enemy's out there! Unionism looks at its heyday as gone. You know, "they were the best of our times." [Whereas for] Republicans, the phrase that was developed inside the blocks was *Tiocfaidh ár Lá*. *Tiocfaidh ár Lá* literally means "Our day will come." So Republicans are looking forward to events, to change, to progress, to winning; however you term it; however you term it. And I think Unionism, sadly, is looking back to what it had, to what it was like, to what it was like then. . . . That's reflected in the garb, the dress of the bands. You know? Very impressive, I have to add. It's also reflected in the big parades. The Covenant parades were almost a step back into history. They weren't a step forward into change. So, you've all of that. (Interview with author, 2014)

The political function of the Somme's commemoration for Loyalists is often (perhaps conventionally) assessed as a consequence of this juxtaposition to and contrast with Republican commemoration of the Easter Rising (cf. Jarman 1999), such that Graff-McRae (2010, 110) has criticized the way in which "a reference to '1916' is first assumed to signify the Rising—the Somme is an addition, made obvious because of its inclusion."

Edna Longley (1994, 69, 75) has suggested that "Irish Catholics and Ulster Protestants not only tend to remember different things, but to remember them in different ways," with Loyalism's "heritage-pack survival kit" opposed to Nationalism's merger of "memory into aspiration." Guy Beiner (2007a, 386) has likewise contrasted the "future perfect" orientation of Irish Republicanism with the "past continuous" of Ulster

Loyalist social memory, suggesting that in constructing the "traumatic memory of the Somme, unionists were taking a leaf out of a *nationalist* book, which had forcefully demonstrated the appeal of political claims based on accounts of suffering" (emphasis added). In what Beiner identifies as a recent defeatist turn in contemporary Loyalist politics, "Protestant loyalists may have *unconsciously* emulated the nationalist republican tradition of triumph of failure" (2007a, 382; emphasis added).

This analysis is emblematic, in the first instance, of a widespread tendency to overemphasize the differences between the two traditions of Unionism and Nationalism (cf. Santino 2001). As suggested in chapter 4, accounts of suffering have long been a defining feature of PUL social memory, while Gerry Adams's comments about breaking the "bastards" demonstrate that Irish Republicans are quite capable of triumphalism. Furthermore, if there has been "unconscious emulation," then it has been reciprocal. Despite some significant differences—particularly in the role of spectator qua spectator at Loyalist parades versus the spectator as participant at Republican processions (see Jarman 1997, 152)—my experience of parades on the Falls and on the Shankill was very similar. For instance, to the untrained ear, there is little to distinguish between a Republican and a Loyalist flute band. Indeed, Ray Casserly (2012) has demonstrated that many marching tunes are replicated across the two parading traditions, and that the chief factors in determining differences in drumming style between bands are socioeconomic rather than ethnonational. More generally, the military-style costume and marching, flag parties, raising and lowering of standards, playing of the last post, minute-long silences, and Christian religiosity in both parading traditions fits a wider and "apprehensible" (Humphrey and Laidlaw 1994, 101) European—even global—commemorative mold.

Crucially, both Loyalism and Republicanism are defined by their incompleteness as political projects. Ulster Loyalism is a protest movement. The claim to be a political community resisting the hegemony of the state in Northern Ireland is certainly problematic for those who carry the state flag as a symbol of that resistance. Nonetheless, Loyalism's historically dominant position in the Orange State (Farrell 1980) was not experienced as such. Rather, it was, and remains, understood as one of perennial embattlement. In a political, social, and economic environment defined by the hegemonic "sharedness" of the "new" Northern Ireland and its "propaganda of peace," Loyalism's status as a (pro-) hegemonic political-cultural formation has become all the more ambiguous. Furthermore, some of the resonances of many social or revolutionary movements of which the Invisible Committee (2009) is explicitly approving are in evidence in contemporary forms of Loyalist cultural expression and political agitation. The footage of masked young men in hooded tops hurling missiles at police in Belfast during the flag protests bears more than a passing resemblance to that of riots in Paris in 2005, Athens in 2008, or London in 2011. The language of civil rights at the Twaddell protest camp resonates with that of movements (including in Northern Ireland itself) in the 1960s, while the tactic of thus appropriating public space for protest owes much to the inspiration of the Arab Spring and Occupy Wall Street (see Graeber 2013).

The reproduction and evolution over time of the "memory" of the Somme for Ulster Loyalism outlined in chapter 5 can usefully be understood as a process of resonance or of *différance*, characterized by its appearance, (near-)disappearance, and reappearance across time and space. At the unveiling of a new war memorial in Coleraine in 1922, then prime pinister of the newly established state of Northern Ireland, James Craig, declared, "Those who passed away have left behind a great message . . . to stand firm and give away none of Ulster's soul" (Jeffrey 1993, 124). In 1934, Craig's oft-(mis)quoted allusion to "carrying on a Protestant Parliament for a Protestant people" was a corollary to his claim that "the Act of 1920 . . . was given to the Ulster people in order to save them from being swallowed up in a Dublin Parliament. Therefore, it is undoubtedly our duty and our privilege, and *always will be*, to see that those appointed by us possess the most unimpeachable loyalty to the King and Constitution" (NIHC Deb [1934–35] 17 Col. 72–73; emphasis added).

Founded on the blood sacrifice of the Ulster Division, "Northern Ireland" is the emancipatory, perennial, and unfulfilled promise of deliverance for the soul of Ulster: Northern Ireland as its promised land, as a home for a covenanting people. While Brian Graham (1997) has described Ulster as "a place yet to be imagined," in Loyalist commemoration I saw and experienced what I felt to be a continuous process of its reproduction and reimagination (cf. Miller 1978; Finlay 2001). The labeling of Northern Ireland as "a Protestant State for a Protestant People" is misattributed to the Viscount Craigavon. But it nonetheless captures something of the (deferred) essence of the Unionist political project. Over the course of my fieldwork, the resonances of this founding promise of Northern Irish nation building kept (re)appearing.

For example, on the evening of 9 May 2015, following the march-past, we sat and talked with some of the members of Jamie's former band at the Harland & Wolff Welders' Social Club (known locally as "The Welders"). I was taken in by the (distinctly homosocial) camaraderie and the genuine affection that underwrote the casual banter and the good slaggin' given and received in equal measure by all those present. The welcome was gruff but not unfriendly. The animated storytelling; the physicality of the bear hugs and greetings between old friends; red-faced, animated, but friendly differences of opinion; arguments about whose was the next round; and the ringing of raucous laughter served to render tangible the idea of the PUL community, giving it form and so-lidity. As I left the bar—much earlier than anyone else seemed intent to—the final line of the slurred karaoke's chorus hung on the air as it fol-lowed me through the door: "And every day's like the Twelfth of July."

In its myriad forms of signification—in the music and color of the marching bands, the camaraderie of The Welders, in homemade (invari-ably by "the ladies") cakes and sandwiches and urns of stewed tea at the Orange Hall, or in the pints of lager, the hot whiskeys, sing-alongs, jokes, and slaggin' of the band hall—I felt I saw Ulster and glimpsed its soul, albeit in ways that were fleeting or ephemeral, not to mention some-times overtly misogynistic or homophobic and occasionally racist or ex-plicitly sectarian. It would take on form and density, only to dissipate and reemerge elsewhere. I sensed the ghosts of the Somme and their de-ferred promise in the lyrics of drunken karaoke—"Oh give me a home/ Where there's no Pope of Rome/And there's nothing but Protestants stay/Where seldom is heard/A discouraging word/And flute bands play the Sash every day"—in the cries of "Let Them Home!" during speeches at Twaddell Avenue, and in the banners at city hall flag protests. In 2014, at one such protest, a banner proclaimed, "Our Forefathers, As We And Our Children, Will Never Surrender Our National Flag." A version of this national flag—reproduced in Taiwanese plastic—fluttered next to it. At its center was J. P. Beadle's famous depiction of those forefathers: the 36th (Ulster) Division leading the charge out of the trenches on the morning of 1 July 1916 (fig. 6.1).

Figure 6.1. "In Memory 36th (Ulster) Division" Union flag.

Thus, while the transient "political life" to which Aughey referred was that of the Republic proclaimed by Padraig Pearse outside the General Post Office on Easter Monday 1916, his argument is also applicable to the Protestant State proclaimed by James Craig in 1934. The Northern Ireland of the 1920 Government of Ireland and 1922 Special Powers Acts is not the Northern Ireland of O'Neill and the Civil Rights movement, is not the Northern Ireland of direct rule from 1972, nor is it the Northern Ireland of the Good Friday Agreement. None of these Northern Ireland's is the "Ulster" of the 1912 Covenant. But to celebrate the fixed community represented in the Somme's sacrifice is to celebrate a never-ending ought to be. Just as the Republic of 1916 remains to come, so too does "Ulster." Both are political projects guided and guaranteed by their own ghosts of 1916.

Through the deferral of the Somme's promise, the stability of Loyalist ontology is itself endlessly deferred, rendering it what Derrida termed hauntological: "To haunt does not mean to be present, and it is necessary to introduce haunting into the very construction of a concept. Of every concept, beginning with the concepts of being and time. That is what we would be calling here a hauntology. Ontology opposes it only in a moment of exorcism. Ontology is a conjuration" (Derrida 2006 [1993], 202). This disruption of being is further compounded in moments of (existential) crisis. The more identity in the present is destabilized, the more hauntology comes to "supplant its near-homonym ontology, replacing the priority of being and presence with the figure of the ghost as that which is neither present nor absent, neither dead not alive" (Davis 2005, 373). Under the conditions of disjuncture and anxiety represented by multiple and overlapping crises of the culture war, Loyalists "conjure up the spirits of the past to their service and borrow from their names, battle cries and costumes in order to present the new scene of world history in this time honoured disguise and this *borrowed* language. . . . [T]he more the period is in crisis, the more it is 'out of joint', then the more one has to convoke the old, borrow from it" (Derrida 2006 [1993], 135–36).

As indicated in chapter 5 (see also Brown 2007, 2011; Viggiani 2014), the culture war, and specifically the period since the signing of the Good Friday Agreement in 1998, has been characterized by a significant increase in Loyalist commemoration. Since 2006, and particularly during the present Decade of Centenaries, a notable feature of these commemorations has been their recourse to reenactment and period costume. At parades to mark both the hundredth anniversaries of both the formation of the Ulster Volunteer Force in East Belfast and their gun-running Operation Lion in Larne, the same speeches delivered by Edward Carson during the original events were (re)delivered word-for-word by Billy Hutchinson, leader of the Progressive Unionist Party. At both of these events, Hutchinson even dressed to resemble iconic images of the legendary Unionist leader, in a top hat, three-piece suit, and long black coat. Vintage cars; replica rifles; the flat caps, black suits, puttees, boots, and bandoliers of the Ulster Volunteers; the white and blue gowns of the UVF nursing corps; and the khaki uniforms of the 36th (Ulster) Division have all been a dominant feature of these commemorations.

During the commemoration of the signing of the Ulster Covenant at Belfast City Hall on Ulster Day in 2012, some of those involved signed replicas of the Covenant in their own blood[4]—a phenomenon reported but never substantiated during the original event in 1912. Jamie, discussing his involvement in the 2012 centennial reenactment of Ulster Day suggested that, for him, the presence of men (re-)signing the Covenant in blood made it more corporeal, visceral, and ultimately more *real* than the original event being commemorated (interview with author, 2015). That the Decade's simulacra have produced meaning—referred but transfigured from, and for some greater than, the "original" events of one hundred years ago—of their own is further demonstrated in a series of murals outside the Shankill Road's Rex Bar (fig. 6.2). Inaugurated in 2014, the murals commemorate the Unionist centenary commemorations themselves. The constant reiteration of memorial tropes in discourse and material culture, and the accretion of commemorative symbolism throughout the marching season, contributes to the sense that the commemoration is truly endless (cf. Jarman 1997). Repetition of these same symbols on murals and memorials serves to transform entire streets into Loyalist *lieux de mémoire*: sites of more or less continuous commemoration, where the customary liminality of remembrance is turned on its head, and the boundary between "ritual" and "normal" time is blurred (cf. Tonkin and Bryan 1996).

Figure 6.2. "A Force for Ulster" murals, Rex Bar, Shankill Road, Belfast.

For many of the Loyalists I interviewed, commemoration during the Decade of Centenaries seemed to have become more a state of being than a form of doing. One of my interlocutors quipped that for Loyalists even "going to the shops for a Mars Bar" is about commemorating their "forefathers" at the Somme. Another spoke of what he termed "professional" commemorators, who will, almost without fail, appear at any talk, exhibit, or other event on the subject of the Somme, even where such events are repeats of others they have attended previously. This was certainly a trend I observed at East Belfast & the Great War events and roadshows. During my interview with Sammy, I felt I received perhaps the clearest indication as to the appeal of this perpetual and repetitive commemorative state.

> JE: What do you think that your remembrance gives you that those people [who are less involved in commemoration] are missing?
>
> S: Peace. It gives me peace. It says to me that, you know, *I* have remembered. Sometimes I remember too often. You know . . . and then you get drawn back to the Menin Gate. And they have it every day. So if they have it every day, why can't we have it every day? So, I've always thought that the Prods, the Unionists, you know, remember too much, and then you say, well, they do it at the Menin Gate every day, so it can't be that bad. But it does, it makes me feel . . . I can go to those graveyards with a clear conscience, so I can. In peace.

The idea of finding peace, purpose, or security in commemoration was echoed by many other Loyalists. It was connected to the claims of (genealogical) authenticity or of ontological certainty, of "knowing" one's identity (see ch. 5).

Through perpetual reiteration, Loyalist commemoration attempts to transcend its own liminality or boundedness, and to restore to Loyalism a sense of stability, presence and permanence. The Somme's ghosts belong to the Golden Age (Smith 1996, 1997; Brown 2007) of a remembered future. They provide a "hidden direction and goal beneath the obscuring present" (Smith 1997, 51), and their invocation during acts of commemoration augurs a security "which has never yet existed" (Derrida 2006 [1993], 135). In the face of the myriad and destabilizing crises of parity of esteem and the culture war, they point to "a glorious destiny, stemming from the true nature revealed in and by [the] golden past," proclaiming "an imminent status reversal: though at present 'we' are oppressed, shortly we shall be restored to our former glory" (Smith 1997, 51). Loyalist commemorators vaunt the 36th (Ulster) Division as the paragon of their *ethnie*, representing the authentic essence from which their community has deviated. During our interview, Scott, who is a member of a Shankill Road Somme Society, lamented:

> Considering where Unionism was in 1905, and the journey that we have made today, I feel that we have let down those men. . . . I think that a lot of people have turned their backs on their sacrifice. They were prepared to break the law—Carson and Craigavon—holding the ground, holding the discipline of the Unionist people at that time. . . . [O]ne wonders what would've happed if Carson *hadn't* have been there. What sort of violence would have ensued? As we can see from the late sixties, early seventies, when there was no coordination, when the Unionist leadership didn't have control, and I think we're slipping back again to that. (Interview with author, 2014)

Salvation is rooted in the resurrection of Unionism's true nature: principled, disciplined, coordinated, and, above all, unified under a coherent leadership. But as Derrida (1986, 58) suggests, "Memory stays with [such] traces, in order to 'preserve' them, but [they are] traces of a past *which has never been present*. . . . Resurrection does not resuscitate a past which had been present. It engages the future" (emphasis added). In each reenactment, the community's return to its authentic essence is deferred, and "Ulster" is propelled always and endlessly into the future. The "standards of [the] golden [age] come to define the normative character of the *evolving* community," and the ghosts of the Somme "define an ideal, which is not so much to be resurrected (few nationalists want actually to return to the past, even a golden past) as to be recreated in modern terms" (Smith 1996, 584; emphasis added). Each commemorative iteration emphasizes the distance the community has yet to travel to reach the Promised Land. It opens up space for reinterpretation or even transformation of the Somme's meaning, into which "doubts about authenticity are liable to creep. . . . This in turn may erode any sense of continuity and hence [the Golden Age's] usefulness as a guide to communal destiny" (Smith 1997, 55). As such, the ghosts of the Somme point to a future in which the instability of the unjust present can be overcome while simultaneously demonstrating that it cannot.

THE BATTLE FOR THE SOMME

The Unionist Centenary Committee (UCC) was established in late 2009 to organize and coordinate commemoration within the "Unionist family" during the Decade of Centenaries. The committee has played a key role in organizing large-scale commemorative reenactments during the Decade, among them, the Balmoral Review in 2011 and the signing of the Ulster Covenant in 2012, as well as the Belfast City Hall march-past in 2015. It boasts a broad range of stakeholders, including the 36th (Ulster) Division Memorial Association, the Grand Orange Lodge of Ireland, the Independent Loyal Orange Institution, the Apprentice Boys of Derry, the Democratic Unionist Party, the Ulster Unionist Party (UUP), Traditional Unionist Voice (TUV), the Progressive Unionist Party, and—not to be confused with the numerous subsidiary groups that form the 36th (Ulster) Division Memorial Association—the Somme Association, which manages both the Ulster Tower in Thiepval and the Somme Museum in Conlig, Co. Down. It also includes representatives of the Ulster Defence Union and the West Belfast Athletic and Cultural Society, organizations established by former members of, and largely synonymous with, the UDA and the UVF, respectively.

The UCC's mission statement is worth quoting here in full:

> The Unionist Centenary Committee (UCC) takes as its Mission Statement the Ulster Covenant, which was the Declaration of Ulster of her right to exist as a free people under God.
>
> Today we must use this decade to establish in Ulster a cultural consensus, irrespective of political conviction, religion or ethnic origin, using a broader perspective of our past to create a deeper sense of belonging to the country of our ancient British ancestors.
>
> For this Land of the Cruthin[5] is our Homeland and we are her children. We have a right to her name and her nationality. We have

a right to belong here, a right to be heard here, a right to be free; free from suspicion, free from violence and free from fear. We must therefore develop the vision of a new and united Ulster, to which all can give their allegiance, so we may achieve a government of all the people, by all the people, for all the people. For only in the complete expression of our Ulster Identity lies the basis of that genuine peace, stamped with the hallmarks of justice, goodness and truth, which will end at last the war in Ireland.

For we are a Risen People and Liberation is our song. (UCC 2009)

Perhaps the primary message of the Golden Age for the present is precisely that of *unity*, of the authenticity of Unionism's common purpose across (arbitrary) divisions including class and gender (Brown 2007). The reclamation and complete expression of a unitary Ulster identity is fundamental to the UCC's mission. To a person, its achievements in this regard have been heralded by those I interviewed who have participated in commemorative events organized by the committee. For instance, when I interviewed him in advance of the city hall march-past, Mike enthusiastically declared:

So far I've been ecstatic. I think we have done our grandfathers and great-grandfathers proud. I think that the Somme Associations, in particular the 36th (Ulster) Division Memorial Association, of which I am a proud member, I think we have been fantastic. And that's not me blowing my trumpet, that's me blowing the trumpet of each and every one of the men who's involved—and women, sorry, I want to make that quite clear, and the women—of the 36th (Ulster) Division Memorial Association: a lot of people, from a lot of different backgrounds who have tried really, really, really hard to get things going, to push our story forward. They've done it magnificently, I think. You only have to look at all the parades that have went ahead. . . . Everything we've done has been for the betterment of Loyalism. I think that what we've done has been fantastic. The parades have been fantastic. They've been well organised. A lot of people from a lot of different walks of life have pulled the finger out and joined in. . . . What I'm trying to get across is the Unionist/Loyalist family are 100 percent behind this. (Interview with author, 2015)

Likewise, reflecting on the centenary commemoration of Ulster Day in 2012, Derek, a member of the Ulster Defence Union, was satisfied that "everything worked in the end and everybody walked and we were all, you know, part of one big happy family! Which was really, really good." Indeed, in Derek's view, the commemoration of Ulster Day had been such an effective display of Unionist unity that it had galvanized Sinn Féin to find ways to disrupt it. This, in turn, had resulted in the change in policy on the flying of the Union flag at city hall that had given rise to the flag protests.

> D: After that it all went pear shaped you know, you had us all walking together, on Ulster Day, in September, and then two months later the flag protest kicked in, and everything just went [whistles] "boom"!
>
> JE: And do you think that was a factor in . . .
>
> D: Oh, aye! Big time. . . . Y'know, you'd seen the whole Unionist . . . every shade of Unionism walking: Orange Order, Apprentice Boys, UVF, UDA everybody! You know what I mean? And then, "poof" . . . I don't believe that's a coincidence. I don't do coincidences. All being there in the city hall, all going in and reenacting signing the Ulster Covenant again, which was a real slick operation . . . it went slick as, slick as hell. Really good, not a hiccup, not a dickie bird.
>
> JE: And then the reaction was . . .
>
> D: Was that. Was the flags.

Despite his lauding of the centenary commemorations as demonstrating the strength of Unionist unity, already implicit in Derek's analysis is the potential or propensity for division within the Unionist "family." He went on to lament the speed of its unraveling as a result of the flag protests: "Unionism *in general* after that's just completely fractured and fragmented. You know, I haven't seen it as bad, probably since the Loyalist feuds, the UDA and UVF feuds in the early 2000s. . . . Generally, you know, Unionists and Loyalists' family's, you know, fragmented; dysfunctional" (interview with author, 2014). While Derek (and many others with whom I spoke) blamed this fragmentation on what he perceived as a deliberate Sinn Féin policy or conspiracy as part of the broader culture war (see ch. 4), forms of intracommunal conflict have been an endemic and defining feature of Ulster Loyalism, the PUL community and its politics. These conflicts exist at multiple and overlapping organizational, geographic, demographic, socioeconomic, and gendered fault lines. And in its very attempt to mask or overcome these ruptures and cleavages, commemoration works to (re)produce them.

Certain of these conflicts belong, or appear to belong, to the realm of the purely logistical or procedural. For instance, one of my interlocutors noted the organizational differences and potential tensions between the Orange Order—whose "demonstrations" conventionally involve both an outward and return parade—and the Apprentice Boys of Derry—whose parades generally consist of only one leg. The purported purpose of the UCC and its committee meetings is precisely to prevent what are, on the surface, such relatively minor organizational differences from derailing the unity that underlies them. In her ethnographic study, *The Meeting* (1989), Schwartzman suggests that the primary function of such minor differences may even be to justify the meeting itself. Expression of divergent opinion is perhaps more for the sake of having expressed it than an indication of profound ideological difference per se. This was certainly something I felt I identified during my observations of UCC meetings in the run-up to the march-past. Objection and dissent were part of what justified the committee as a social formation and the meeting as a social event, providing committee members with an opportunity to engage in discussions, debates, and arguments that were visibly enjoyed for their own sake.

However, many of the conflicts revealed in the organization of Loyalist commemorations are far from trivial, and those that on the surface appear to be often reflect deeper discord or have real-world consequences that are divisive beyond their apparent inconsequence. At stake are claims to authenticity and leadership in and of the community. Commemoration, particularly of the Somme, provides the symbolic capital through which these claims are both established and challenged. Among the most significant of the cleavages in which it is mobilized is that between the UVF and the UDA. Intermittent feuding between the two organizations has been a prominent feature of Loyalist paramilitarism since the 1970s. In 2000, a particularly bloody feud centered on the Shankill Road. Significant among its multiple causes were ideological differences over the Good Friday Agreement, with Jonny Adair's Lower Shankill–based UDA C Company taking a staunchly anti-Agreement line, in contrast to the UVF's ongoing commitment to the peace process (see Cusack and McDonald 2008; Wood 2004; Gallagher and Shirlow 2006). The legacy of the 2000 feud, which involved a series of shoot-outs and murders and the displacement and resettlement of a number of Shankill households (including that of former UVF chief of staff, Gusty Spence) is to be found in entrenched forms of territorial control on the Shankill and in other "Loyalist" areas of Belfast and in patterns of segregation between areas controlled by the UVF and those controlled by the UDA.

Claims to moral authority are central to these patterns of segregation. And these claims are often made or mediated through commemorative symbolism. As Bryan has pointed out:

> On the upper part of the Shankill from Agnes Street for the half-mile to Lanark Way, references to the UVF and the Battle of the Somme adorn almost every lamp-post and gable end in the form of flags, bannerettes, posters and murals. . . . In stark contrast is the half-mile of the Shankill that runs into the centre of Belfast. . . . In September 2009, other than a small mural with the Titanic on it, there was no symbolic representation here. The flags flying in July had been removed and there was not a single depiction of the Somme. . . . So one half of the 'loyal' Shankill Road is a shrine to 'the fallen' of World War I, whereas the lower part, judging by the lack of representations, remembers nothing. (2014, 300–302)

The UVF has employed the symbolism of the 36th (Ulster) Division and the Somme in order to define its territorial jurisdiction and to stake a claim to rightful authority within it. And this legitimacy is derived from an assertion of continuity across time and space.

The fusion of the imagery and iconography of the contemporary organization with the UVF of 1913 in murals, memorial gardens, and the regalia of marching bands is well documented (Graham and Shirlow 2002; Brown 2007, 2011; Bryan 2014; Viggiani 2014), and it is perhaps best demonstrated in a (recently updated) mural on Glenwood Street on the Shankill (fig. 6.3). On Cherryville Street in East Belfast, a service of remembrance is held each 1 July at a memorial dedicated to the members of the 2nd Battalion (Willowfield) East Belfast Regiment of the Ulster Volunteer Force who "made the supreme sacrifice in the Great War 1914–1918" and to members of the East Belfast UVF who "without fear or reward fought militant Republicanism on its own terms" during the recent conflict (fig. 6.4). Likewise, at ceremonies across Northern Ireland on Remembrance Sunday and at commemorations for individual volunteers "killed in action" during the Troubles, the evolution of the organization is traced in sequential rows of parading men, first in the garb of the original UVF, followed by the khaki of the 36th (Ulster) Division, then the black leather jackets of the distinctive 1970s "blackneck" uniform[6], and finally the boots, combat trousers, and ribbed knit jumpers of the UVF's "active service" battle dress uniforms.

Figure 6.3. UVF A Coy mural, Glenwood Street, Belfast.

Figure 6.4. UVF Memorial Garden, Cherryville Street, Belfast.

While, as I discuss in more detail below, this narrative is disputed, including by (former) members of the UVF itself, it enjoys a certain level of acceptability in the PUL community and particularly in working-class Loyalist areas (Graham and Shirlow 2002; Brown 2007). Mike, for instance, asserted:

If you take 1912, you had insurrection, you had bringing guns into the country, you'd the Loyalist people standing up to the British government, you had men who were prepared to fight and die to maintain what they seen as their right to be British. Fast forward fifty, sixty, seventy years, you have a band of men who are prepared to form an organisation in open rebellion against the British government: to fight and die for what they believe and to make that stand. You can quite easily see how the similarities are between both. Whether you agree with it or disagree with it, you can see that there is a similarity. No matter how loose, that similarity's there very strong. If you've guys who formed the UVF in 1912 and who were quite prepared to go to any lengths to keep their Britishness, if you take it forward to now, or to 1969, 1970, does the same thing not really apply? I think it does. It doesn't mean I'm right. But it's my opinion.

I can't speak for the UVF [but] their relatives done the same as what my relatives done: signed the Covenant, joined the UVF and were prepared to fight and die to keep their Britishness and to defend their country and to do everything that they done. And, like I say, fast forward down the line and these guys done the same thing. (Interview with author, 2015)

As Bryan (2014) has argued, this claim to the Somme and its symbolism has lent the UVF a certain respectability within the Unionist mainstream that the UDA has never attained. Despite, for instance, the fact that the Orange Order is officially opposed to paramilitary membership, the inclusion of "1912" in the corner of a UVF flag grants it a certain historical validity that makes it permissible in Orange parades. This is reinforced by the Parades Commission, which has made it clear in successive determinations that these flags are not deemed to represent support for a proscribed organization. It is virtually unheard of for representatives of either of the two largest Unionist parties to actively challenge the UVF on their use of the heraldry of the Ulster Volunteers or the 36th (Ulster) Division, or publicly object to the use of "official" symbols such as the poppy or the Union flag at paramilitary commemorations.

During our interview, one DUP representative did express some disquiet about the UVF's association with (and appropriation of) the Somme but also suggested that it was politically expedient to allow space for "the Somme thing" so as not to "give the impression that [the DUP] are trying to take something away" and thereby avoid "getting a red card from [that section of] Loyalism" while also avoiding direct involvement or association with particular forms of Somme commemoration (interview with author, 2015). This may help to account for what Sammy bemoaned as a relatively hands-off approach to the centenary commemorations on the part of the DUP: "It doesn't help when the major Unionist political party has no interest in the centenary events. [The DUP] don't commit themselves in any shape or fashion to the centenary events. Now, they all turned up at the city hall on Ulster Day 2012, to get their photographs taken . . . but put that all aside, did the DUP take much part in anything? No" (interview with author, 2014).

When politicians from the main Unionist parties have participated in commemorations during the Decade of Centenaries, it has often served to bolster the UVF's symbolic capital. For example, at the reenactment of the 36th (Ulster) Division city hall march-past, the role of Carson—as it had been at the centenary commemorations of the formation of the UVF and of its 1914 gun-running Operation Lion—was played by the UVF former prisoner and leader of the PUP, Billy Hutchinson, who led the parade up Belfast's Royal Avenue and then received the salute of the marchers at city hall. Other Unionist politicians—including two UUP MPs and the DUP deputy lord mayor of Belfast—were consigned to positions lower down the parade's running order. On East Belfast's Newtownards Road in July 2015, a poster in the window of a DUP constituency office depicting the silhouettes of First World War soldiers (fig. 6.5) was displayed directly below a photographic mural of an East Belfast UVF show of strength (fig. 6.6). Whether or not this was intended, the effect was to signal the DUP's participation in a symbolic landscape controlled and maintained by the East Belfast UVF, on the UVF's terms.

The UVF's relative success in establishing and legitimizing its place in the Unionist pantheon by monopolizing "ownership" of the 36th (Ulster) Division has served to complicate and disrupt the UDA's relationship with its symbolic lexicon. The UVF's proprietorship over the "Road to the Somme" story—and UDA resentment thereof—both reflects and provides fuel for the bitter rivalry between the two organizations. According to Derek, negotiating UDA buy-in for the Balmoral Review and Ulster Day commemorations (in 2011 and 2012, respectively) had been difficult, and for commemorations of the formation of the Ulster Volunteers in 2013 and Operation Lion in 2014 it had been impossible. Discussing the exclusion of the UDA from these commemorations, he complained to me:

There was no space there for UDA men, even if they'd have wanted to [participate]. Even though, you know, *historically*, *my* family fought on the Somme and were part of the UVF, but because the

Figure 6.5. Commemorative poster in DUP Constituency Office, Newtownards Road, Belfast.

modern-day UVF have took that as part of their history, y'know, and just grabbed it, you know what I mean? . . . When it came to the formation of the Ulster Volunteer Force, and the landing of the guns and stuff, the modern-day UVF took over *outside* of the UCC. Outside of that, the modern-day UVF took over, called rank on all their men, and said, "This is what you're doing." This is what you're

Figure 6.6. "East Belfast UVF on Parade" mural, Newtownards Road, Belfast.

doing, this is what you're getting involved in, we're organising this. And they just took it away from us. There was nothing we could do about it. (Interview with author, 2014)

This is not to say, however, that the UVF's claim on the Somme has gone wholly uncontested. In recent years, the UDA has sought to appropriate some of the symbolic capital of the First World War in general and of the Somme in particular through what Viggiani (2014, 157–62) has termed a process of symbolic "accretion" in its murals and memorials. In this mural on the Highfield estate in West Belfast, for instance, an equivalence is drawn between the Ulster Division and the UDA as "Ulster's Defenders past and present" through the juxtaposition of the image of the Ulster Tower at Thiepval with the crests of the UDA and its military wing, the UFF (fig. 6.7). The mural also includes a representation of the Irish Tower in Messines and thereby makes a version of the Loyalist claim of "inclusivity" discussed in the previous chapter.

During my interview with Andy, a senior UDA former prisoner from West Belfast and one of the sponsors of the Highfield mural, he was keen to stress that the UDA had just as much entitlement to this First World War heritage as the UVF *and* that its less "obsessive" relationship with the Somme made it more in tune with the real history of the war and the broader nature of its sacrifice for King and Empire (including by Irish Nationalists), beyond that of the 36th (Ulster) Division on "one day in July."

The UDA is not the only group forced to negotiate or compete with the UVF for access to the Somme story. The Somme Associations can trace their heritage to the UVF, its political evolution in the cages of Long Kesh and its demobilization strategy in the wake of the 1994 ceasefires. However, despite the resultant linkages (real and perceived) between the two organizations and the common assertion—particularly on the part of UDA men—that they are one and the same, rivalry over claims to the Somme also exists between the UVF and the groups that constitute the 36th (Ulster) Division Memorial Association. When I asked Sammy about this conflict, he sighed regretfully before pointing out the pains to which the latter have gone to distinguish themselves as distinct and separate. Again, these claims were framed in terms of authenticity and inclusivity.

> On the gun-running parade, we carried a banner right at the front of us which said, "We are the 36th (Ulster) Division Memorial Association." We are not the UVF, we *aren't*. But if people don't want to believe us, then there's nothing we can do. . . . Some people now believe us. Some people don't believe us. And some people will never believe us. 'Cause they just think, with closed minds, that we're the UVF. What saddens me is that they think *I'm* in the UVF. . . . But we've UDA men in the 36th (Ulster) Division Memorial Association! We have people who have no affiliation to anything else in the 36th (Ulster) Division. We've UVF men in the 36th (Ulster) Division Memorial Association. We have everybody and we exclude no one. It doesn't matter what religion you are, what color you are, if you're disabled, whatever, it's irrelevant. If you're there to remember the sacrifice of the 36th (Ulster) Division, you're one of us. (Interview with author, 2015)

Figure 6.7. "Ulster's Defenders" mural, Highfield Drive, Belfast.

Other Somme Association members spoke of heated or angry exchanges between the two groupings as they jostle for position on parade days, as well of the conflicted loyalties of those who are members of both who may be expected to be in two places at once or forced to choose between two contradictory sets of demands. Including at the city hall march-past, these conflicts are mirrored and replicated in contentious subdivisions within parades that outwardly manifest and are usually represented as unified and whole. In his analysis of the 2012 reenactment of Ulster Day, Sammy suggested that what was treated and widely regarded as one unitary procession may really have been as many as three separate, competing parades.

> My spiel on all this is that on Ulster Day 2012, 100,000 Unionists put their feet on the ground. It may have been three parades, but 100,000 people bothered their arse to do something about it. So that's the positive. Now, if you want to go into the negatives: the UVF walked from South Belfast to city hall, stood there like planks while row upon row of Orangemen walked past them, who don't want anything to do with the UVF, but the UVF stood there like, "Hi lads, how are yas?" Whereas the Unionist Centenary Committee, which was primarily on that day the 36th (Ulster) Division Memorial Association and the UDA, formed up in front of the Orange Order, who didn't want us anywhere near them, and paraded up to Stormont. Now we didn't go in the gates. They wouldn't let us in, you see, to Stormont. They made sure the gates were closed. They wouldn't let us in. (Interview with author, 2015)

Sammy hinted at another important contest over the Somme and its legacy: that between the Orange Order and the other groups within the UCC. This was sometimes represented as a split between the rural and the urban, which is how it was explained by Daniel.

> D: It was very clear at the time of the Covenant that the Unionist Centenary Committee would have liked one large event with everybody present. The Grand Lodge of Ireland knew that that would not work because half of our membership would not be there. And

that's the reality of it. There was quite a robust discussion at the UCC about that one . . .

JE: Half of them wouldn't come if certain other groups were involved?

D: If certain other people were there, yeah. And that's just the reality of it. And a lot of it is an urban and rural thing.

Far more significant than the rural-urban divide, however, is that on an organizational level the leadership of the Orange Order does not want to be seen to be entering into joint endeavors with representatives of the Loyalist paramilitaries. The Orange Order's governing body, the Grand Orange Lodge of Ireland, is officially opposed to paramilitarism and, to some extent, the "blood and thunder" marching tradition with which it is associated (Jarman 1997).[7] The Grand Lodge's concern with setting itself apart from these aspects of Loyalist political culture is indicative of broader concerns about maintaining its "respectability" (Bryan 2000). Ultimately, the issue is arguably what Bourdieu (1984; see also Ramsey 2011) would term one of distinction: it is about taste and the politics of class prejudice. As Daniel suggested:

> It's an issue for perhaps the more middle-class Protestant community, as to how do they relate to these [i.e., working-class] people? The flag protests and so on are an example of all of that. Do people who are in the shady suburbs just turn away from all of that? Do they wash their hands of it? Or do they actually say, "Well, what's wrong here, what's actually *wrong*? Why do these people feel they have to do this?" Because there's clearly something not right in how they feel things are. So we *all* have to, and that's not going to be an easy journey, I don't think, for the Protestant community to make, and I've seen some examples of that, in terms of these commemorations. (Interview with author, 2014)

During our interview, Matthew, another senior Orangeman, suggested that in his view the Somme Associations represent a short-term deviation from an authentically Orange commemorative tradition.

The Somme Associations, and this is a controversial comment, [but] it's the Orange Order without the religious part. It's "For God and Ulster" without the "God" . . . the Orange Order has ritual, tradition—for a lot of people, that doesn't appeal to them nowadays. They just want to remember the Somme, it's "let's go and do that without having to join or having to be required to be seen to be a bit more churchy." So to me they're the Orange Order without the ceremony.

They're not massive organizations. They're serving a good purpose, they do a good job. They've formed their own parades. You know, why do you need a parade for other days, battles and all? I think they're a bit of a fad. I don't mean that in a negative sense. I think they'll live . . . the Somme, the Battle of the Somme commemoration in East Belfast will go as long as there's one Orange Lodge left. Some of those other parades I think will die out. (Interview with author, 2014)

Here again, commemorative possessiveness forms a key part of claims to represent or speak for the PUL community. The true or authentic nature of that community as revealed in its golden past, and therefore who or what constitutes its true voice, remains contested.

Underwriting all of the permutations of this contest, however, is a unifying politics of gender. While profound disagreement persists between the groups and individuals who make up the UCC as to who may rightfully claim to speak with and for the Somme's ghosts, there seems to be at least tacit agreement that that voice is definitively masculine. As Sales (1997, 140) notes, "The imagery of the Protestant community is masculine, whether it is bowler-hatted Orange-men celebrating Protestantism's triumph at the Battle of the Boyne, the archetypal Protestant worker (the skilled manual worker), the harsh fundamentalist rhetoric of Ian Paisley or the balaclava-hooded Loyalist paramilitaries" (see also Racioppi and O'Sullivan See 2000; Ashe and McCluskey 2015). Jane McGaughey (2012) has demonstrated how the language of blood sacrifice at the Somme has contributed to thus framing the essential nature of the Ulsterman as precisely that of the militarized hard man.

Rachel, who has had some involvement in organizing commemorative activity during the Decade of Centenaries, reflected on the contrasting roles of men and women in PUL commemorations:

> I think it is down to the fact that what that community seek to celebrate is World War I, and specifically the Somme. Well, for the majority, it's the Somme. And women *didn't* go and fight. And I hear, "Oh, we have to tell the women's story at home," and I'm like, yeah, absolutely. But the woman's story was sitting home looking after the kids. I'm not taking anything away from that, but, you know . . . I'm being terribly generalistic here, but I would say that a lot of [Loyalists], their respect for a woman isn't great.

While women are represented on and involved in the UCC, it is a distinctly patriarchal social formation, and its meetings involve a degree of the banter and other forms of social behavior that are the stuff of male bonding. This is reflected in the gender roles defined for men and women on parade, with women conventionally filling the role of auxiliary. Reenactments during the Decade of Centenaries have involved a small number of women in black uniform carrying replica weapons, but for the most part, women are represented on parade by contingents of UVF nurses or by the Ladies' Somme Associations.

This process of gendering the Somme and its legacy is mapped on to the other battles over rightful claims to it. For example, in 2011, the UCC held a community consultation to assist in drawing up its plans for the centenaries of the Balmoral Review, Ulster Day, the formation of the UVF and its gun-running Operation Lion, the 36th (Ulster) Division march-past, and the Battle of the Somme,[8] which Laura attended.

> I can remember, I was put in a group. There was ten of us in this wee group, and I was the only female! And here's me, "Christ! I'm gonna get ridiculed here now!" I'm gonna get this, and I'm gonna get that! Now, all the Orange Order wanted was this: "church service, church service, church service, church service, church service!" . . . But I was trying to say, "Well, what about people that don't want to have church services?" "Well, it's in the name of the Lord! It's the name

of the Lord!" And I'm like, "Right, here we go!" I don't even know where to *start* with this conversation here!

But this is how it all started, and we were like, "Well, why don't we have parades to celebrate it?" Get the kids to learn: exhibitions, educate them. "Ah, how can you educate heathens?" And I can see matey going out a window in a minute! And then it was coming down to the sexism of it: "Well, what do females know?" So things got a wee bit uptight there. And I started rhyming off quite a bit about my family history, y'know, asking, "Have you any family members in France?," y'know. "No." "Well, then don't you sit there and tell me that this is all to do with men, when you haven't a *fucking* clue what you're talking about." (Interview with author, 2014)

Generally, women's role in the Loyalist community—which reflects more general (ethno)national imaginings of the feminine, women's role as auxiliary, and women's "purity" as that which the masculine must seek to protect (Yuval-Davis 1989; Enloe 1988)—is reinforced through commemorative practice. However, Laura's confrontation with the Orangeman at the community consultation suggests that particular gendered assumptions, patriarchal relations of power, and the hegemony of particular forms of masculinity can also be challenged through commemoration in general and through appeals to authenticity in particular. Access to the "truth" of the Somme—particularly by blood—provided an important means by which Laura has been able to disrupt her and others' understanding of her place and role in Loyalism's social order. As she suggested, emphatically:

Now, don't get me wrong, there's a couple of women's Somme groups out there. But they wouldn't be as active as what I would be. But I think it's because I'm not scared to get up and talk in front of the men. I mean, they go to talk and I'm like, "You're wrong!" I wouldn't feel intimidated by a man. Y'know, I could walk into a room and it's full of men and I'd be quite quick with themmuns. They'll not put me down. I think I get a lot of respect out of the Somme groups and the men. But I think it's because I do know what I'm talking about, because I do take the time to learn what I am talking about, and I'm not scared to ask questions either. (Interview with author, 2014)

DISEMIA AND THE WORK OF MEMORY

"Nothing could be worse," Derrida (2006 [1993], 9) warns, for the "work of mourning, than confusion or doubt." But Loyalist memory work is defined by it. Deconstruction of Loyalist commemoration of the Somme reveals fierce competition among different unofficial historiographies and memorial narratives for recognition as authentic (cf. Chatzipanagi-otidou 2012). The ghosts of the Somme thereby "figure the impossibility of mastering, through either knowledge or action, the past or the present" (Brown 2001, 146). If the true nature or authentic essence of the PUL community is revealed at the Somme, then the battle for it reveals that this essence is fundamentally irrecoverable. The contested claims to the Somme's story destabilize the very notion of authenticity. None of these claims is without some validity, but equally, if all have some right to the Somme's inheritance, then none are its true heirs. And this is per-haps the defining feature of the Somme's role in what Herzfeld (1996, quoted in Jansen 2003, 227) might term Loyalism's "disemia": the ten-sion between its "labour of representation" and "what goes on in the pri-vacy of collective introspection." The Golden Age never was; nor, crucially, will it ever be. Parity of esteem and the culture war make at-tempts to reclaim it all the more futile, but the imagined virtue of the Somme's ghosts was already, by its very nature, unmatchable and their promise of a glorious destiny, irredeemable.

As suggested appositely, and with some sympathy, by Seosamh, Loy-alists are, therefore, "whistling in the dark. You know, you put on a big parade, you come out in your best clothes, you put your chest out, you have as many flags as you can, big bands, all of that. And you hope that if you beat the drum loud enough the bogeymen will go away" (inter-view with author, 2014). But they will not. Of course, Seosamh and his colleagues in Sinn Féin (see, e.g., Adams 2016) are apt to stress that the Orange State is gone and is "never, ever coming back." But, as outlined in chapter 4, its passing is only partly a result of the ascendance of Irish Republicanism as such, and is guaranteed as much, if not more, by broader and even global political, economic, and cultural trends. The bogeymen are not exclusively or even predominantly those of the Republican movement.

As we sat in Jamie's living room on a warm May evening, the laughter and the intense but good-humored discussion about the state of Loyalism that characterized so many of our conversations subsided. "My fear would be that the rest of society laughs at us, you know," Jamie began solemnly.

Dressing up as these—[my girlfriend] calls us "toy soldiers." Dressing up like toy soldiers to go out and play our flutes and pretending to be someone from a hundred years ago: there's something a bit sinister and a bit menacing and a bit morbid in it. Whenever I went to France with the band in 2011, we went in the "authentic" World War I uniforms. So I have a picture of me and my brother at the Ulster Tower in the World War I uniforms. We had no family connection that we knew of.

I subsequently learned that I had a family connection to the Great War, someone who would have been wearing the same uniform as me who would have died on that ground. And I felt angry and sad and proud and everything all at the same time. Because I was there on that spot, my blood was in that ground, and there I was standing dressed up like him, you know?

I could almost put myself in his shoes and watch him looking at me, just shaking his head and going, "What are you doing? Why would you want to do that?" At the time I felt proud: you were at the cutting edge and this is how it was done and this is how you commemorate it, and that was from someone who didn't have a family member. And other people who were there who did have a family member still thought they were at the cutting edge and still thought they were doing it right and it was good to be there on the ground, where your blood was shed.

Now, looking back on it, I look at that photograph and I cringe actually. Because when I look at it now I think of the person who died who has the same surname as me, and whose body was out there somewhere and was never recovered. And I probably trampled all over it wearing the same uniform. And I probably dishonoured him more than honoured him actually. And then I think about my behaviour when I was there as well, and I think about the behaviour of my brother and the people that I was with, and I don't like it. . . . He was blown to bits there and then we went over and wore that uniform. The whole thing is just bizarre, it is just bizarre. (Interview with author, 2015)

In this chapter, I have demonstrated how Loyalist commemoration of the Somme—what I have called its ghost dance—ultimately functions to reproduce the insecurity and division that it claims to have overcome. However, while the disemia of the ghost dance reflects the irretrievability of Loyalism's Golden Age, Jamie also hints at the opportunities this irretrievability offers for the renegotiation of Loyalist "knowledge." Loyalists' quarrel with the ghosts of its imagined past, and also "with one another about them—their shape, their meaning, their significance, their longevity" (Brown 2001, 146), forms a vital part of an ongoing and intracommunal conversation about politics and "the political" (Edkins 2003) as such. Crucially, as I discuss in the following chapter, this process of renegotiation, rooted precisely in Loyalism's experience of and knowledge about violence, suffering, and loss, has political consequences beyond those for which the "shared" historiography of commemorative orthodoxy in the "new" Northern Ireland—which seeks to exclude, preclude, or otherwise delegitimize particular truths or forms of knowledge about violence and its consequences—allows.

CHAPTER SEVEN

"Dupes no more"?

Loyalist Commemoration and the Politics of Peace-Building

S: And the Battle of the Somme is . . . you know, obviously it was the worst military day in history, but it was something—and of course it was a hundred years ago and there's obviously nobody still living who fought there—but our uncles, our great-uncles, our grand-fathers were there. And we still commemorate that as a part of something glorious! Even though we never saw the squalor or the dirt, or the fear. But the fact that they were brave enough to go over the top, and they were Ulstermen, and we can pick up on the glory of that.

P: It should be used—

S: [Interrupting] We can pick up on the glory of that—the fact that it was men from my village, my town, my street that went and I have the same blood in me now. I always have to ask myself, if I was lying there, 1 July 1916 . . . and somebody blew the whistle. I don't think I could . . . they hadn't the beauty of hindsight. They didn't know what was in front of them. They went there to fight, for ad-venture . . .

P: [Frustrated] But they were duped! "Dupes no more"! I think, for me, the young Loyalist getting political, I think for me, that's the importance of the Somme. Because never again do I want to see . . . I don't want to raise children in a community where they have to fight a war. I don't wanna die. I want to live. I wanna have a good life. And I want my community to live a good life. And I think *that's* the importance of the Somme. (Exchange between Stevie and Paul at focus group conducted by author, 2015)

Shortly before 6:00 p.m., 4 August 2014: one hundred years to the day since the United Kingdom of Great Britain and Ireland entered what would become the First World War. As Jamie and I waited at the front doors of Belfast's St. Anne's Cathedral ahead of the service of remembrance organized by the Northern Ireland First World War Commemoration Committee, a group of press photographers began to gather at the foot of the stone steps, waiting on the arrival of the secretary of state and the first minister. An elderly gentleman who had come a long way to attend the ceremony waited ahead of us in the queue. Pinned to his lapel were a number of service medals. He had no invitation, but staff in the cathedral managed to find some space for him. We followed him in, and found the last remaining seats. Maybe it was just our position at the back of the church, but it seemed that we were quite intentionally being kept apart from the dignitaries, including Prince Andrew, Duke of York; the secretary of state for Northern Ireland, Theresa Villiers; the first minister of Northern Ireland, Peter Robinson; and, significantly, Heather Humphreys, then minister for arts, heritage, and the Gaeltacht in the Republic of Ireland. Led by a British Legion color guard and flanked by clergy from both the Roman Catholic and main Protestant churches, as well as senior representatives of other faith communities in Northern Ireland, they processed in during the first hymn. It was, I felt, a somewhat officious affair.

The service was reminiscent of the hours spent on hard, cold pews in the village church of my youth. The choir's singing was perfectly pleasant, and I found the readings broadly in keeping with the solemnity of the occasion. However, the radical message of the Sermon on the Mount was lost somewhat: that "the meek shall inherit the earth" seemed an ironic claim for a duke. During the sermon, my simmering unease with the pomp and circumstance of this state-sponsored officialdom came to full boil. From the pulpit, Richard Clarke, archbishop of Armagh, opened with the suggestion that "only somebody with no sense of history, or no sense at all, would seek to suggest neat and simple answers to the political, social and indeed moral questioning that has always surrounded this First World War."

> There are of course . . . myths to be debunked. It was not only foot soldiers who died in battle. Indeed, if one was an officer, one's chances of dying on the western front were fifty percent greater than for those in other ranks. The British generals were for the most part not the total incompetents they are presented as being in popular mythology. Many of them too died in battle; they were not relaxing in beautiful chateaus miles behind the front lines. And personally I can well remember as a child knowing a number of veterans of the First World War whose memories of the conflict were not uniformly terrible. (Clarke 2014)

In the archbishop's attempted "debunking" were echoes of Michael Gove's controversial argument that the "truth" about Britain's role in the First World War renders it worthy not merely of solemn commemoration, but of active celebration one hundred years hence. Presented as dispassionate and apolitical, the suggestion that the Great War had not been as bad, or the generals as donkey-like as "popular mythology" would lead us to believe is anything but. In his recourse to fact (itself highly contested), the archbishop failed to capture the *affective* gravity of the moment. Above all, it seemed morally inconsistent with his subsequent claim that "war must *always* represent the abject failure of the human spirit and of humanity itself. It can never be other and we should never pretend it is other." The particular politics of the archbishop's claims became clearer in the distinction between "monuments of hatred" and "monuments of beauty":

> Yes, we can create easily monuments of hatred (it takes no effort at all), or we can painstakingly and even painfully build monuments of beauty, even to a horrifying past. We can allow the ruins of what others have made of our hopes and longings to stand there, bare and broken, as a symbol of our hatred. We can build monuments to darkness, and it is only too easy to do. We can, and it is by far the

more painful option, seek to restore beauty and even restore relationships, and allow light to shine in the darkness. . . . Memorialis-
ing can be a crude, self-obsessive and vengeful thing—an empty
shell of past hatreds that seeks to demonise an enemy forever—or it
can become, with forbearance, integrity and true spiritual courage,
a thing of beauty. (Clarke 2014)

Mirroring the language on commemoration and its role in the perpetuation of conflict in the propaganda of peace, as outlined in chapter 3, allusions to the violence of the Troubles, its legacy, and its divisive
memorialization were thinly veiled. We could infer that those of us
present in the cathedral that evening were participating in building a
monument of beauty, juxtaposed to the memorial to hate built by those
in Northern Ireland for whom commemoration forms part of their
contentious politics of identity or community. In the cross-communal
service at St. Anne's were to be found forbearance, integrity, and true
spiritual courage, whereas the murals, memorial gardens, parades, and
other partisan forms of Loyalist (or, for that matter, Republican) commemoration are crude, obsessive, and vengeful.

As the service came to an end, we were allowed to leave the church
only once the VIPs had been escorted past us. We filed out into the late
summer twilight, and Jamie and I quickly headed over the river to the
Newtownards Road—the heart of Loyalist East Belfast—and the Westbourne Presbyterian Community Church, for a candlelight vigil. Here,
I felt a cup of tea and a slice of apple pie said more about the significance
of this definitive centennial moment than all of the grandstanding at
St. Anne's. The church was filled with the chat of neighbors and friends,
young people and old. Tea and buns were generously dished out in poly-
styrene cups and on paper plates. The suits, choreography, and chatter
of the Northern Irish glitterati were replaced by something at once
more sentimental and more meaningful, a sense of togetherness or belonging. The experience was intimate and comfortable.

And then it was very moving. At 10:00 p.m. we made our way across
the road to Pitt Park. Towering above us were the Harland and Wolff
cranes, Samson and Goliath. All those present carried candles, which
they lit as the service began. As the light of the evening rapidly faded, the
flickering light of hundreds of candles danced in the dusk. The opening

prayer was raw and impassioned: "War is the death of humanity, of sanity and of dignity." The words and the intonation signaled that this was no celebration but an acknowledgment of something more disquieting. An accordion player played for too long, and a rendition of "It's a Long Way to Tipperary" to electric keyboard accompaniment was kitsch. But poems and letters of love and loss both to and from the Western Front, read by a local actor, Dan Gordon, were evocative. Shortly before 11:00 p.m., he delivered a passionate reading of Wilfred Owen's "Anthem for Doomed Youth" (1917):

> What passing-bells for these who die as cattle?
> Only the monstrous anger of the guns.
> Only the stuttering rifles' rapid rattle
> Can patter out their hasty orisons.
> No mockeries now for them; no prayers nor bells;
> Nor any voice of mourning save the choirs,—
> The shrill, demented choirs of wailing shells;
> And bugles calling for them from sad shires.
>
> What candles may be held to speed them all?
> Not in the hands of boys, but in their eyes
> Shall shine the holy glimmers of goodbyes.
> The pallor of girls' brows shall be their pall;
> Their flowers the tenderness of patient minds,
> And each slow dusk a drawing-down of blinds.

In the uncanny stillness that followed, Reverend Mervyn Gibson, minister at the Westbourne Presbyterian Church, read Edward Grey's famous lamentation: "The lamps are going out all over Europe. We shall not see them lit again in our life time." The incompetence of the council workers struggling to find the light switch for Pitt Park risked interrupting the solemnity of the moment, but as hundreds of candles were simultaneously blown out, the streets lights (eventually) extinguished, and the pronouncement made that "their name liveth forever more," an eerie and arresting calm descended: a tranquility interrupted only by the muted calls of seagulls and the comforting sound of young children, too young to understand, playing somewhere out of sight. In the shadow of the shipyard cranes, in a place scarred by decades of social and political upheaval, deindustrialization, deprivation, violence, and conflict, it was profound, and, in its way, it was beautiful.

As discussed in chapter 3, the prevailing assertion in political discourses during Northern Ireland's Decade of Centenaries is that sectional Loyalist (and Republican) commemorative forms pose a particular threat to peace, to which the cross-communal reorientation of commemoration can provide a remedy. In this chapter, I propose instead that Loyalist commemoration plays an important—albeit ambiguous or counterintuitive—role in conflict transformation. The emphasis in the propaganda of peace is on the role that Loyalist commemorations play in maintaining and fostering division between the two communities in Northern Ireland. However, as revealed in chapters 5 and 6, commemoration—particularly of the Somme—is also integral to a series of ongoing intracommunal debates, conflicts, and negotiations in a community defined by fear and uncertainty, as discussed in chapter 4. One such negotiation is precisely that between the pull, on the one hand, toward revanchism and violence and, on the other, toward transformative and progressive politics.

Crucially, this negotiation draws on a lived understanding of violence and its consequences that is less contradictory than that promoted by peace propagandists and the newly hegemonic narrative on shared sacrifice. I argue that the emotional and political authenticity of Loyalist commemoration transcends the historical accuracy demanded by peace propagandists during the Decade of Centenaries, which is at any rate contested. The vilification of particular commemorative practices risks the further alienation of members of a community who already perceive themselves as engaged in a culture war, arguably enhancing the revanchist over the (potentially) transformative aspects of Loyalists' commemorative politics.

LOYALIST TRUTH AND CONFLICT TRANSFORMATION

On 12 May 2016, the Loyalist Communities Council (LCC) held a press conference to announce its adoption of a new protocol on the flying of flags and to unveil their new, "official" flag for the upcoming Battle of the

Somme centenary commemoration. The LCC is an umbrella organization for the three main Loyalist paramilitary groups: the UDA, the UVF, and the Red Hand Commando. Its formation was announced in October 2015, as part of an initiative—supported by, among others, Jonathan Powell, who had been Tony Blair's chief of staff during the negotiations that led to the Good Friday Agreement—to facilitate the final phases of their demobilization. The new protocol, which includes proposed restrictions on the flying of paramilitary flags,[1] was cautiously welcomed by many, including Secretary of State Theresa Villiers and Irish Foreign Affairs Minister Charlie Flanagan (*Belfast Telegraph* 2016a).

However, the new commemorative flag was derided by a number of high-profile commentators. The *Irish News* journalist Allison Morris accused the LCC of making a mistake in printing the flag with a left rather than a right red hand insignia.[2] On Twitter, the question, "Has the Loyalist flag commemorating the Somme got the wrong red hand? Does it matter?," was posed by BBC Radio Ulster's lunchtime chat show, "Talkback," and @frwhiskeyblog responded, "Yes it does, getting it right implies that they actually care about the history, rather than the bigotry." In perhaps the best summation of a prevalent attitude toward the LCC's announcement among members of the (Northern) Irish commentariat on the day of the LCC press conference, @belfastbarman, who regularly contributes to the popular political blog, *Slugger O'Toole*, tweeted:

1: not another flag
2: in what way is this news.
3: yet again the PUP associate with terrorists
4: see point 1

It is the perceived paramilitary ownership of Loyalists' Somme culture with which the proponents of the public transcript on commemoration in Northern Ireland take greatest issue. It is this, above all, that they seek to censure by asserting that it has no basis in "fact." In a 2016 letter printed in the *News Letter*, for instance, Trevor Ringland, former deputy chairman of the NI Conservatives and member of the board of the peace-building charity Co-operation Ireland, wrote:

Many of those who died during the battle [of the Somme] came from working class areas of Ulster, but that's where any similarity with modern paramilitary groups ends. While loyalists may be well-meaning, they are demeaning the memories of soldiers in the 36th Ulster Division, by trying to link it to their organisations. . . . Ensuring their organisations take a step back from these commemorations might go some way to recognising the grace bestowed on them by so many and might begin to help heal some of the hurt of the past.

Owing in no small part to their function in promoting a "shared future," the men of the 36th (Ulster) Division are vaunted by peace propagandists like Ringland as heroes while those of the UVF and the UDA are readily dismissed as terrorists.

Indeed, the Loyalist paramilitaries' record of (sectarian) murder during the Troubles of some 1,027 people, including 878 (mostly Catholic) civilians (Sutton 2002), and their association in particular with the barbarity of the Shankill Butchers and atrocities including the McGurk's Bar, Dublin, and Monaghan bombings and the Greysteel and Loughinisland massacres, marks the violence of these organizations as qualitatively different from that of the 36th (Ulster) Division (see Bruce 1992). To be completely clear, moral outrage at the scale and nature of Loyalist violence during the Troubles is entirely justified, and even the most cursory reading of accounts and analyses of Loyalist paramilitarism (see, e.g., Edwards 2017) affirms beyond doubt or question its visceral brutality, viscous cruelty, and moral vacuity. However (albeit with hesitation and some difficulty) I contend that the dismissal or attempted circumscription of all Loyalist commemoration of the Somme on this basis is nonetheless flawed.

In the first instance, such a dismissal is representative of a tendency to conflate all forms of Loyalist commemoration, and those who engage in them, with paramilitarism. Loyalist commemoration of the Somme is demonstrative not merely of paramilitary Loyalism's claim of ownership of the Somme but also of an intracommunal conflict—a series of hidden transcripts—over the veracity or authenticity of this claim. Many Loyalists reject not only the UVF's claim over the Somme, but, by extension, the organization's claim to be truly representative of Loyalism as such. Laura, for example, told me:

A lot of people I think, you see, associate the 36th (Ulster) Division with the UVF, which is wrong. The Ulster Volunteer Force, the way it was formed in 1913, that then went in to the 36th (Ulster) Division: that is nothing to do with the UVF nowadays. Nothing. I can sit here now and a lot of people say to me, "You're a wee blackneck," and I'm like, "How am I a blackneck? How am I a blackneck?" "You're in a Somme group." "And what's that got to do . . . what's that got to do with the 36th (Ulster) Division?" The UVF today has nothing to do with the UVF then. And I think that's what sometimes people need to realise. (Interview with author, 2014)

Commemorations during the Decade of Centenaries are not merely paramilitary shows of strength. They reveal the complex negotiations involved in Loyalism's politics of identity, part of which is an ongoing debate about the role and ethics of paramilitary violence in communities from which it draws its support (see Hayes and McAllister 2000; Reed 2015) but in which it is also met with vocal opposition. That they are central to both establishing and rebuking claims of continuity or ownership demonstrates the deep rootedness of the commemorative patterns that Ringland is keen to dismiss in the lifeworlds not only of paramilitary members, but of the wider Loyalist community in and from which he fails adequately to locate or differentiate them.

Second, this condemnation of the "men of violence" is a difficult or even contradictory position to maintain for those who seek to vaunt some forms of violence as exemplary. Sincere ethical concerns about the violence of Loyalist paramilitarism both during and since the recent conflict in Northern Ireland notwithstanding, to argue that the violence of the Western Front was legitimate or honorable—in direct contradistinction to that perpetrated by paramilitary Loyalism during the Troubles—is not *simply* an issue of available evidence. "Terrorism" is not an empirical category. It is—however valid—an interpretive label, a political ascription (see Cramer 2006; Schinkel 2010; Bryan, Templer, and Kelly 2011). Likewise, the issue of continuity (or lack thereof) between Carson's Army and Loyalist paramilitarism in general and the UVF in particular is ultimately as much one of interpretation, perception, and argument as it is of verifiable fact. As Bowman (2007) has identified, attempts to draw a direct line of descent from the original Ulster Volunteers to the UVF (re-)formed in 1965 are tenuous. But this does not render these attempts any less meaningful to those who claim this connection between incarnations of the UVF, who construct and negotiate those claims through genealogy or commemorative ritual and many of whose ancestors were members of the original organization. The interesting questions are why and how institutional and ideological continuity is established, maintained, and negotiated and what forms of social action—both violent and nonviolent—this precipitates rather than whether the claim of continuity is true per se.

Crucially, analysis of the kind typified by Ringland tends to negate that debates about the efficacy and morality of violence are intrinsic to Loyalist paramilitary discourse itself (see Shirlow 2012; Novosel 2013; Reed 2015). These debates have not been least among the factors contributing to ongoing conflict between the UDA and the UVF. Commemoration, particularly of the Somme, provides one means by which this conflict is perpetuated, but it also provides space for mediation. In particular, while its significance should not be overstated, coordination between senior figures in the UDA and UVF in the design of the new commemorative flag for the centenary of the Somme and their joint sponsorship of a new flag protocol represents a new development in attitudes within and relations between the two organizations.[3]

An assessment of paramilitary activity in Northern Ireland commissioned by the secretary of state in 2015 found that at a leadership level the main Loyalist paramilitary organizations "remain committed to transforming the purpose of [their groups] from violent crime to community focused initiatives" (NIO 2015), and while valid questions about their effectiveness, worth, or moral validity persist, attempts at disarmament, demobilization, and reintegration (DDR) are ongoing. The redirection of volunteers from active service to commemorative activity has been an important aspect of these processes. For example, through Action for Community Transformation (ACT), a DDR initiative for the UVF conceived and directed by former prisoner William Mitchell, former combatants have been engaged in coordinating commemorations for fallen comrades and for significant centennial events as part of a broader program designed to foster volunteerism and promote education, civic pride, and community leadership (*Balaclava Street* 2014c).

Ironically, the very possibility of the First World War's use as a parable for peace-building during the Decade of Centenaries itself owes much to Loyalists' having kept the commemorative flame alight when it otherwise looked in danger of being extinguished. As demonstrated in chapter 5, while commemorative culture was blossoming in the cages of Long Kesh, in the world outside it was in (apparently terminal) decline. Its reinvigoration can be traced, at least in part, to the kinds of community and political work undertaken by paramilitary prisoners upon their release. In his rebuttal of Ringland's letter, also printed in the *News Letter*, David Campbell (2016), chairman of the LCC and founding trustee of the Somme Association argued that "it was the lobbying from the loyalist community which ensured the restoration and rededication of our national war memorial—The Ulster Tower at Thiepval, after it lay neglected and forgotten by 'middle Ulster' for twenty years or so." As noted in chapter 3, Glenn Barr, joint architect of the Island of Ireland Peace Park and the International School for Peace Studies' Fellowship Program, is himself a former UDA brigadier. Many of the school's first cohort of fellows were paramilitary former prisoners.

In the years since the formation of the Somme Association and the dedication of the Peace Park, and particularly since the beginning of the Decade of Centenaries, there has been a perceived attempt at excluding from the official commemorative space the very people responsible for some of the developments in the cultural and symbolic landscape of remembrance that now define that space. For instance, Scott, a member of a Somme Society based on the Shankill Road, lamented:

I think that the [Somme Association], what they do, they do for money, that's my concern. I'm concerned about working-class Loyalism being excluded or marginalised in 2016. I think they just want to keep these people away from it all. . . . There's rumours that they want the Taoiseach to attend the Ulster Tower for 2016 and things like that, and they want to keep these people away in case somebody says something. I was there one year and Paisley had arrived—three or four years ago—and this gentleman shouted at him, "Traitor!," when he was walking up. He'd some face on him! He'd some face on him, and the man explained to me, the man explained to me why he done it. And I can understand why.

2016 worries me, what way it's going to be commemorated. Are they going to involve the Irish government at the Ulster Tower? Certainly I'd imagine they'll be invited to the Anglo-French events. But it worries me, who's going to be used here? It worries me that our people are being used for someone else's agenda. Instead of going over and respecting the dead, I think there's going to be a gloss put on it. (Interview with author, 2014)

Scott's comments echo a widespread view among Loyalists that it is new forms of cross-communal commemoration that represent a "crude, obsessive, and vengeful" distortion of—or playing politics with—a commemorative tradition whose sanctity and authenticity they have sought to protect. This concern was reflected in the criticism leveled by many Loyalists at the decision to extend an invitation to Deputy First Minister Martin McGuinness to attend the 1 July ceremony at the Ulster Tower in 2016. In an interview with the *Belfast Telegraph*'s Adrian Rutherford (2016), Phil Hamilton of the Rathcoole Friends of the Somme Association stated that if McGuinness attended, he would be unable to participate: "I think it's very insensitive, particularly at that time of the year, to invite someone with the baggage that Martin McGuinness brings. . . . He has declined invitations in the past, and turning up to the 100th anniversary to me would be solely political point-scoring. We need to keep politics out of commemorations." Although McGuinness ultimately declined the invitation, the "spirit of reconciliation" in which he and his Sinn Féin colleagues Declan Kearney and Mary Lou McDonald stepped "out of [their] comfort zone[s]" (BBC News 2016b) to lay a wreath at the Ulster Tower during a visit to the Somme in June 2016 was likewise rejected by many Loyalists as a cynical politicization and insulting debasement of the memory of the 36th (Ulster) Division.

During my interview with Mike, he argued that there was really no place for Republicans like Martin McGuinness at Loyalist commemorations of the Somme, as the politics of their attendance would diminish its "credence."

JE: What if someone who had been in the IRA wished to walk in [a 36th (Ulster) Division Memorial Association] parade?

M: [Pauses] Not welcome.

JE: They're not welcome?

M: No. They, uh, their contribution, would be tainted to say the least. . . . They would have no reason to be there, they'd have no credence to be there. An ordinary innocent Catholic who has nothing to do with Sinn Féin and the Republican movement? No problem, but I wouldn't accept [IRA former prisoner and Sinn Féin MLA] Gerry Kelly if he asked could he walk at it. I would find it insulting. I would find it hypocritical and insulting for a Republican to want to be at it even! There again, if Sinn Féin wanted to lay a wreath at the cenotaph when Belfast City Councillors are laying a wreath at it, that's up to them. Doesn't affect me. It's not the 36th (Ulster) Division [Memorial Association] organising it, they can do what they like. . . . That's dirty and political! They're a political grouping down there and they can do what they like!

The Loyalist critique of "sharedness" recognizes (and rejects) the public transcript on commemoration during the Decade of Centenaries as (anti-)political in a way that its authors are keen to deny. Of course, in so doing Loyalists often fail to acknowledge the politics of their own position: the alleged apolitical integrity of *their* "remembering" the Somme for *what it really was*—and their claim to "genuine" inclusivity that stems from it—is juxtaposed to the manipulation or distortion of this memory, its repackaging as a (political) exercise in good relations and its contrived or false claims to inclusivity or parity of esteem. As asserted by Matthew, an East Belfast Orangeman:

Where I find the cynicism is at play is in people using this to try and make it something that it's not. You know, that it was all "huggy huggy" in the trenches. [Unionists and Nationalists] didn't all go [to France and Belgium] and all of a sudden discover that they loved each other! It wasn't, as people are making it out here, that they sat around the campfire singing Kumbayah, you know, "we're all together here"! You know, that's what annoys me: making it something it's not. . . . That's not denying what happened. That's not denying the stories about Redmond's brother being carried by the UVF man from North Antrim.[4] That's not denying those stories. In fact, those stories should be told and held up. But not for something that

they're not. Not to be transposed into today's community relations
market just for that purpose. They deserve to be remembered because they're acts of heroism, or they're acts of compassion, or
they're acts of comradeship. That's why they deserve to be remembered. Not to, to shore up somebody's idea of what should go today.
Not to be re-invented. They're memories in their own right. (Interview with author, 2015)

Asserting the truthfulness of the memory and forms of Loyalist knowledge of which they are representative, Loyalist commemorations therefore function as sites at which the peace settlement, its "rewriting" of
history and its cross-communal hermeneutics, are contested.

However, as Kris Brown (2007, 2011) has demonstrated, they nonetheless function as sites where a new commitment to conflict resolution
can be negotiated (see also Graham and Shirlow 2002; Viggiani 2014).
For example, during the much-maligned commemoration for Joe Bratty
and Raymond Elder that I witnessed in 2014, a senior UDA former prisoner and member of the South Belfast UPRG used his oration to reassert his commitment to the peace and political processes (see ch. 3).
Addressing a sizable crowd from a rickety, makeshift platform in the "hijacked" Annadale garden of remembrance, he conceded that his initial
refusal to support the Loyalist cease-fires of 1994 had been a mistake and
that the decision to call a cessation of military activity had been the right
one. Was he angry about the culture war, the flag at city hall, or the parades impasse at Twaddell? Yes, but not as angry as he had been when,
twenty years ago to the day, he had received the news of the murder of
his friends and comrades. He expressed a sincere hope that the young
people listening never had to experience anger or sadness like it. His
challenge to those listening was that they ask themselves, "Because of the
cease-fires and the work that has gone on since, how many lives have
been saved?" The ultimate aim of that work, which includes, however
unfortunately, maintaining relationships and engaging in political
dialogue with Republicans, is "to save lives . . . and make sure I never
have to do this again." Despite some grumblings in the crowd about
the need to go back to war, many people I spoke with at the bar after the
commemoration begrudgingly conceded that the orator had a point.

A mural on the Shankill's Disraeli Street (fig. 7.1) may provide further indication that Loyalist commemoration that invokes the kind of

partisan social memory of the First World War criticized in the propaganda of peace is not necessarily antithetical to peace as such. The incorporation of antiwar verse from Siegfried Sassoon's poem "Suicide in the Trenches" in this memorial dedicated to Trevor King—a senior member of the Shankill Road UVF shot and killed by the Irish National Liberation Army (INLA) in 1994—is indicative of the intimate, visceral understanding of the true human cost of violent conflict that is borne by those whose lived experience has been defined by it. Drawing on firsthand knowledge of violence and its consequences, the negotiations that take place at Loyalist commemorations are founded on an understanding and repudiation of it in a way that is arguably less inconsistent or incoherent than approaches to peace-building that celebrate the First World War's violence as a form of "shared sacrifice." Personal experience of hurt and loss, and the ability to situate—through genealogy and commemorative ritual—this experience within the wider Loyalist communal experience across time and space, is arguably a far better tool for those seeking to negotiate Loyalism's rededication to peace and conflict transformation than is the historical "fact" of the First World War's "sharedness."

Figure 7.1. Trevor King mural, Disraeli Street, Belfast.

"SHOTS IN THE BACK AND DIRT IN THE DARK"

Talking about the Troubles during our interview, Bill was keen to stress that "there's no way you can compare this dirty, squalid, sordid little war with what happened in the trenches." When I asked, "Why not?," he replied:

> Well, number one is that both sides had uniforms. And both sides fought each other, sometimes man to man in the trenches. Here, innocent souls on their way to work were murdered, you know: shots in the back and dirt in the dark. Sordid, incestuous and squalid: that's how you would describe this forty years in Northern Ireland. There was nothing honourable about it. Nothing honourable. In fact, it was disgusting. And it's got nothing to do with the Ulster Volunteer Force who, number one, declared war on the British Army and were ready to go for them, and also the men who went to the Somme and fought at the Somme. It's a world of difference. But you have to say also, you have to say. You have to sort of qualify that by saying that I believe the *British establishment* turned it into a dirty, filthy little war. . . . Governments don't have friends, they only have interests. And if you are in line with their interests, you're their friend, if not they'll ditch you. They'll throw you to the dogs. (Interview with author, 2014)

On first reading, Bill's claims do not differ radically from Ringland's. Both are keen to stress particular discontinuities between the violence of the First World War and that of the Troubles. However, Bill's comments provide important insight into Loyalists' analysis of the role and culpability of the state in directing or perpetuating that violence and how the state's (class-political) relationship with its citizens is understood by Loyalists. Crucially, this analysis challenges prevailing norms and assumptions in the propaganda of peace about the causes and nature of conflict in Northern Ireland.

As suggested in chapter 4, the (British) state is seen by many Loyalists, with some validity, as essentially duplicitous: prepared to use, abuse, manipulate, and then discard as suits its interests. For many Loyalists, the Somme and the Troubles are equally significant in evidencing this view of the state—as well as the wider British and Unionist establishments—and its treatment of the Loyalist community as dupes or puppets. For instance, one East Belfast UVF member quoted by Graham and Shirlow in their article, "The Battle of the Somme in Ulster Memory and Identity," contended:

> The Somme and the Troubles are the same in a way. Both are about working class Prods [Protestants] giving their lives for Britain, the Empire and all that. It's about defending Britain at the Somme and about us defending our right to be British over the last 30 years. But you see it's more than that. We used to always give. We fought for Britain in two wars; we worked for nothing to support unionism and the rich Prods. We fought republicans to a cease-fire and what did we get? Nothing, we got nothing. It's like after the First World War the saying "Homes fit for heroes". What did men get after the wars, crap housing, bad schools, poor wages? What did we get after the Troubles? Not a thing you could hang your hat on! So we are proud that we gave. Our crime was loyalty. For we were always loyal and we got nothing. (2002, 894)

This analysis is at the heart of what Graham and Shirlow (2002) have defined as a form of working-class Protestant "Sinn Féinism" (Ourselves Alone) that prevails in sections of the Loyalist community and is represented in particular by the social democratic trend in the politics of the PUP and their foundational *Principles of Loyalism* (PUP 2002).

As an interpretation of the Somme's symbolism, this narrative draws on the message originally propounded by Gusty Spence and the Spence University in the cages of Long Kesh. For instance, in a Remembrance Day speech in 1977, Spence drew on the same Siegfried Sassoon verse used in the Trevor King mural to argue:

> In the name of the Government we are expendable and simply cannon fodder. . . . When we are labelled 'terrorist' we will simply smile the smile of the knowing and know that in a so-called legitimate war we would be dressed in a uniform of their choosing—having been stupid enough to have volunteered in the first place and

having listened to their impassioned patriotic and intimidating appeals questioning our manhood if we had not willingly volunteered. (Spence 1977)

He encouraged Loyalist prisoners to refuse to be cannon fodder, to sue for peace and reconciliation with their Republican enemies, and to seek a political solution to the conflict (see Novosel 2013).

While Spence's arguments eventually went on to form the basis of the UVF's political strategy and its approach to the peace process, as Novosel (2013) demonstrates, at the time his Remembrance Day oration fell largely on "deaf ears" both within and without the Long Kesh prison camp. The UVF's (sectarian) war would continue unabated until its cease-fire in 1994, and the organization did not declare an official end to hostilities until 2009. The influence of the Spence University is seen today in forms of grassroots politics, conflict transformation and community development initiatives, self-reliance, and autonomous organization in Loyalist communities (see Gallaher 2007; Smithey 2011; Shirlow 2012). But some aspects of contemporary Loyalism, its Somme cult and wider political culture, would appear to represent a significant deviation from Spence's core message. The use of images from the Somme on the flags of Northern Ireland supporters' clubs at the 2016 EUFA European Football Championship (fig. 7.2), for example, is surely more celebratory and in poorer taste than he would have condoned. More seriously, the forms of chauvinistic, virulent, and discursively violent nationalism—manifest in sectarianism, racism, and xenophobia and the backlash against the cultural transformations of postcolonial Britishness—that have been definitive of much of my encounter with Loyalism cannot be ignored. However comprehensible, they are difficult to justify and at times have come close to giving the lie to the social democratic or "progressive" politics espoused by some Loyalists.

Ethnic machismo and bigotry are among the defining traits of Loyalists' Somme culture that official commemoration during the Decade of Centenaries has sought, ostensibly, to neutralize. But perhaps the ultimate paradox of the Decade's propaganda of peace is precisely that it is has fostered an environment in which the service of working-class Irishmen, Protestant and Catholic, during the First World War is celebrated and heralded as exemplary rather than condemned as nation-

Figure 7.2. "Off to France Our Boys Were Sent" Northern Ireland football flag.

alistic folly or imperial misadventure. "Official" commemoration and its lauding of sharedness is no less (or perhaps even more) a celebration of violence—of Girardian (1977) "sacrifice"—than is represented by Loyalists' "unofficial" commemorative forms and discourses. Through their circumscription or condemnation, all forms of Loyalist commemorative discourse and practice are maligned and marginalized equally, even where they play an important role in reconfiguring or mediating Loyalist attitudes toward peace, conflict, reconciliation, and the repudiation of violence.

Crucially, criticism of the role of the British state in particular—and by extension, the state in general—in the instigation and perpetuation of violence either during the First World War or in subsequent conflicts has been almost wholly absent from public discourse and the prevailing official narrative of Northern Ireland's Decade of Centenaries. Of the Community Relations Council's 2012 lecture series, "Remembering the Future," for instance, a number of lectures focused on Ireland's role in the Great War, but none focused on the role of the British imperial state in causing it. The war is not condemned as a brutal interstate conflict to protect the competing and selfish interests of violent European empires but celebrated, at the most reductive, as "a war that stopped a war" in

Ireland. This, in turn, reinforces representations of the problem of violence in Northern Ireland as being one that exists between two hostile communities that have yet to be reconciled rather than as a question of state violence and its role in the politics of community (cf. McVeigh 2002; Rolston 2010). Simply put, the ethics of the British state's role in violence during the period 1912–22 and any continuity with its role during the Troubles has not been scrutinized to the same extent as the extra-, anti-, or pro-state violence of the period.

As suggested by President Michael D. Higgins at the RTÉ "Remembering 1916" symposium at Dublin's Mansion House in March 2016,[5] the Decade of Centenaries has fostered

> a great deal of critical reassessment of aspects of the [Easter] Rising and, in particular, of the myths of redemptive violence that were at the heart, not just of Irish nationalism, but also of Imperial nationalism. My view is that the latter has not, perhaps, been revisited with the same fault-finding edge as the former. Indeed, while the long shadow cast by what has been called 'the Troubles' in Northern Ireland has led to a scrutiny of the Irish Republican tradition of 'physical violence', a similar review of supremacist and militarist imperialism remains to be fully achieved. (Uachtarán na hÉireann [President of Ireland] 2016)

Succor has been given to particular forms of commemorative practice that reinforce jingoistic assertions about the justness of Britain's role in the First World War at the expense of alternate interpretations, including from within Loyalism itself. These assertions work to reinforce the current political settlement in Northern Ireland by seeking to silence the ghosts who would seek to disrupt it, and to exclude those who convene with them.

THE FACT OF THE MATTER AND THE GHOSTS AT THE FEAST

The modern nation state works by processes of exclusion, and it can change the definition of who precisely will be excluded at any time. . . . The state as sovereign power produces its obverse, the bare life of the citizen-soldier trapped in the battlefield of the Somme. (Edkins 2003, 6, 109)

One hundred years ago, the men of the 36th (Ulster) Division began their march into no-man's land. Today, their ghosts march on: on banners, drum skins, and gable walls throughout Northern Ireland. In the intervening century, these ghosts have given witness to the rupture of their homeland in the violent birth of two states, years of hurt and bloodshed on their native streets, and now they stalk the "shared" future of the "new" Northern Ireland. The Somme groans under the weight of a symbolism that far exceeds the boundedness of the event itself. Arguably, it is symbolically overburdened (cf. Burke 2013). It is the defining moment of Ulster's Golden Age: its imagined past and remembered future. It is the blood sacrifice which guarantees the never to be fulfilled promise of its soul's salvation. As the ghosts of the Somme continue their disruptive march, it is fitting that we seek to understand those who march with them, to hear rather than seek to silence them.

Loyalist commemoration is often—perhaps conventionally— represented as an exercise in ethnosectarian coat-tailing based on a willfully inaccurate reading of the past. It is definitive of the alleged danger of allowing memory to take primacy over history, which received critical treatment in chapter 1. This allegation is certainly not without foundation. The will to empathy, which I identified as being central to my methodology in chapter 2, cannot disguise or mask that Somme commemorations manifest forms of exclusionary and even repugnant politics; and they can and do function as paramilitary shows of strength. Through commemoration, paramilitary Loyalists attempt to assert their legitimacy as the guardians of the PUL community, and to stake particular territorial, political, and moral claims through assertions of heritage that are not empirically verifiable per se. As such, insistence on "starting from the historical facts" on the part of "peace propagandists," as examined in chapter 3, is understandable and even commendable.

Efforts to wrest control of Somme commemoration from Loyalism in general, and the UVF in particular (including by former Loyalist paramilitary members who are involved in initiatives like the Fellowship of Messines Association [Grayson 2010]), by asserting the primacy of "the facts" have yielded some reconciliatory results. But empathetic engagement with the ghosts of the Somme and their followers has also revealed that paramilitary use of the Somme's symbolism is only one part of the wider internal politics of a community that has suffered the adverse consequences of the modernist project in Northern Ireland: war, deindustrialization, economic decline, and a "lost" sense of identity, purpose, and ontological security. As revealed in chapter 4, Loyalists' "knowledge" is characterized as much, if not more, by fear, existential crisis, and the instability of their relationship with the state as it is by supremacism and ethnic chauvinism.

Loyalism's Somme culture is redolent with forms of "postcolonial melancholia" (Gilroy 2005) and attendant forms of militarized masculinity, ethnic hypernationalism, and virulent sectarianism. But in chapter 5 I argued that rather than reflecting uncomplicatedly Loyalism's "obsession" with (former) imperial dominance (and associated forms of ethnic chauvinism and sectarian bigotry), Loyalists' connection to the Somme through genealogy and its representation through commemoration speaks to their experience of ontological instability in the liquid (Bauman 2000) present. As discussed in chapter 6, the reiterative projection of the "Golden Age" that the Somme signifies is an attempt to overcome—though it ultimately functions to reproduce—Loyalist concerns about the uncertainty of the future.

The Somme's ghosts play a role in perpetuating division and conflict, but, as argued in this chapter, they also provide a source of knowledge through and from which Loyalists are able to (re)negotiate their position in the unstable present. Commemoration provides a means by which Loyalists are able to mobilize this knowledge to mediate and reassert their place in a social, political, and economic order in which they perceive themselves—with some justification—as marginal(ized). Above all, I contend that this knowledge is no more based in particular (however disagreeable) ideological assumptions, represents no more willful a manipulation of "the facts," and perhaps even communes more closely with the real (Lacan 1982) than does the Decade of Centenaries' public transcript on shared history, which valorizes shared sacrifice and lauds particular forms of violence rather than repudiating it per se.

"We forget," as Jenny Edkins (2003, 14, 229) asserts, "that a complete, non-antagonistic society is impossible. . . . Too often what we call politics in the contemporary world is evacuated of antagonism. Most of what is accepted onto the agenda of discussion is already delimited to such an extent that it contains no properly political disagreements." Couched in the language of history (or, more properly, what Benjamin [(1968] termed historicism) and its presumed superiority over memory, the project of promoting narratives on the war's shared sacrifice is an exercise in (disciplinary) power that attempts, ultimately, to circumscribe oppositional politics and to depoliticize the social order. It is, as argued in chapter 3, anti-political (Ferguson 1990). While the aim of creating an "inclusive and accepting society" (CRC and HLF 2013, 4) is benign and meritorious, it nonetheless requires the active negation of alternate narratives and dissident transcripts, particularly those that are critical of the role and nature of the state, or that question the violence at the heart of the state's relationship with its citizens. This violence is the subject of what Edkins (2003; see also Graff-McRae 2010) terms the political, which exists in moments where state power, authority, and the social order are revealed as contingent and arbitrary (cf. Agamben 1998; Žižek 1999, 2005): the political, that is, as "the arena of innovation and revolution, a field of unexpected and abrupt change, a point at which the status quo is challenged" (Edkins 2003, xiii). As Edkins argues, "Politics is part of what we call social reality. It exists within the agendas and frameworks that are already accepted within the social order. The political, in its 'properly traumatic dimension', on the other hand, concerns the real. . . . The political takes place at a moment when major upheavals occur" (12). The public transcript on commemoration during the Decade of Centenaries seeks to prevent just such revelations, challenges, or upheavals. In Northern Ireland, where the open wounds of more than thirty years of violent upheaval have yet to heal, this imperative is understandable and even commendable. But the commemorative landscape is stalked by disruptive ghosts (Pearse 2012 [1915])—those of Easter Week and the Somme—who refuse to simply acquiesce to this project of depoliticization. And their invocation through commemoration is a central part of political life in Northern Ireland.

In its insistence on starting from the historical facts, the Decade of Centenaries' public transcript insists on the primacy of certain facts, and on a particular interpretation of them as true. But as Wendy Brown (2001, 141) asserts, "The complex *political* problem of the relation between past and present, and of both to the future, is resolved by neither facts nor truth" (original emphasis). Crucially, in promoting a particular version of shared history, official commemoration of the war in the United Kingdom and Ireland has risked becoming divorced from communal, vernacular, and properly political understandings of the disposability of human life and the pity of war, which are acute in working-class communities in Northern Ireland—both Protestant and Catholic, Republican and Loyalist—where violence has been central to lived experience throughout the twentieth and early twenty-first century. It is these understandings that are vital to "contesting the depoliticisation which goes under the name of politics, and in keeping open a genuine political challenge by encircling . . . trauma, rather than attempting to gentrify it" (Edkins 2003, 15).

Rather than seeking to "gentrify" the violence of (Northern) Ireland's twentieth century: evacuating it of its political content for the sake of telling a cross-communal story of shared sacrifice, in its practices of genealogy and commemorative ritual—its ghost dance—Loyalism returns the Somme to the political. It restores to the ghosts of the Somme a politics denied to them by the propaganda of peace and locates them within wider analyses of Loyalism's relationship with state (bio)power. However disruptively or disjointedly, it also explicitly acknowledges that there are deep, significant, and irreconcilable differences between the Loyalist and Republican projects, stemming from and reflected in their divergent analyses of the politics and resonances of Irish involvement in the First World War and the nature of the conflict in Northern Ireland in the decades since. These contradictions cannot simply be dismissed or annulled through apolitical or cross-communal reorientation of commemorative ceremony. "Loyalist" and "Republican" are not merely communal labels; they are (oppositional) political positions.

Perhaps paradoxically, this acknowledgment may even create spaces for more meaningful forms of political transformation than exist in the narrative of shared sacrifice and its insistence on good relations between two communities in Northern Ireland. Through commemoration, the political is able to intrude into the (mundane) realm of politics (Graff-McRae 2010). In creating this space for opposing experiences and political understandings of violence to be viewed as opposite and equal, rather than seeking to circumscribe this opposition, it allows for the possibility of new conversations and new forms of understanding between the proponents of political projects that, however opposed, are of equal political validity. While the Decade of Centenaries' public transcript is principally concerned with encircling or enclosing the political, it is in acceptance of the validity and significance of profound political disagreement that more properly democratic politics becomes possible (cf. Mouffe 2005). Simply put, normative questions about the nature of the nation, the relationship between the state and its citizens, the ethics of empire, and the moral validity of violence—which are definitive of the political as such—are not addressed by simply acknowledging the fact of Irish involvement in the First World War. On the night of our interview, Jamie talked about opportunities he had had to discuss and debate these questions with Irish Republicans and spoke to their transformative potential.

> I went into [it] a sort of raving DUP supporter . . . I would have been your traditional "super Prod," if you know what I mean. And I [ended up] a PUP member . . . and that was purely because I was introduced to debate with people who were different than me and whom I hadn't met or discussed or debated with before . . . my thinking at the time was, understand your enemy, but it was also an interest just in the period. But I found a [new] connection with it; there were things being said about equality and civil rights and things like that. (Interview with author, 2015)

Couched in the language of culture war, Loyalists perceive and treat the present political settlement in Northern Ireland as an attempt to consign them, finally, to the "dustbin of history." The roots of this perceived marginalization are all too real. In communities defined by socioeconomic vulnerability, precarious relations in employment, and chronic educational underachievement, the ameliorating effects—the promised and much vaunted "peace dividend"—of Northern Ireland's double transition (McCabe 2013) have arguably failed to materialize at all. By and large, with some notable exceptions (e.g., Nolan et al. 2014; Burgess and Mulvenna 2015), attempts at voicing disaffection with these conditions—albeit incoherent or sectarian and often riotous and violent—are met with derision in public discourses and accusations by politicians, academics, and public commentators of wrecking or spoiling rather than seen as meaningful attempts at empathy or comprehension.

At times during the course of my fieldwork I was tempted to write off Loyalist protestations of a culture war as the jealous convulsions of a community that has lost a dominant position within the social order to which it was never entitled. But to do so negates not only that for many Loyalists this position was never perceived as such, but that many have never experienced the supposed material benefits of their socioeconomic, political, and cultural "ascendancy" or "ethnic dominance" (Kaufmann 2004b). In *Politics Out of History*, Wendy Brown (2001, 144) argues that "Derrida aimed to deprive the present of its sense of triumph over Marxism, its sense of being done with Marxism." A key aim of this book has been likewise to seek to deprive the "new" (anti-political) Northern Ireland of its sense of being done with Loyalism.

The Decade of Centenaries' public transcript is demonstrative of broader attempts to exclude particular forms of properly political knowledge and experiences from the realm of politics. Whether or not it corresponds to Loyalists' claims about a culture war, the prevailing official or dominant approach to commemoration during the Decade of Centenaries is based on the occlusion of particular unofficial forms of knowledge about the political: the violence of the past and its relationship with both the present and the future. While the logic of this process of exclusion is that of promoting peace, it may ultimately have the opposite effect. Instrumentally, for many Loyalists it provides the very validation they are seeking for their claims of a culture war. What is at times active and at others subtler exclusion of Loyalists or the watering down of their story about the Somme in official commemorations provides further evidence of their alienation from the state and the wider establishment. Denigration of Loyalists' commemorative practices on social media and their dismissal as paramilitary pageants in the press signal to Loyalists that they will never be respectable (Bryan 2000). And, as Gary suggested to me mournfully during our interview, "If they think we're monsters, well then, let's just *be* monsters."

More intrinsically, Loyalist commemoration is part, however disruptively, of the politics of Northern Ireland: the means by which Loyalists' place in the social order is understood, negotiated, and contested. For good or ill, meaningful debate about the shared future of Northern

Ireland must surely involve the ghosts of the Somme and those who follow them. And the contentious politics revealed by and negotiated
through Loyalists' commemoration of the Somme are not always or
necessarily as antithetical to peace as its propagandists might lead us to
believe. To be opposed to the present settlement is not to be opposed to
peace as such. Loyalists' myth of the Somme and their representations
of it have evolved over time in response to changes in the political, cultural, and economic environment in Northern Ireland. Certainly, in part
this evolution represents attempts by some Loyalists to justify past,
present, or future violence. But it also represents Loyalists' attempts to
mediate their intracommunal relationships. Crucially, this mediation involves reflecting on and challenging violence from within, and relies on
the ability to base these challenges in communal experiences, understandings, and knowledge of it. The Somme story is—and is likely to
remain—central to Loyalist ideas about peace, conflict, and the political.
Attempts during this Decade of Centenaries to exorcise the ghosts of the
Somme may ultimately serve only to prolong their restless dance.

Postscript

"All changed, changed utterly"?

JE: [2016] already feels like such a long time ago.

W: It does.

JE: To me it feels like a long time ago because, I think, the world has changed. This transformation—or what I perceive as these profound political transformations—have perhaps outstripped the commemorative moment . . .

W: OK, yes, that's a good point actually. Commemoration changes its meaning whenever there's more stuff happening, doesn't it? Or there's less space for it. . . . I think events have sort of overhauled the commemoration. . . . What I did want to say is though, is that of course the tours are still going out to the Somme. The tours will continue, and money's been set aside for them. There will be an attempt to continue doing all of that. It won't go away. But, you know, you're not going to be able to do a civic dinner at the City Hall or organise a jamboree of events about what comes next.

We're going to have to renegotiate what commemoration is I think. The first two letters of commemoration—*co*-mmemoration—how do you do that when the thing you remember is the thing that pulled you all apart? (William, interview with author, 2017)

Watching him announce his government's plans for the First World War centenary at the Imperial War Museum in 2012, who would have anticipated that it would be a much-diminished David Cameron who would eventually be laying the centennial wreath at the Somme's Thiepval Memorial, mere days after losing a referendum on the United Kingdom's continued membership in the European Union had resulted in his resignation as prime minister? In the run-up to 2016, nowhere was it predicted that by the end of the centennial year there would be as much, if not greater, political capital for Sinn Féin in a botched renewable energy scheme than in the commemoration of the Irish Republic's sacrificial founding during Easter Week. In the event, politics in Northern Ireland in 2016 weren't really about commemoration at all. As the 1916 centenaries themselves recede into memory, historians may attribute their relative lack of political volatility to the years of cumulative work undertaken by advisers, civil servants, and policy makers in preparing for them. Or perhaps they will ask what all the fuss (such as it was) had been about: whether the dedication of all those column inches, journal pages, and conference papers to exhaustive discussion about their discipline's confrontation with commemoration during the Decade of Centenaries had been strictly necessary. More likely, they will be far too preoccupied dissecting the more enduring political shifts and upheavals of 2016, by which the centennial commemorations of both the Easter Rising and the Battle of the Somme have been, arguably, dramatically upstaged and overshadowed.

It would always have been a truism to say that Northern Irish politics in 2017 were not what they had been when I began this research in 2013, but the rate and scale of change has felt precipitous, vast, and at times overwhelming. Elections to local councils and the European Parliament; three seminal referenda (on the issues of Scottish independence, marriage equality, and Brexit, respectively); one Irish and two U.K. General Elections within the space of two years; and two Northern Ireland Assembly elections only nine months apart have both mirrored and resulted in rapid and unpredictable realignments of political gravity across the British Isles. The deaths of both Ian Paisley and Martin McGuinness have provided space in which to reflect on the profound political, social, and cultural transformations that have characterized postconflict

Northern Ireland. Conversely, ongoing paramilitary violence; the ascendant politics of language, culture, and identity; the impasse on issues such as sexual equality and reproductive rights; the resurgent question of the border; and the collapse of power sharing have all raised questions about the true extent, longevity, and trajectory of those transformations. More broadly, Brexit, the election of Donald Trump to the office of president of the United States, and the rise of a so-called post-truth regime in Western political culture have shaken the foundations of the international (neo)liberal consensus and its Northern Irish avatars: the double transition and its propaganda of peace.

Given the intensity of this politico-cultural ferment, at this distance it is difficult to judge with any great precision the impact or consequences (either short- or longer-term) of 2016's centennial commemorations: of either the Easter Rising or the Battle of the Somme. Some of the worst fears—evoked by the ghosts of 1966—about their likely association with violence appear not to have been borne out, though the murder of prison officer Adrian Ismay by the dissident New IRA in March 2016 was explicitly linked by PSNI investigators to an increase in the group's activity in the run-up to the centenary of the Rising (see McDonald 2016b). Generally, though not unanimously (see Kennedy 2016), official marking of the centenaries has been heralded by the political, academic, and media establishments on both sides of the Irish Sea as having been broadly and sufficiently solemn, reconciliatory, and embracing of all "traditions" on the island (see, e.g., Godden and Palli 2016; Humphreys 2016; McDonald 2016a). Predominant themes in public commentary on the commemorations have included celebration of their historical "accuracy" and self-congratulation for having "maturely" avoided replicating the supposed mistakes or triumphalism of which O'Brien (1972) accused the 1966 Golden Jubilees (see, e.g., Kenny 2016; Humphreys 2016; Dudley Edwards 2016a, 2016b).

There can be little doubt as to the broad appeal of official approaches to the 1916 centenaries: it is evidenced by the literally thousands of commemorative events organized, in the main, at the local level across the island of Ireland in 2016.[1] Grounded in the genealogical logics and impulses that I examined in chapter 5—the quest to affirm identities in the present by locating their roots in the past—much of this vernacular commemorative activity sought to explore individual, familial, and communal connections to the events of 1916 (and, indeed, the period 1912–23 more widely). North and South of the border, an expansive range of lectures, panel discussions, workshops, and exhibitions was supported by a boom in publications by historians covering myriad aspects of 1916 (see Hanley 2016) and in the availability of digital and digitized resources, including for teaching, for community projects, and to support genealogical research (see Decade of Centenaries 2016; Creative Centenaries 2017).

Fintan O'Toole has suggested that also in 2016, "official Ireland trusted its artists." Lauding both the quantity and quality of artistic production during the centenary, he wrote:

> Perhaps for the first time in its history, the State gave artists the floor and left them to their own devices, trusting them to come up with responses to 1916 that would somehow hit the right note. Implicit in this trust is the embrace of a literal revisionism. Art, if it is any good, is always a re-visioning of the given materials, in this case the Rising and its legacy. (O'Toole 2016)

So defined were the 2016 commemorations by the levels of public engagement with artistic, theatrical, and literary reappraisals of 1916 that this cultural "creativity" was identified by the Irish government as the key achievement of the centenary year. A legacy program, Creative Ireland, was launched in December 2016, with the express aim of building on the success of the centenary and "mainstreaming creativity in the life of the nation" (Creative Ireland 2017). Its creativity was also seen to have been intimately associated with another of the key perceived successes of the centenary: its multivocality and firm commitment to narrative plurality and inclusivity (Humphreys 2016).

Prior to 2016, overzealous adherence to this commitment had almost derailed the entire official commemorative project before it had left the station. When the Irish government launched its commemorative program at the end of 2014, it did so with a video presentation that made no meaningful reference to the Easter Rising but did feature footage of or references to Queen Elizabeth II, Ian Paisley, U2 frontman Bono and former Irish rugby captain Brian O'Driscoll, Facebook and Twitter (whose European headquarters are located in Dublin), and, crucially, David Cameron and Enda Kenny's joint visit to the First World War battlefields. The video was roundly condemned, including by the historian Diarmaid Ferriter—a member of the Decade of Centenaries Expert Advisory Panel—who called it "embarrassing, unhistorical shit" (Feeney 2015). Sinn Féin withdrew what tentative support they had lent to the Irish government's program for 2016 and committed to delivering a rival schedule of commemorative events, which was launched in February 2015.

However, the Irish government moved quickly to regain the initiative. The *Ireland Inspires* video was pulled, and this was followed by a rapid renewal and repackaging of the official approach to the commemorations. A series of public consultations, North and South; a rebranding exercise; and a new yearlong program sought to further devolve the centenary to local communities while retaining its (albeit recalibrated) focus on pluralism and partnership, peace and reconciliation. The extent to which the organizers of the official commemorations eventually succeeded in recapturing the national(ist) imagination was illustrated to me when I stopped in at a pub on the Falls Road on Easter Sunday, 2016. I was struck by how many people had crowded into the bar to watch the RTÉ broadcast of the state ceremony at the GPO, even as the National Graves Association parade was passing by outside.

In line (broadly) with the prediction made by Heartfield and Rooney (2015, 150) in their polemic, *Who's Afraid of the Easter Rising?*, the architects of the centenary seemed to have "given up on trying to control the event, and [had] chosen instead to decentre and dilute it." Perhaps paradoxically, the devolution of commemoration to local communities, and, thereby, the encouragement of a "creative" islandwide commemorative cacophony, seems to have allowed for greater narrative control than would have been possible under similar conditions of tighter state management as had prevailed—in various forms and on both sides of the border—in 1966, 1976, or 1991 (Higgins 2012; Bean 2016; O'Callaghan 2016). Particular forms of critique or dissidence were, I felt, often absorbed, crowded out, or rendered otherwise indiscernible by the sheer volume of commemorative activity, much of it lacking in explicitly political content or even revelling in its apoliticism. For example, wandering around RTÉ's busy, sprawling (and undoubtedly quite enjoyable)

"Reflecting the Rising" jamboree in Dublin on Easter Monday, 2016, it was often difficult to discern what, precisely, the many pageants, performances, and (in one particularly perplexing exhibit) horticultural displays had to say about 1916—about either the Rising or the Somme—at all.

If the peace propagandists' relative success in their attempts to regain control of the commemorative agenda from other expressly political interests can largely (and counterintuitively) be attributed to the "democratization" of the centenary, then it should be noted that this *did* also rely, in part, on processes of circumscription, prohibition, and co-optation.[2] It is important, too, to note the ways in which discord, dissent, and division—the political as such—nonetheless found ways to intrude into the centenary(-ies) of 1916. The politics of gender, for example, was foregrounded in the aftermath of the Abbey Theatre's announcement of its program for 2016. Titled "Waking the Nation," it contained only one play written by a woman and only three directed by women. In response and through a series of discussions both on- and off-line, a group of theater professionals came together under the banner #WakingThe Feminists to put pressure on the Abbey Theatre and other cultural institutions to develop comprehensive policies on gender equality. #Waking TheFeminiists evolved into a broad-based social movement that has achieved some considerable and enduring successes in challenging malignant forms of misogyny and the male domination of the arts in Ireland (see #WakingTheFeminists 2016).[3]

Already bruised and shaken, though not dealt a killing blow, by the fiasco of the *Island Inspires* video, the "inclusivity"—the reconciliatory urge—at the heart of official commemorations also faced renewed forms of hostility, contestation, and destabilization in 2016. Throughout the centenary year, divisive ghosts continued to stalk the commemorative landscape, and there were moments when the political dissociations between British and Irish, Unionist and Nationalist, threatened, decisively, to reveal themselves. For example, in April 2016, one person was arrested during a protest against the unveiling of a new Wall of Remembrance in Dublin's Glasnevin Cemetery. The controversial Necrology Wall is inscribed with the names of all those killed during the Easter Rising: civilians, Republicans, and British Army personnel are listed side by side, ranked only according to date of death and then in alphabetical order.

Described by the chair of the Glasnevin Trust, John Green, as "simply [a] record [of the] historical facts of those who died as a result of political conflict" (McDonald 2016c), the memorial wall has been condemned by descendants of the "men and women of 1916" and by both Sinn Féin and their "dissident"rivals as promoting a false equivalence between Republican volunteers and members of the British Armed Forces. In April 2017, it was damaged when vandals covered it in paint (Keena 2017).

In Northern Ireland, at the very outset of the centenary year, newly anointed leader of the DUP and soon-to-be first minister, Arlene Foster, ruled out participating in any event she deemed to be a celebration of the Easter Rising. In an interview with the *Impartial Reporter*, she termed the Rising a "[direct] attack [on] the state to which I owe my allegiance. I don't think I'd be invited but even if I was invited I certainly would not be going to commemorate a violent attack on the United Kingdom" (Manley 2016). True to her word, Foster did not accept the invitation to attend the state ceremony in Dublin on Easter Sunday. Unionist councilors followed her lead and chose to boycott a civic dinner held to commemorate the Rising at Belfast City Hall. This, in turn, led to Irish president Michael D. Higgins pulling out of the event, which he had understood to have enjoyed cross-party support (Black 2016). Coupled with Loyalist rejection—as examined in chapter 7—of the reconciliatory overtures of Sinn Féin's 2016 visit to the battlefields of the Somme and Flanders as insincere, callous, and politically jarring, these boycotts created pockets of deconstructive repoliticization of the centenary commemorations, however fleeting or transitory.

As noted by William, by and large, Loyalist commemorations in 2016 proceeded in parallel with official commemorative program, North and South. He suggested that in his view, these programs (we discussed, in particular, the Belfast City Council's Belfast Somme 100 project) amounted to "a pretty formidable bunch of stuff. To what degree Loyalism found itself involved in it is another matter. Loyalism did what Loyalism does. You know, it put crosses in the ground, and all the band parades and things like that. . . . I think at the end of the day people didn't flock in to the city hall to hear [lectures] and stuff like that" (interview with author, 2017). He spoke specifically about one event he attended at Belfast City Hall in 2016: a "hedge school" organized by the Fellowship of Messines Association:

They managed to get, as they do, a bit of a cross-community audience. [Some Loyalists] were there. But the talks proceeded right the way through—it was a Somme 100 event, right? [One speaker] talked about women, but there was hardly any mention of the Somme. [Another speaker] talked about Nationalism. I realised these Loyalist guys were there sitting in the audience, had been there an hour, and there had been no mention *whatsoever* of anything to do with [the Somme], really, to be honest. . . . They've come out for this, and there's not going to be anything about them! (Interview with author, 2017)

The perpetuation of what has herein been termed the greening of the Great War and an emphasis on the 16th (Irish) Division's role in the latter stages of the Battle of the Somme appear to have been key features of official commemorative events that sought to stress the cross-communal sharedness of 1916's sacrifice.

This having been said, it should be noted that none of the official programming sought actively to hold back a tide of Loyalist commemoration that reached its high-water mark in June and July 2016. Indeed, several prominent Loyalists were themselves involved in developing the Belfast Somme 100 program highlighted by William, and included in its events schedule were parades and exhibitions organized by the Orange Order and the UCC (see History Hub Ulster 2016). The parade and reenactment in Woodvale Park on 18 June—a description of which provided the opening vignette for this book—was listed as a flagship event. As custodians of Belfast Somme 100, History Hub Ulster and the Belfast City Council also worked with the parade organizers to ensure new (though very particular and militarized) forms of representation of women in the parade (see *Focal Point* 2016). With some estimates putting the number of participants in the events of 18 June at around fifteen thousand (Cunningham 2016), the reenactment was notable for its use of professional pyrotechnics, its high production values, and its cinematic quality. Thinking back on the day, Sammy was keen to stress, "It was a great day. The weather was terrific, so it was. . . . Overall I thought the day was just terrific. The parade itself, with the period costume and all that was first class. In 2015 we'd had a large parade through Belfast as well, and that set a standard. And then 2016 sort of surpassed that, so it did. It was fantastic" (interview with author, 2017).

While the success of 18 June has thus been widely heralded, for many of my respondents, it nonetheless came a relatively poor second to the main event: the centennial pilgrimage to the former battlefields of the Western Front. Indeed, the parade and reenactment had been organized on 18 June—some two weeks before the centenary of the first day of the Battle of the Somme—precisely so as not to interfere with the travel plans of those making the journey to the Somme for 1 July. Sammy estimated that at least a thousand men and women traveled from Northern Ireland to participate in commemorative events organized by the 36th (Ulster) Division Memorial Association in France and Belgium (interview with author, 2017). These included wreath-laying ceremonies at the 36th (Ulster) and 16th (Irish) Division memorial stones on the outskirts of the village of Wytschaete and a parade from Ypres's Cloth Hall to the Menin Gate on the evening of 30 June, which featured four Loyalist flute bands. Most, though not all, of those participating in these events had also been allocated tickets in a public ballot for the ceremony hosted by the Somme Association at the Ulster Tower on 1 July itself.

As expressed throughout this book, some of my respondents had feared that the pomp and bureaucracy of official ceremonies in France in 2016 would result in (or perhaps had been designed to ensure) people effectively being excluded from them. As it transpired, strict restrictions were indeed imposed on those attending the Ulster Tower on 1 July 2016, though they were perhaps of a different magnitude and nature from those that had been anticipated. In the wake of a series of terror attacks, including shootings and bombings that had claimed the lives of 130 people in Paris in November 2015, attendees were subjected to a rigorous and heightened regime of security checks, searches, and controls. Sammy talked about what it was like at the Ulster Tower.

> S: Not everybody *wanted* to go [to the Ulster Tower for 1 July] because they were gonna have to be in the Ulster Tower area for endless hours. . . . You had to go and get searched first of all, and your bus had to be searched from top to bottom, the boot and all—everywhere. And then you were taken to the Ulster Tower and dropped off and then the bus drove away and didn't come back for . . . oh, I mean, it was, it wasn't easy for them but they did it well.
> JE: Did it feel worth it?

S: I think that to be there, one hundred years later, to the—not quite to the hour obviously—but to the day, just to be there and mark that and remember it. It's worth it every time, but to be there on the centenary was *definitely* worth it, like. But it was a lot of hassle. You had to be patient.

When I asked whether he felt that the presence of dignitaries had resulted in other kinds of restrictions on Loyalist participation in the official ceremony at the Somme on 1 July, he responded prosaically:

You know, the dignitaries will always get the best seats. The bigwigs will always get an umbrella when it starts raining—which it did. But to be fair to the Somme Association, and I think they were the main organisers, along with the Northern Ireland Office, they did look after us. You know, we got a packed lunch and we got drinks and they gave us sun chairs and stuff. And I can't complain about it to be honest with you. Apart from the weather, like. (Interview with author, 2017)

Thomas, who had also traveled to the Somme for the 1 July ceremony at the Ulster Tower, gave a thick description of an experience he termed "kaleidoscopic": vivid, multisensory, and perhaps a little overwhelming.

T: The amount of effort we had to go through to get there, you know, big bus journey—so many buses! We were conscious of the big thing happening over at the Thiepval Memorial,[4] so they were driving past us. And there was the archbishop of Canterbury walking around; all these other dignitaries. I was very conscious of that going on, but it was over there somehow, you could hear the sounds of it going on as we were at the Tower.

And the whole ceremonial thing [at the Ulster Tower] was very Orange. People were wearing their collarettes from early in the day . . . as I looked around I knew so many people there. I knew so many people. The Orange, all [the Somme Societies] were there. It was just like transportation of Loyalism to this site!

And then, whenever the royalty turned up, you know, there were barriers all along there, the royalty went by, shaking hands and all the rest of it. . . . People were going off into the corn fields around to get pictures of themselves with the poppies in the corn fields and then somebody was saying to me, "D'you know, this is really part of Northern Ireland here, you know this is the one place where the French have allowed us to fly the flag." And all the time, endless French police. It was very militarised: helicopters in the distance.

JE: That separation [between dignitaries and other attendees], were people put out by that, do you think?

T: No. I think everybody was very happy. There was reverence. You know, people were waiting very patiently for their buses and whatever else.

As highlighted by both Thomas and Sammy, the amount of time, organizational effort, and money invested by those who participated in the centennial commemorations of the Battle of the Somme provides evidence of their profound and enduring prepolitical and personal significance (interviews with author, 2017). But in addition to this, they also served as a way marker for what, during most of the centenary year, appeared to be a relatively ascendant cultural and political trajectory for Loyalism (and wider Unionism).

In January 2016, DUP First Minister Peter Robinson departed from the political front line after cashing in the last of his dwindling political capital to secure the Fresh Start Agreement. The DUP went into the 2016 Assembly elections with a renewed and more popular leadership (see LucidTalk 2016, 3) and emerged with both the largest vote share and the largest number of seats (see BBC News 2016c). The election was therefore heralded as having been good for Unionism in general and for the DUP in particular (see, e.g., *Guardian* 2016). By contrast, in the wake of a number of high-profile controversies—including revelations by former activist, Máiría Cahill, that her rape by an alleged member of the PIRA had been covered up by senior members of the party (see BBC News 2014d); and the arrest and questioning of party president, Gerry Adams, over the 1972 disappearance and murder of Jean McConville (see BBC News 2014f)—the 2016 election was widely understood to have been difficult for Sinn Féin. The party experienced a 2.9 percent drop in its first preference vote share, a net loss of one seat, falling voter turnout in core constituencies like Belfast West and Foyle, and an insurgent challenge on the left flank from the People Before Profit Alliance (BBC News 2016c). Sinn Féin's position was further weakened by the resignation in August 2016 of one of its most talented MLAs, Daithí McKay, amid accusations that he had "coached" Loyalist blogger Jamie Bryson before the latter had given evidence to Stormont's Finance Committee—of which McKay was then the chair—in 2015 (see O'Doherty 2016).

The summer of 2016 saw thousands of Northern Ireland football fans travel to France to watch their team perform unexpectedly well at the UEFA European Championship, gaining a reputation (and indeed, an award) for their infectious enthusiasm and love for the game and their team. "Will Grigg's on Fire"—a supporters' chant about Northern Ireland's star striker sung to the tune of Gala's 1996 dance hit "Freed from Desire"—became an anthem of the tournament as a whole (see *Belfast Telegraph* 2016b).[5] Following a relatively peaceful marching season, and as the anger of the flag protests of 2012 and 2013 continued to dissipate, an accommodation was reached between the Orange Order and the Crumlin and Ardoyne Residents Association that finally ended the Twaddell parades impasse. The protest camp was dismantled, and the Ligoniel Lodges completed the return leg of their 2013 parade in October 2016 (see BBC News 2016e).

Perhaps most significantly, the unanticipated victory of the campaign(s) in favor of leaving the EU in the U.K.-wide referendum held on 23 June 2016 appeared to herald—at the national level—the vindication of a Loyalist cultural-political project defined by its postcolonial melancholia and the attendant rejection of forms of globalization, multiculturalism, and liberal cosmopolitanism. In the lead-up to the referendum, a mural appeared in the Loyalist Tiger's Bay area of North Belfast imploring residents, "Vote Leave EU." The mural included a reference to a biblical passage—Revelations 18:4—which urges, "Come out of her, my people, that ye not be partakers of her sins, and that ye receive not of her plagues." Among the 52 percent of voters across the United Kingdom who eventually elected to leave the EU were 60 percent of Protestant voters in Northern Ireland. Of Northern Ireland's eighteen constituencies, seven (all Protestant majority areas) had majorities in favor of leaving (see McCaffery 2017). Analysis of an ESRC survey of over four thousand Northern Irish participants in the referendum conducted by John Garry and John Coakley (2016) revealed that a majority of supporters of the two main Unionist political parties, the DUP (70 percent) and even the pro-Remain UUP (54 percent), voted "Leave," as did the majority of TUV supporters (89 percent). Crucially, Garry and Coakley (2016) found that of the working-class Protestants in Northern Ireland who participated in the referendum, fully 71 percent put their crosses in the "Leave" box. Describing his feelings about the referendum result, Gary remembered fondly:

> I'll tell you what, see, the next day, after the vote? I didn't think the vote would go in our favour. I was driving home, and just happened to look up at the sky, and a big grin came over my face. And I just felt, for the first time, of being or having a sense of freedom which I'd never had before. . . . I didn't feel like my vote counted that much. But suddenly, now, I feel like the country's *ours* again. (Interview with author, 2017)

This celebratory mood would, however, be short-lived. Indeed, from the outset, Loyalists' satisfaction with the referendum result was awkwardly juxtaposed to the inconvenient truth that a majority in Northern Ireland (56 percent)—as well as a majority in Scotland (62 percent) and a very substantial, angry, and vocal minority across the United Kingdom as a whole (48 percent)—had voted "Remain" (BBC News 2016a). Amid the ensuing lack of clarity about what Brexit really means—ambiguity as to its consequences for the United Kingdom's only land border and uncertainty about the future shape of trade, diplomatic, and geopolitical relationships between the United Kingdom and its European neighbors—the border, the specter of partition, and the constitutional question have once again become salient in Northern Irish politics in a way not seen since the height of the Troubles. As suggested by William:

> It had looked not so long ago like the Sinn Féin vote was going down. And it *was* going down! And was that because people were getting comfortable . . . people on the Nationalist side of the fence seemed quite happy in [a] Northern Ireland [within the U.K.] and to

be getting happier. And now that's been reversed. And it's all the more of a shock. And Brexit is part of that because Brexit here is not so much about, you know, loads of Romanians coming to Kent and Essex, or "flooding" Boston in Lincolnshire. . . . Brexit here is going to mean the border at the end of the day. That's where it's going to be really problematic. And I think in its heart and core, Loyalism is worried about that: worried about what that might entail. (Interview with author, 2017)

If the Brexit referendum result had already represented somewhat of a pyrrhic victory for the Loyalist political project, then events of late 2016 and early 2017 were nothing short of a crisis. In December 2016, a BBC Spotlight investigation alleged that concerns about serious flaws in the Northern Ireland Executive's Renewable Heat Incentive (RHI) scheme, raised by whistleblowers as early as 2013, had been summarily and deliberately ignored by Arlene Foster, then minister for enterprise, trade, and investment. In what was dubbed the "Cash for Ash" scandal, the scheme—which ran from 2012 until it was eventually closed down in 2016—overspent by more than £400 million (BBC News 2016d). Foster, now first minister, faced sustained criticism for her belligerent, bellicose, and uncompromising handling of the affair. Eventually, following repeated demands for Foster to temporarily step down as first minister while an inquiry examined the bungled scheme—and also in the wake of a decision by DUP communities minister, Paul Givan, to cut a £50,000 Gaeltacht bursary scheme for Irish-language learners in late December 2016 (Meredith 2016)—Martin McGuinness resigned his position as deputy first minister in January 2017, effectively unseating Foster and collapsing the devolved institutions.

In his resignation letter, McGuinness alleged:

The equality, mutual respect and all-Ireland approaches enshrined in the Good Friday Agreement have never been fully embraced by the DUP. Apart from a negative attitude to nationalism and to the Irish identity and culture, there has been a shameful disrespect towards many other sections of our community. Women, the LGBT community and ethnic minorities have all felt this prejudice. And for those who wish to live their lives through the medium of Irish, elements in the DUP have exhibited the most crude and crass bigotry. . . . [T]he refusal of Arlene Foster to recognise the public anger or to exhibit any humility in the context of the RHI scandal is indicative of a deep seated arrogance which is inflicting enormous damage on the Executive, the Assembly and the entire body politic.[6] (*Belfast Telegraph* 2017b)

By now in terminally poor health, the former deputy first minister was replaced as Sinn Féin's Northern leader by Michelle O'Neill, who had previously served first as minister for agriculture and rural development and then as minister for health in the Northern Ireland Executive. O'Neill led the party into the Assembly election triggered by the collapse of the Executive, which was held on 2 March 2017. During the election campaign, the arrogance of which McGuinness had accused Arlene Foster and the DUP became a prominent theme. This was not helped by several gaffes on the part of the former first minister, among them, a press conference in which she referred to proponents of an Irish language act in general and Sinn Féin in particular as "crocodiles" who, if fed, would "keep coming back for more" (Gordon 2017). The crocodile motif was quickly co-opted as a badge of honor by Republicans and Irish-language campaigners.

The 2017 Assembly election saw a rapid reversal of the electoral fortunes that had prevailed in 2016. On an increased voter turnout (64.78 percent, nearly 10 percent higher than the turnout in 2016), Sinn Féin's first preference vote share rose by 3.9 percent, while the DUP's dropped by 1.1 percent (BBC News 2017b). In an Assembly reduced from 108 to 90 seats, this translated into a net loss of 10 seats for the DUP, including those that had been held by party grandees, Nelson McCausland and Lord Morrow, and rising star, Emma Little-Pengelly (who would go on to win the Belfast South seat in the 2017 General Election). With 28 seats, the DUP fell below the 30-seat threshold required to unilaterally trigger a petition of concern[7]—which it had traditionally used to veto legislation on marriage equality—while Sinn Féin's tally of 27 seats brought it within one seat of becoming the largest party in the Assembly. Crucially, Unionism had lost its majority in the Northern Ireland Assembly, and for the first time since the state was founded in 1921, Unionist candidates failed to gain a majority either of votes cast or of seats available in an election in Northern Ireland (BBC News 2017b).

Neatly summarizing the nature of the position in which Loyalism (and Unionism more widely) found itself following the Assembly election in 2017, Sammy lamented:

> The simple fact is that in 2016, Unionism was in a position of strength. Unionism in 2017 is f'ing not in a position of strength. It's been fucked by the political parties, and even in the General Election, they've fucked us as well. The DUP made an absolute horlicks of the Assembly elections; the UUP made a horlicks of the Assembly elections, in how they presented themselves and in what they said. They didn't give leadership, they made bollocks, after bollocks, after bollocks, and just made themselves out to be total and utter fools. So we paid the price for that. Then in the General Election, for example, in South Belfast and East Belfast, they're running two candidates. And there's a distinct possibility the SDLP will retain South Belfast, and in East Belfast maybe [the liberal-centrist, cross-community] Alliance [Party] will get in. Instead of having two safe Unionist seats, my fear is we won't have any.[8] (Interview with author, 2017)

The electoral success of a resurgent Irish Republicanism was largely unanticipated during most of the centenary year. It has resulted in an intensive process of soul-searching within the PUL community and has been met with renewed calls for Unionist unity. In particular, the DUP's claims that they are best (indeed, uniquely) placed to guarantee the long-term security of Northern Ireland's position in the United Kingdom (cf. DUP 2017a, 7; 2017b, 3–4) appear to be gaining traction. For example, ahead of the 2017 General Election, the Loyalist Communities Council issued a statement urging Unionist and Loyalist voters to cast their votes for the DUP over other Unionist candidates in the three key marginal seats of Belfast North, Belfast South, and Belfast East (LCC 2017).[9] Following a disastrous election for Prime Minister Theresa May and the loss of the Conservatives' parliamentary majority, having succeeded in increasing their share of the vote by more than 10 percent since the

2015 General Election, and with a net gain of two seats (taking their total to 10) in the House of Commons (BBC News 2017a), the DUP's new position as king makers in a hung Parliament may yet signal that the pendulum is swinging back in Unionism's favor, at least in the short to medium term.

However, the longer-term trajectory is still far from certain. Unionism failed to regain its electoral majority in the 2017 General Election (BBC News 2017a), and it is unclear when or if it will do so, particularly given contemporary demographic trends and the renascent issue of the border. It should not be assumed—as it has been in some quarters (see, e.g., Meagher 2016)—that either an increasing Catholic population or a new regime of customs checks will lead inevitably or inexorably to a United Ireland. Likewise, the "threat" that Brexit poses to the peace process makes for sensational headlines, which, I think, tend to misrepresentation or overstatement (see, e.g., Greenwood et al. 2016). But it does appear that Brexit has served to repoliticize the politics of Northern Ireland: reactivating and recalibrating the long-running conflicts and deep-seated animosities that the propaganda of peace had sought to neutralize. At the time of writing, Anglo-Irish relationships seem to be deteriorating rapidly as negotiations about the terms of the United Kingdom's terms of departure from the European Union become increasingly tense and volatile, and it remains ambiguous as to whether the current climate will be conducive to establishing a new, durable, power-sharing Executive in the North.

Against this backdrop, Loyalist factionalism and paramilitary feuding have claimed three lives since August 2016 (see McDowell 2017), and ongoing conflicts in and over the symbolic landscape—in 2017 the issue of eleventh night bonfires has proven particularly vexatious—have sustained and renewed Loyalist claims about a culture war (see BBC News 2017c). Concurrently, a steady stream of allegations and revelations about collusion between Loyalist paramilitaries, the police, and security services during the Troubles has raised new and profoundly troubling questions about Northern Ireland's sordid past, and the nature of Loyalists' relationship with the state (see, e.g., Cadwallader 2013; Urwin 2016). The increasingly apparent depth of this relationship and the seemingly pathological violence at its heart raise further ethical concerns as to the legitimate extent of (the already qualified) empathy I have argued that it is possible or desirable to extend to Loyalism.

Where and how the remaining centenaries sit in this context is unclear. The much-vaunted conciliatory potential of the centenary of the 1917 Battle of Messines—at which the 36th (Ulster) and 16th (Irish) Divisions fought side by side—appears to have been overtaken by events. A joint Anglo-Irish ceremony was held at the Island of Ireland Peace Park on 7 June 2017, and participants included Prince William, Duke of Cambridge, Taoiseach Enda Kenny, and representatives from across the Northern Irish political spectrum (including the DUP's Arlene Foster and, significantly, Sinn Féin's Alex Maskey) (*Belfast Telegraph* 2017a). However, Messines's place in the news cycle—which, on the eve of a U.K. General Election, was at any rate fairly marginal—was defined as much by its being Enda Kenny's last overseas engagement as Taoiseach as by its reconciliatory symbolism.

Already likely to be more highly charged, upcoming centenaries will surely be even more fraught in the current political climate. In particular, the centenary of partition and of the founding of the Northern Irish state in 2021 is bound to take on enhanced significance for Ulster Loyalists seeking to reassert their status as integral members of a Union that is itself in a state of flux. The DUP has made the marking of this centenary a key policy commitment in subsequent elections (DUP 2016, 31; 2017b, 22). And led by a "reinvigorated" and "rejuvenated" UCC, discussions are already under way at the grassroots about how the centenary of partition can be marked with a view to ensuring that Northern Ireland's membership in the United Kingdom is guaranteed for another one hundred years (Sammy, interview with author 2017).

During our follow-up interview in 2017, William and I discussed one of his recent projects, which had involved a visit to the Somme battlefields following the 1 July ceremonials. His description of the experience was arresting and posed a (if not the) centrally important question for Loyalism and its politics of commemoration in the final years of the Decade of Centenaries:

It was grey, and there was nobody there. You'd had this *huge* crowd [on 1 July], and now there was nobody there. And suddenly it felt more real, you know? Far, far more real than all the pomp and stuff for me. . . . What has happened is the corporatisation of the whole thing—if you compare the poetry on the Ulster Tower to the poetry on Helen's Tower, one is "Ulster's grief," which has taken over from personal grief. It's a cold, colder kinder of thing that.

And I thought, "We've had the Somme, 2016. What's next?" Will Loyalism forget about it or move on from it? Or will it seek to continue with it? I think people will *always* come here, to remember. But things have changed. [There's] Brexit, and the alterations there. . . . Courage [is] required of Loyalists at this moment. Courage was required of the men who came up these slopes with bayonets and guns. What's required now of Unionism and Loyalism? What is required now for the future? What is required now for a changed world? (Interview with author, 2017)

Loyalist commemoration of the Somme may have reached its apotheosis in July 2016, and its ghosts may even have enjoyed a little respite in the days and weeks following. But in a world transformed, the ghost dance will surely continue. What new forms and meanings will it manifest in an uncertain, unstable future? For now, only the ghosts are given to know.

NOTES

Introduction

1. Unless indicated otherwise, all emphases are in the original.

2. The "Decade of Centenaries Timeline" funded by the Northern Ireland Community Relations Council (CRC) and produced by Digital Key covers the forty-year period between 1885 and 1925. It is available at http://centenaries timeline.com/.

3. Another execution—that of Sir Roger Casement, who had been apprehended attempting to smuggle weapons into Ireland in advance of the Rising—took place in London's Pentonville Prison on 3 August 1916.

4. Though under the terms of the Government of Ireland Act 1920, three of Ulster's nine counties—Donegal, Monaghan, and Cavan—would eventually be ceded, first to the (short-lived and abortive) state of Southern Ireland, then to the Irish Free State, and finally to the Republic of Ireland. The loss of these three counties of the historic province of Ulster and the drawing of a border around the six counties of Antrim, Down, Armagh, Tyrone, Fermanagh, and Londonderry guaranteed a permanent Protestant majority in the new state of Northern Ireland.

5. On the evening of 3 December 2012, a motion was passed by Belfast City Council that placed new restrictions on the flying of the Union flag above Belfast City Hall, reducing the number of days on which it is flown from 365 to no more than 18 "designated" days per year. On the night of the vote, Loyalist protesters gathered outside the city hall and some engaged in violent clashes with police. Flag protests, several of which became riotous, continued nightly in Belfast for several days and weeks, and Loyalists continued to protest the city council's new flags policy for several months into 2013. To date, a weekly flag protest is held outside the city hall every Saturday, though the number of protesters has reduced markedly week after week since the height of the protests. For a full account of the flag protests and their aftermath, see Nolan et al. 2014.

ONE.   (Re)theorizing Commemoration

1. Creative Centenaries is a project led by the Derry-based media and arts organization the Nerve Centre. It was initially supported by the Northern Ireland Department for Culture, Arts and Leisure (DCAL), until the latter was closed and its functions and duties distributed to other executive departments in 2016. The aim of Creative Centenaries is to "[bring] together information and resources about the Decade of Centenaries and the work of Northern Ireland's creative sector in commemorating these events." See creativecentenaries.org.

2. East Belfast & the Great War is an HLF-supported community project examining the impact and legacy of the Great War on and in East Belfast. I joined the project as part of my fieldwork in 2013, and have helped to organize a number of its events and activities, working in partnership with the Living Legacies 1914–1918 Research Center, based at Queen's University Belfast. See the project website at www.eastbelfastww1.com.

3. Historical and social scientific research in and on (Northern) Ireland demonstrates a particular preoccupation with memory. The recent publication of Oona Frawley's four-part edited *Memory Ireland* series (2011, 2012, 2014a, 2014b) is the latest in a tradition that includes Ian McBride's seminal edited volume, *History and Memory in Ireland* (2001); Tom Dunne's *Rebellions: Memoir, Memory and 1798* (2004); Eberherd Bort's edited volume, *Commemorating Ireland: History, Politics, Culture* (2004); and Guy Beiner's *Remembering the Year of the French: Irish Folk History and Social Memory* (2007b). Arguably, the tradition of Irish memory studies predates the present memory boom, with F. X. Martin's 1967 essay, "1916—Myth, Fact and Mystery," providing an early example of the intertwining of revisionist history and examination of popular memory. In fact, a number of key studies of Irish memory have focused on the meaning and memory of Easter 1916—Ireland's memorial site par excellence (Ní Dhonnchadha and Drogan 1991; Daly and O'Callaghan 2007; Graff-McRae 2010; Higgins 2012).

4. Deleuze and Guattari (1988, 16–23) criticize what they call "root and branch" readings of history, which "inspire a sad image of thought that is forever imitating the multiple on the basis of a centred or segmented higher unity. . . . History is always written from a sedentary point of view and in the name of the unitary state apparatus." They argue instead for a more "rhizomatic" reading based on "lines of segmentarity and stratification" (21) rather than of cause and effect.

5. All states are involved in the construction and dissemination (including through the sponsorship of "heritage" projects and in the design of school curricula) of official histories. It is perhaps one of the key features of the state as such. For an interesting and specific example of the role of the state and edu-

cation policy in the construction of official history, see Onta 1996 on Nepal. More generally on the co-construction of history and identity in the nation-state, see Bryan 2016.

6. As argued by Bryan (2016), an important caveat to this assertion is provided by historians of commemoration, whose work is explicitly concerned with these questions. Pertinent examples are Beiner 2007b; Daly and O'Callaghan 2007; and Higgins 2012. The contribution of these histories of commemoration to understanding the social function of the past in the present may suggest that the issue is with what questions historians seek to answer rather than with their method per se. However, as Bryan (2016, 40) suggests, it remains the case that "the role of the discipline of history in . . . the understanding of memory and remembering is problematic as it [ultimately] lacks the conceptual tools for the task. It . . . profiles particular types of transmission over others, thereby disguising the extent to which commemoration is necessarily, and fundamentally, a synchronic process."

7. On the idea of the public space and its politics, see Lefebvre 2009.

8. In fact, poststructural forms of analysis have only ever occupied a fairly marginal position in wider academic and political discourses on the Northern Irish question, or "problem" (see Zalewski and Barry 2008).

9. More information on "Remembering the Future," including videos of the series, is available at CRC's website: www.community-relations.org.uk /programmes/marking-anniversaries/.

10. As a historical materialist, Benjamin's implicit assertion is that that which must inevitably be reversed, the specific set of injustices that must be overcome, are those injustices that inhere in the contradictory relations of capitalist production.

11. In a post–Cold War global order defined by the ascendance of (neo)-liberal, capitalist democracy, it is unclear where certain political movements—which define themselves as opposed to the liberal project of globalization but are also definitionally racist, sexist, homophobic, or otherwise intolerant or exclusionary—fit within this dichotomy. Good examples are Afrikaner Nationalism in South Africa (Davies 2009), the Tea Party in the United States (Skocpol and Williamson 2013), and the UK Independence Party (UKIP) in the United Kingdom (Ford and Goodwin 2014).

TWO.   "What does it mean to follow a ghost?"

1. Entwined Histories is a cross-community schools project that has been run by the peace-building charity Co-operation Ireland since 2012. Its expressed aim is to "examine and compare different interpretations of our shared history,

encouraging dialogue and positive remembrance." I have been involved with the project—first as a project assistant and facilitator and later as project coordinator—since 2013. See www.cooperationireland.org/programmes/youth-education-programmes/entwined-histories/.Batt.

2. Although a number of interviews were also conducted with other stakeholders in the Decade, including representatives of the Northern Ireland Office, charities, community groups, and political parties, such as the DUP and Sinn Féin.

3. Any content from Facebook contained herein was obtained from public pages and is available to view without the need to create a Facebook profile or to add an individual as a friend. I have not made use of any content from individual profiles, private pages, or closed or secret groups. Likewise, all quoted content from Twitter is openly and publicly available.

4. The "Famine Song" has its origins on the terraces of the Glasgow Rangers football club. It refers to the large number of Irish migrants to Scotland to find work during the Great Hunger of the 1840s, with the most provocative rejoinder being, "Well the famine is over, why don't they go home?" Some versions of the song include accusations about stealing, rape, or pedophilia on the part of Irish Catholics. The song made headlines in 2012, when the Young Conway Volunteers flute band was filmed playing it provocatively outside St. Patrick's Catholic Church on Donegall Street in North Belfast.

5. In 2011, a set of taped interviews by former paramilitaries, collected as part of the oral history Belfast Project led by the researchers Ed Moloney and Anthony McIntyre and housed in Boston College's Burns Library, were successfully subpoenaed by the U.S. attorney general and returned to the United Kingdom for examination by the Police Service of Northern Ireland (PSNI) (see Palys and Lowman 2012).

THREE.   Policy, Peace-Building, and "the Past" during the
Decade of Centenaries

1. Although the Orange Hall was marked as the designated starting point for the parade, it is important to stress that the Orange Order itself had no role in organizing and did not sanction this commemoration.

2. The UDU provides what one member described to me as a "legal identity" for the Ulster Defence Association, which is a proscribed organization. It takes its nomenclature from an organization originally formed in 1893 in opposition to the Second Home Rule Bill. The standards of the UDU are either sky blue or black, colors conventionally associated with the UDA.

3. *The Wombles* was a 1970s children's television series about a group of furry, hedgehog-like creatures who lived on London's Wimbledon Common. Members of the UDA were nicknamed Wombles owing to the furry hoods of the parkas they wore on parade in the early 1970s (Wood 2006).

4. "Re-imaging" is the term used to describe the process of replacing (para)military murals, memorials, or other installations in the public space with imagery identified as less violent or divisive. It is also the specific name given to the project(s) through which funding is distributed for this purpose (see Rolston 2012).

5. The symbol of the red hand of O'Neill is used in heraldry to denote the Irish province of Ulster, and it features heavily in the symbolic lexica of all of the main Loyalist paramilitary organizations.

6. According to its website, the Junction, based in Derry, "acts as an 'access point' and 'gate keeper' guiding, resourcing and supporting individuals and organisations in community relations work. . . . The influencing of policy at the local, regional, national and international levels are among its core functions."

7. Although the extent to which the Somme *actually* occupied a central position in the Orange Order's commemorative lexicon until the 1990s is questionable. This is discussed further in chapter 5.

8. Formally the largest of Northern Ireland's Nationalist parties, until it was overtaken by Sinn Féin in the early 2000s, the SDLP has had a growing presence at the Remembrance Sunday service at the cenotaph since the late 1980s. In 1994, councilor Alex Attwood led the first official SDLP delegation to the ceremony, and in 1995 he laid a wreath. In 1997 Alban Maginness became Belfast's first Nationalist Lord Mayor, and he went on to play a full, formal role in commemorative events, including at the 1 July Somme commemoration and on Remembrance Sunday (Grayson 2010, 331).

9. That representatives of the Irish government choose to lay laurel—as opposed to red poppy—wreaths at remembrance ceremonies reveals ongoing difficulties in attempts to establish shared symbolism. The red poppy, inextricable from its association with British militarism, remains a symbol imbued with particular historical-political significance and with which Irish nationalists continue to have a difficult relationship.

10. Though as Richard Grayson (2010) has demonstrated, Republican and Nationalist engagement with the "sharedness" of the First World War's "sacrifice" has often belied and even served to reinforce underlying intercommunal conflicts over the war's meaning, morality, and legacy.

11. For a full explication of the Gramscian concept of hegemony, see Bates 1975; Mouffe 1979.

12. For example, the "programme of events" promised in the Executive's Statement on the Decade of Centenaries—which included a series of talks and

exhibitions—never materialized, having been canceled in advance of the first such event (Good Relations professional, interview with author, 2014).

13. Although the Haass-O'Sullivan process ended without agreement, talks between the parties on these and other contentious issues continued. In December 2014 an agreement was reached. While the justificatory language of this Stormont House Agreement is less florid than that of Haass and O'Sullivan's draft agreement, the proposals for dealing with the past in Stormont House reproduce almost exactly those in Haass-O'Sullivan.

14. Under the terms proposed in Haass-O'Sullivan, and as agreed at Stormont House, information retrieved by or provided to the ICIR would be inadmissible in court.

15. This has been acknowledged and argued by many historians, including members of Arkiv itself. The entries in the commentary section of Arkiv's website provide a number of more nuanced claims and critical understandings as to the limits of history in solving the "problem" of the "the past" than does the group's submission to the Panel of Parties. A 2016 report from the Conference of Irish Historians in Britain states emphatically, "What divides the people of Northern Ireland is not so much disagreement over particular facts as clashing perceptions of the responsibility for violence, the motives of the principal agents in the conflict, and the meaning of victimhood."

16. This is not to deny the soundness of the moral judgment that underwrites the will to characterize or even dismiss particular narratives on Northern Ireland's violent past as "terroristic," though this can be and has been subject to critique (see McEvoy and Shirlow 2013). Rather, my aim is to demonstrate the subjectivity, implications, and political consequences of such a characterization.

17. By contrast, this transcript goes some way in both implicitly and explicitly legitimating the role of the state in the violence of the Troubles, as well as claims on the part of the Unionist establishment (so-called middle Unionism) to blamelessness (cf. Lawther 2011). A fuller discussion of ongoing debates about postconflict "truth recovery" in Northern Ireland lies just beyond the scope of this study. However, it is important to note that Loyalists remain distrustful of proposed mechanisms for dealing with the past, in part because they fear being scapegoated or betrayed by both a state and a domestic political elite that refuses to acknowledge its own role in the conflict while simultaneously pursuing what is perceived as a policy of Republican "appeasement" (Lawther 2014; Faulkner 2014; cf. Lundy and McGovern 2008). This trope in Loyalist political culture receives further treatment below; see esp. chs. 4 and 7.

FOUR.   Peace as Defeat

1. At the time of writing, this mural has been removed, as the building on which it was located has been redeveloped.

2. "Working-class" Unionists refers to those belonging to the Ipsos MORI social grade bracket C2DE (see Ipsos MediaCT 2009).

3. The Civil Rights Camp at the junction between the Crumlin Road and Twaddell Avenue (an area commonly known as the Ardoyne shops), was established by members of the Ligoniel Orange Lodges and their supporters in July 2013 in protest of the Parades Commission decision not to allow a return parade to pass this volatile interface on the Twelfth of July. It remained in place—with first nightly and eventually weekly protest parades proceeding to it—for just over three years. It was eventually disbanded following an agreement between the Orange Order and the local Crumlin and Ardoyne Residents Association (CARA) in September 2016.

4. "The bru," or "the brew," is slang for the state unemployment benefit. It is a jocular reference to cultural attitudes that regard those receiving the benefit as lazy or work shy and liable to spend most or all of the money on alcohol.

5. Though this accommodation has long been characterized by tensions and was by no means always stable. The involvement of Protestants in the Northern Irish Labour movement has been far from insubstantial, and class antagonism has been a persistent feature of internal Unionist politics. The split between the Orange and Independent Orange Orders, for instance, is a demonstration of this antagonism (Bryan 2000, 52–54).

6. Section 75 of the Northern Ireland Act (1998) requires that public authorities must, of necessity, pay "due regard to the need to promote equality of opportunity" between persons of different religious belief or political opinion. Coupled with other legislative and statutory instruments that seek to promote "parity of esteem," this has contributed to increasing material and symbolic equality between Protestants and Catholics in terms of political representation and access to jobs and housing, the public space, and civic life in Northern Ireland (see Nolan 2014).

7. James Mackie & Sons—Mackie's for short—was a textile machinery engineering plant and foundry in West Belfast. Historically, it was one of the city's largest employers, but, in line with broader trends in British manufacturing since the end of the Second World War, its closure in 1999 followed a period of sharp decline in demand and output (see *Mackie—Built to Last* 2012).

8. Roughly equivalent to the U.S. high school diploma, General Certificates of Secondary Education (GCSEs) are academic qualifications undertaken by British secondary school pupils across a broad range of subjects over two years, beginning at age fourteen and culminating in final examinations at age sixteen. GCSEs are letter graded, with an A* being the highest available grade, a G representing the lowest passing grade, and a U (unclassified) representing an outright fail. Grades falling between A* and C are considered "good," and generally a student requires a minimum of five good GCSEs, including in the core subjects of English, Science, and Mathematics, in order to progress to further or higher education.

9. In 2001, the Newry and Mourne Council voted to rename a Newry playground after the PIRA Hunger Striker Raymond McCreesh. Following a series of complaints and a report by the Equity Commission, the council voted to retain the name in 2012.

10. In fact, disputes and violent confrontations over parades in Portadown are traceable to at least 1873, and protests over the specific part of the contentious parade route on the Garvaghy Road had taken place since the late 1980s (Bryan, Fraser, and Dunn 1995).

11. On the Twelfth of July in 2012, members of the Young Conway Volunteers Loyalist flute band were filmed playing the "Famine Song" outside St. Patrick's Catholic Church on Belfast's Donegall Street. Subsequent parades on Donegall Street in 2013 had restrictions imposed on them by the Parades Commission and were protested by local residents and members of the congregation (see BBC News 2012).

12. The green flag is the symbol of the international Eco-Schools program. Schools are awarded the flag in recognition of their efforts to promote environmentalism and sustainability. More information is available on the Eco-Schools Northern Ireland website: www.eco-schoolsni.org.

13. In November 2014, two men were killed while changing the tire on a farm vehicle in Co. Donegal. The news was reported in Northern Ireland by the BBC (BBC News 2014e).

14. Though increasing electoral support for the UK Independence Party (UKIP) across the "mainland," the promotion of "British values" in British schools by the Conservative government, and recent polling that suggests some 43 percent of Britons believe that the British Empire was broadly a "good thing" all provide some indication that this melancholy and resistance to the project(s) of postcolonial Britishness are not confined to Northern Ireland (see Ford and Goodwin 2014).

15. In an interview with the *Irish News* in May 2014, then DUP leader and Northern Ireland First Minister, Peter Robinson, refused to condemn Pastor McConnell's remarks about Islam, stating, "I'll be quite honest, I wouldn't trust [Muslims] in terms of those who have been involved in terrorist activities. I wouldn't trust them if they are devoted to Sharia Law. I wouldn't trust them for spiritual guidance. Would I trust them to go down to the shops for me, yes I would, would I trust them to do day-to-day activities . . . there is no reason why you wouldn't" (*Belfast Telegraph* 2014a).

FIVE.   "Our culture is their bravery"

1. "Let Them Home" is the slogan of the ongoing campaign by the Ligoniel Orange Lodges and their supporters at the Twaddell Civil Rights Camp

to allow them to "complete" their return parade, which was restricted in a Parades Commission determination in 2013.

2. Memorial plaques were issued to the families of all British and Empire soldiers killed during the First World War. Cast in bronze, these round plaques look like large pennies, measuring approximately twelve centimeters in diameter. Known colloquially as "death pennies," they were often regarded by my respondents as treasured family heirlooms, and they often provided an entry point into more extensive family history research for amateur genealogists.

3. The Farset Somme Project, established in the late 1980s, was a cross-community initiative that worked to restore the Ulster Tower in Thiepval. The project receives further treatment below.

4. In 2014 the trial of John Downey for his suspected role in the IRA's 1982 Hyde Park bombing was dismissed when Downey produced a letter he had received from the British government in 2007 stating, "There are no warrants in existence, nor are you wanted in Northern Ireland for arrest, questioning or charging by police. The Police Service of Northern Ireland are not aware of any interest in you by any other police force." Although Downey had received the letter in error, the judge ruled that it nonetheless amounted to a guarantee that he would not face trial. A subsequent inquiry into the so-called On the Runs scheme led by Lady Justice Dame Heather Hallett found that 192 Republicans suspected of being connected to Troubles-related offenses had received similar letters of assurance (see McKevitt 2015). While the Hallett Review found that the scheme did not amount to an amnesty or "get out of jail free card" for Republican On the Runs, it has been widely regarded as such by Loyalists.

5. Since 2012, the 36th (Ulster) Division Memorial Association has been involved in organizing a program of annual commemorative concerts at the iconic Ulster Hall.

6. B&Q and Homebase are both chain DIY and home improvement retailers and garden centers.

7. Formed in 1972, the RHC is a small Loyalist paramilitary organization. Although the group has maintained its own distinct identity and structure, it has been closely linked to the UVF almost since its inception. As detailed by Tony Novosel (2013), inside the "cages" of Long Kesh the UVF and the RHC shared a common command structure and members of both organizations reported to Gusty Spence as their commanding officer.

8. In ways that receive further treatment in later chapters, it is arguable that the kind of celebration of the Somme that has come to define Loyalist cultural production during the culture war represents a deviation from its role in the construction of the "puppets no more" politics of Gusty Spence and the early PUP.

9. I am grateful to both Neil Jarman and Jason Burke for affirming that this has been an observable trend in Loyalist parading and band culture since 2006.

10. The West Belfast Athletic and Cultural Society was founded on the Shankill Road in 1998 by UVF former prisoners. It provides sports facilities and a gym, as well as programs on culture, heritage, and identity (Philip, interview with author, 2015).

SIX. The Ghost Dance

1. The Shankill Historical Society and Shankill Band Shop occupy the premises of what was formerly the Eagle chip shop, over which the UVF had its headquarters during the Troubles. Upstairs are now the editorial offices of the *Purple Standard*.

2. The 2016 Committee of the West Belfast Athletic and Cultural Society is responsible for organizing and coordinating the organization's commemorative activity during the Decade of Centenaries. It provided costumes and replica weapons for reenactors, in addition to organizing rigorous drilling practices ahead of the main event on 9 May 2015.

3. The National Graves Association is an Irish Republican organization aligned with the Provisional Republican movement. It is responsible for the care and maintenance of the graves of Irish Republican Army volunteers. The Belfast branch of the organization maintains three plots in Milltown Cemetery in West Belfast, including the New Republican Plot, in which are buried PIRA volunteers killed on active service or on Hunger Strike since 1972. Among its core duties is the organization of an annual Easter Rising commemoration on the Falls Road. The commemoration organized by the National Graves Association is the largest of the three main commemorations in Belfast on Easter Sunday and ends with an oration from a senior Sinn Féin figure at the New Republican Plot.

4. Despite some discussion within the Unionist Centenary Committee at an early stage of the planning process about adopting a reworded and updated text for the reenactment of Ulster Day in 2012, it was decided to use the original text, as it was deemed both to be of ongoing relevance and to be more authentic and historically accurate (Jamie, in conversation with author, 2016).

5. The Cruthin legend, propounded in particular by Ian Adamson, a former Ulster Unionist Party politician, founding chair of the Somme Association, and author of the UCC mission statement, posits that Ulster Protestants are descended from a pre-Gaelic people—the Cruthin—who were driven from their ancestral homeland in the North of Ireland by the Gaelic tribes. As such, the seventeenth-century Plantation of Ulster signaled a return to the ancient homeland rather than the "settlement" of Irish nationalist mythology (see Adamson 1974).

6. According to an article on the blog *Balaclava Street*, which is dedicated to exploring the Loyalist paramilitary experience of the Northern Irish Troubles, the UVF "had a regulation outfit—black trousers, boots, black polo neck sweater,

cap comforter, sunglasses, and most famously a black leather jacket—designed by Gusty Spence and which all volunteers were expected to possess. . . . [T]his getup led to the UDA calling them 'blacknecks'" (*Balaclava Street* 2014b).

7. Despite the rhetoric, there has nonetheless long been some crossover in membership between the Orange Order and both the UVF and the UDA, particularly in Belfast (see Taylor 2000).

8. This list of significant anniversaries had been decided after "lengthy discussions" by the committee in advance of the consultation.

SEVEN.   "Dupes no more"?

1. It should be noted that despite the adoption of this protocol, there has been little discernible decrease in the flying of paramilitary flags from lampposts in Belfast. In fact, at a rough estimate, in my view, the practice had become more prevalent in 2017, one year after the introduction of the new protocol, than it had been prior to 2016.

2. Despite some debate about which version is "correct," the emblem can be either a left or a right hand. The heraldry of the 36th (Ulster) Division, for example, used both (*News Letter* 2016b).

3. Though it should be noted that in the buildup to and aftermath of the Somme centenary in 2016, flying of the commemorative flag designed by the LCC was more prevalent in UVF-controlled areas of Belfast than in those controlled by the UDA. This may be indicative of ongoing tensions within and between the two organizations about "rightful" claims to the Somme and its symbolism.

4. A leading proponent of Home Rule, Major William "Willie" Redmond was the brother of the Irish Parliamentary Party leader John Redmond and the party's MP for East Clare from 1892 until his death in 1917. At the outbreak of war in 1914, he enlisted as an officer in the predominantly Nationalist 16th (Irish) Division. John Meeke, a native of Ballymoney, Co. Antrim, had joined the UVF in 1913 and became a stretcher bearer in the 36th (Ulster) Division. At the Battle of Messines in 1917, under heavy fire, Meeke tended to Redmond after the latter had sustained grave injuries, refusing to leave his side until he had been evacuated from the field of battle. Willie Redmond later died of his wounds. He is buried in Loker, Belgium.

5. While Higgins's analysis here is prescient, it should be noted that he has also had a hand in promoting the particular forms of "Imperial nationalism" that he condemns, for example, through his role in the inauguration of the Commonwealth War Graves Cross of Sacrifice at Glasnevin Cemetery. Emilie Pine (2014) has fittingly described Irish state commemoration of the First World War as transitioning from the "merely perfunctory" to the "openly celebratory."

Postscript

1. By way of illustration, according to figures published on the Ireland 2016 website, more than 3,500 centenary events were held on the island of Ireland, with a further 1,200 organized internationally (Ireland 2016/Éire 2016 2016).

2. For example, as part of their program of commemorative events for 2016, Sinn Féin had included a proposed Son et Lumière production: a day-by-day portrayal of key events during the Rising, to be projected onto the facade of the GPO nightly between 24 and 29 April. However, plans for the projection were rejected by An Post—amid accusations of intervention by Communications Minister Alex White—because of their overtly (party-)political nature (Kelly 2015; *An Phoblacht* 2015).

3. Indicative of the particular forms of co-optation at the heart of official commemorations of 1916, such was the impact of #WakingTheFeminists that footage of its protests were included in a retrospective film produced by Ireland 2016 to celebrate the successes of its centenary program (see Ireland 2016/Éire 2016 2016).

4. A larger, international service of remembrance at the Thiepval Memorial for the Missing of the Somme preceded the ceremony at the Ulster Tower on 1 July 2016. In attendance were, among others, members of the British Royal Family, Irish president Michael D. Higgins, and then Prime Minister David Cameron. The Thiepval Memorial is approximately a mile south of the Ulster Memorial Tower.

5. For some of my respondents—particularly Jamie—it was the European Championship and not the centenary that provided the most significant emotive experiences and enduring memories of 2016. The Somme commemorations seem to have been somewhat of an anticlimax by comparison (correspondence with author, 2017).

6. Of course, being equal partners in devolved government, it seems unlikely that Sinn Féin can be entirely absolved of responsibility for the RHI debacle. Indeed, Michelle O'Neill has received criticism for her involvement in the scheme during her tenure as minister for agriculture and rural development (see O'Driscoll and O'Boyle 2017).

7. Intended to guarantee effective power sharing at Stormont, the petition of concern is designed to prevent the dominance of one community over another. A petition of concern can be brought to the Speaker in advance of any vote in the Northern Ireland Assembly. To be accepted, it requires the signatures of 30 MLAs. If a petition is successfully lodged against a particular motion, for that motion to pass requires the assent of a weighted majority (60 percent of those present and voting) and of at least 40 percent of each of the Unionist and Nationalist designations present and voting (see Smyth 2016).

8. In the event, both Belfast South and Belfast East returned DUP MPs to the House of Commons in the 2017 General Election.

9. Though it should also be noted that the LCC did endorse one UUP candidate in the 2017 General Election, Tom Elliot in Fermanagh and South Tyrone. The seat was won by Sinn Féin's Michelle Gildernew.

BIBLIOGRAPHY

Adams, G. 2016. "Ard Fheis Presidential Speech by Sinn Féin President Gerry Adams TD" [Online], 23 April. www.sinnfein.ie/contents/39626.

Adamson, I. 1974. *Cruthin: The Ancient Kindred*. Newtownards: Nosmada.

Agamben, G. 1998. *Homo Sacer: Sovereign Power and Bare Life*. Stanford, CA: Stanford University Press.

Alexander, J. C., and J. L. Mast. 2006. "Introduction: Symbolic Action in Theory and Practice: The Cultural Pragmatics of Symbolic Action." In J. C. Alexander, B. Giesen, and J. L. Mast, eds., *Social Performance: Symbolic Action, Cultural Pragmatics and Ritual*, 1–28. Cambridge: Cambridge University Press.

Anderson, B. 2006 [1983]. *Imagined Communities: Reflections on the Origins and Spread of Nationalism*. London: Verso.

Andrade-Rocha, J. 2015. "The Temporariness of Selling "Northern Irishness": Tourism and Identity in Post-Conflict Northern Ireland." Paper presented at Explorations of Northern Irishness, Belfast, 12 March.

An Phoblacht. 2013. "Video Interview with Mayor—Armistice Day Participation in Belfast 'a Gesture of Respect and Reconciliation'" [Online]. www.anphoblacht.com/contents/23556.

———. 2015. "1916 Sign Goes Up in O'Connell Street as Government Tries to Stop GPO Light Show," 2 November. www.anphoblacht.com/contents/25447.

Appleby, J., L. Hunt, and M. Jacob. 1994. *Telling the Truth about History*. New York: Norton.

Arendt, H. 2005 [1954]. "On the Nature of Totalitarianism: An Essay in Understanding." In J. Kohne, ed., *Essays in Understanding 1930–1954: Formation and Exile*, 328–60. New York: Schocken Books.

Arkiv. 2013. "Submission to the Panel of Parties in the NI Executive" [Online]. http://arkivni.wordpress.com/submission-to-the-panel-of-parties-in-the-ni-executive-on-behalf-of-arkiv/.

———. 2014. "The Past—Practical and Historical" [Online]. https://arkivni.wordpress.com/2014/02/09/the-past-practical-and-historical/.

Armstrong, J. 2010. "On the Possibility of Spectral Ethnography." *Cultural Studies: Critical Methodologies* 10 (3): 243–50.

Ashe, F., and C. McCluskey. 2015. "'Doing Their Bit': Gendering the Constitution of Protestant, Unionist and Loyalist Identities." In T. P. Burgess and G. Mulvenna, eds., *The Conflicted Identities of Ulster Protestants*, 55–69. Houndmills: Palgrave Macmillan.

Ashplant, T. G., G. Dawson, and M. Roper. 2000. "The Politics of War Memory and Commemoration: Context, Structures and Dynamics." In T. G. Ashplant, G. Dawson, and M. Roper, eds., *The Politics of War Memory and Commemoration*, 3–85. London: Routledge.

Assman, A. 2010. "Re-framing Memory: Between Individual and Collective Forms of Constructing the Past." In K. Tilmans, F. van Ree, and J. Winter, eds., *Performing the Past: Memory, History and Identity in Modern Europe*, 35–50. Amsterdam: Amsterdam University Press.

Augé, M. 2004. *Oblivion.* Minneapolis: University of Minnesota Press.

Aughey, A. 1991. "What Is Living and What Is Dead in the Ideal of 1916?" In M. Ní Dhonnchadha and T. Dorgan, eds., *Revising the Rising*, 71–90. Derry: Field Day.

Bairner, A. 1999. "Masculinity, Violence and the Irish Peace Process." *Capital & Class* 23 (3): 125–44.

———. 2006. "The *Flâneur* and the City: Reading the 'New' Belfast's Leisure Spaces." *Space and Polity* 10 (2): 121–34.

Baker, S. 2014. "Belfast: New Battle-Lines in a Post-Conflict City." *New Left Project* [Online], 11 March. www.newleftproject.org/index.php/site/article_comments/belfast_new_battle_lines_in_a_post_conflict_city.

———. 2015. "Loyalism on Film and Out of Context." In T. P. Burgess and G. Mulvenna, eds., *The Contested Identities of Ulster Protestants*, 83–97. Houndmills: Palgrave Macmillan.

Balaclava Street. 2014a. "Apples and Orangies: The UVF and the UDA Compared, Part 1" [Online], 1 March. https://balaclavastreet.wordpress.com/2014/03/01/apples-and-orangies-the-uvf-and-uda-compared-part-1/.

———. 2014b. "Apples and Orangies: The UVF and UDA Compared, Part 2" [Online], 20 July. https://balaclavastreet.wordpress.com/2014/07/20/apples-and-orangies-the-uvf-and-uda-compared-part-2/.

———. 2014c. "'The Fallen and the Brave,' 5th September 2014: A Review" [Online], 14 September. https://balaclavastreet.wordpress.com/2014/09/14/the-fallen-and-the-brave-5th-september-2014-a-review/.

Barthes, R. 1981. *Camera Lucida.* Trans. R. Howard. New York: Hill and Wang.

Basu, P. 2005. "Macpherson Country: Genealogical Identities, Spatial Histories and the Scottish Diasporic Clanscape." *Cultural Geographies* 12 (2): 123–50.

Bates, T. R. 1975. "Gramsci and the Theory of Hegemony." *Journal of the History of Ideas* 36 (2): 351–66.

Bauman, Z. 2000. *Liquid Modernity*. Cambridge: Polity Press.

———. 2006. *Liquid Fear*. Cambridge: Polity Press.

BBC. 2014. "iWonder: The Irish Question and the War That Stopped a War" [Online]. www.bbc.co.uk/timelines/zgwjjxs.

BBC News. 2012. "Loyalist Band Filmed outside North Belfast Catholic Church" [Online], 13 July. www.bbc.co.uk/news/uk-northern-ireland-18829447.

———. 2013a. "Northern Ireland Orange Order Leaders Warn of Cultural War" [Online], 12 July. www.bbc.co.uk/news/uk-northern-ireland-2326 7038.

———. 2013b. "Theresa Villiers: Union Flag Protest Violence 'Damaging NI Image'" [Online], 4 January. www.bbc.co.uk/news/uk-northern-ireland -20915975.

———. 2014a. "Annadale UDA Memorial 'Not Funded by Housing Executive'" [Online], 1 August. www.bbc.co.uk/news/uk-northern-ireland-28599146.

———. 2014b. "HMS *Caroline*: Belfast-Based Warship to Become Museum" [Online], 15 October. www.bbc.co.uk/news/uk-northern-ireland-29630240.

———. 2014c. "Máiría Cahill: Timeline of 'IRA Rape' Allegations" [Online], 24 November. www.bbc.co.uk/news/uk-northern-ireland-29786451.

———. 2014d. "Pastor James McConnell's Islamic Remarks Investigated by Police" [Online], 21 May. www.bbc.co.uk/news/uk-northern-ireland-27501839.

———. 2014e. "Seamus Hegarty and Kevin Woods Killed in Donegal Farming Accident" [Online], 22 November. www.bbc.co.uk/news/world-europe -30154464.

———. 2014f. "Sinn Féin Leader Gerry Adams Held over Jean McConville Murder" [Online], 1 May. www.bbc.co.uk/news/uk-northern-ireland-2723 2731.

———. 2015. "'Gay Cake Row' in Northern Ireland: Q & A" [Online], 19 May. www.bbc.co.uk/news/uk-northern-ireland-32065233.

———. 2016a. "EU Referendum: Results" [Online]. www.bbc.co.uk/news /politics/eu_referendum/results.

———. 2016b. "Martin McGuinness 'out of Comfort Zone' as He Lays Somme Wreath" [Online], 2 June. www.bbc.co.uk/news/uk-northern-ireland-3643 8976.

———. 2016c. "NI Election 2016: Results" [Online]. www.bbc.co.uk/news /election/2016/northern_ireland/results.

———. 2016d. "RHI Scandal: How Does the £400m Overspend Add Up?" [Online], 16 December. www.bbc.co.uk/news/uk-northern-ireland-38344185.

———. 2016e. "Twaddell: Agreement Reached over Long-Running Parade Dispute" [Online], 24 September. www.bbc.co.uk/news/uk-northern-ireland -37458065.

———. 2017a. "Election 2017: Results" [Online]. www.bbc.co.uk/news/election /2017/results.

———. 2017b. "NI Election 2017: Results" [Online]. www.bbc.co.uk/news /election/ni2017/results.

———. 2017c. "Sinn Féin Accused of 12th July 'Cultural War' by DUP and PUP" [Online], 10 July. www.bbc.co.uk/news/uk-northern-ireland-4055 6732.

Bean, K. 2007. *The New Politics of Sinn Féin*. Liverpool: Liverpool University Press.

———. 2016. "New Roads to the Rising: The Irish Politics of Commemoration since 1994." In R. S. Grayson and F. McGarry, eds., *Remembering 1916: The Easter Rising, the Somme and the Politics of Memory in Ireland*, 224–40. Cambridge: Cambridge University Press.

Beiner, G. 2007a. "Between Trauma and Triumphalism: The Easter Rising, the Somme, and the Crux of Deep Memory in Northern Ireland." *Journal of British Studies* 46 (2): 366–89.

———. 2007b. *Remembering the Year of the French: Irish Folk History and Social Memory*. Madison: University of Wisconsin Press.

———. 2011. Review of *Remembering and Forgetting 1916: Commemoration and Conflict in Post-Peace Process Ireland* by Rebecca Graff-McRae. *Irish Historical Studies* 37 (147): 514–15.

———. 2013. "Disremembering 1798? An Archaeology of Social Forgetting and Remembrance in Ulster." *History and Memory* 25 (1): 9–50.

———. 2017. "Troubles with Remembering; or, the Seven Sins of Memory Studies." *Dublin Review of Books* [Online]. www.drb.ie/essays/troubles-with -remembering-or-the-seven-sins-of-memory-studies.

Belfast Telegraph. 2014a. "Peter Robinson: I Wouldn't Trust Muslims Devoted to Sharia Law . . ." [Online], 29 May. www.belfasttelegraph.co.uk/news /northern-ireland/peter-robinson-i-wouldnt-trust-muslims-devoted-to -sharia-law-but-i-would-trust-them-to-go-down-to-the-shops-for-me -30313447.html.

———. 2014b. "Shameful Hijacking of Commemoration by the UDA" [Online], 2 August. www.belfasttelegraph.co.uk/opinion/editors-viewpoint/shameful -hijacking-of-commemoration-by-the-uda-30478164.html.

———. 2016a. "Paramilitary-Backed Loyalist Umbrella Group Issues New Flag Protocol" [Online], 12 May. www.belfasttelegraph.co.uk/news/northern -ireland/paramilitarybacked-loyalist-umbrella-group-issues-new-flags -protocol-34709109.html.

———. 2016b. "Passion of Northern Ireland Fans Helped Make Euro 2016 a Celebration of Football: UEFA" [Online], 16 September. www.belfasttele graph.co.uk/news/northern-ireland/passion-of-northern-ireland-fans -helped-make-euro-2016-a-celebration-of-football-uefa-35055125.html.

———. 2017a. "Battle of Messines Centenary Commemoration: Political Representatives from across Northern Ireland and Republic Pay Respect in

Belgium" [Online], 7 June. www.belfasttelegraph.co.uk/news/northern
-ireland/battle-of-messines-centenary-commemoration-political
-representatives-from-across-northern-ireland-and-republic-pay-respect
-in-belgium-35800273.html.

———. 2017b. "Martin McGuinness' Resignation Letter in Full" [Online],
9 January. www.belfasttelegraph.co.uk/news/northern-ireland/martin
-mcguinness-resignation-letter-in-full-35353349.html.

Bell, D. 1987. "Acts of Union: Sub-Culture and Ethnic Identity amongst Protestants in Northern Ireland." *British Journal of Sociology* 38 (2): 158–83.

———. 1990. *Acts of Union: Youth Culture and Sectarianism in Northern Ireland.*
Houndmills: Macmillan.

Benjamin, W. 1968. *Illuminations.* Ed. H. Arendt. Trans. H. Zohn. New York:
Schocken Books.

———. 2002. *The Arcades Project.* Trans. H. Eiland and K. McLaughlin. Cambridge, MA: Harvard University Press.

Berliner, D. 2005. "The Abuses of Memory: Reflections on the Memory Boom
in Anthropology." *Anthropological Quarterly* 78 (1): 197–211.

Besteman, C. 2015. "On Ethnographic Love." In R. Sanjek, ed., *Mutuality: Anthropology's Changing Terms of Engagement,* 259–84. Philadelphia: University
of Pennsylvania Press.

Black, R. 2016. "Irish President Pulls out of Dinner in Belfast to Mark Rising."
Belfast Telegraph [Online], 1 April. www.belfasttelegraph.co.uk/news
/northern-ireland/irish-president-pulls-out-of-dinner-in-belfast-to-mark
-rising-34588963.html.

Blee, K. 1993. "Evidence, Empathy and Ethics: Lessons from Oral Histories of
the Klan." *Journal of American History* 80 (2): 596–606.

———. 1998. "Managing Emotion in the Study of Right-Wing Extremism."
Qualitative Sociology 21 (4): 381–99.

———. 2003. "Studying the Enemy." In B. Glassner and R. Hertz, eds., *Our
Studies, Ourselves,* 13–23. Oxford: Oxford University Press.

Bloch, M. 1986. *From Blessing to Violence.* Cambridge: Cambridge University
Press.

Bolton, M., and A. Jeffrey. 2008. "The Politics of NGO Registration in International Protectorates: The Cases of Bosnia and Iraq." *Disasters* 32 (4):
586–608.

Bort, E., ed. 2004. *Commemorating Ireland: History, Politics, Culture.* Dublin: Irish
Academic Press.

Bourdieu, P. 1984. *Distinction: A Social Critique of the Judgment of Taste.* Trans.
R. Nice. Cambridge, MA: Harvard University Press.

———. 1986. "The Forms of Capital." In J. Richardson, ed., *Handbook of Theory
for the Sociology of Education,* 241–58. New York: Greenwood.

———. 1989. "Social Space and Symbolic Power." *Sociological Theory* 7 (1): 14–25.

———. 1991. *Language and Symbolic Power*. Cambridge: Cambridge University Press.

Bourgois, P. 1995. *In Search of Respect: Selling Crack in El Barrio*. Cambridge: Cambridge University Press.

Bowman, T. 2007. *Carson's Army: The Ulster Volunteer Force 1910–22*. Manchester: Manchester University Press.

Boyce, G. 2001. "'No Lack of Ghosts': Memory, Commemoration and the State in Ireland." In I. McBride, ed., *History and Memory in Modern Ireland*, 254–71. Cambridge: Cambridge University Press.

Brettell, C. B., ed. 1996. *When They Read What We Write: The Politics of Ethnography*. Westport, CT: Praeger.

Brewer, J. 2000. *Ethnography*. Buckingham and Philadelphia: Open University Press.

Brown, B. 2012. *Daring Greatly: How the Courage to Be Vulnerable Transforms the Way We Live, Love, Parent and Lead*. New York: Avery Publishing.

Brown, K. 2007. "'Our Father Organisation': The Cult of the Somme and the Unionist 'Golden Age' in Modern Ulster Loyalist Commemoration." *Round Table* 96 (393): 707–23.

———. 2011. "'Bound by Oath and Duty to Remember': Loyalism and Memory." In J. W. McAuley and G. Spencer, eds., *Ulster Loyalism after the Good Friday Agreement: History, Identity and Change*, 226–43. Basingstoke: Palgrave Macmillan.

Brown, W. 2001. *Politics Out of History*. Princeton: Princeton University Press.

Browne, B. 2016. "Choreographed Segregation: Irish Republican Commemoration of the 1916 Easter Rising in 'Post Conflict' Belfast." *Irish Political Studies* 31 (1): 101–21.

Browne, B., and R.-S. McBride. 2015. "Politically Sensitive Encounters: Ethnography, Access and the Benefits of 'Hanging Out.'" *Qualitative Sociology Review* 11 (1): 34–48.

Bruce, S. 1992. "The Problems of 'Pro-State' Terrorism: Loyalist Paramilitaries in Northern Ireland." *Terrorism and Political Violence* 4 (1): 67–88.

———. 1994. *The Edge of the Union: The Ulster Loyalist Political Vision*. Oxford: Oxford University Press.

Bryan, D. 2000. *Orange Parades: The Politics of Ritual, Tradition and Control*. London: Pluto Press.

———. 2006. "The Politics of Community." *Critical Review of International Social and Political Philosophy* 9 (4): 603–17.

———. 2014. "Forget 1690, Remember the Somme: Ulster Loyalist Battles in the Twenty-First Century." In O. Frawley, ed., *Memory Ireland*, vol. 3: *The Famine and the Troubles*, 293–309. Syracuse, NY: Syracuse University Press.

———. 2016. "Ritual, Identity and Nation: When the Historian Becomes the High Priest of Commemoration." In R. S. Grayson and F. McGarry, eds.,

Remembering 1916: The Easter Rising, the Somme and the Politics of Memory in Ireland, 24–42. Cambridge: Cambridge University Press.

Bryan, D., T. G. Fraser, and S. Dunn. 1995. *Political Rituals: Loyalist Parades in Portadown*. Coleraine: University of Ulster.

Bryan, D., S. Templer, and L. Kelly. 2011. "The Failed Paradigm of 'Terrorism.'" *Behavioural Sciences of Terrorism and Political Aggression* 3 (2): 80–96.

Bryson, J. 2014. *My Only Crime Was Loyalty*. Bangor: CreateSpace Independent Publishing.

Buckland, P. 2001. "A Protestant State: Unionists in Government 1921–39." In D. G. Boyce and A. O'Day, eds., *Defenders of the Union*, 211–26. London: Routledge.

Burgess, R. 1984. *In the Field: An Introduction to Field Research*. London: Routledge.

Burgess, T. P. 2002. *Community Relations, Community Identity and Social Policy in Northern Ireland*. Lampeter: Edwin Mellen Press.

Burgess, T. P., and G. Mulvenna, eds. 2015. *The Contested Identities of Ulster Protestants*. Basingstoke: Palgrave Macmillan.

Burke, J. 2013. "Are We on the Verge of a Somme Burnout?" *Long Kesh Inside Out* [Online], 2 July. www.longkeshinsideout.co.uk/?p=2072.

———. 2016. "Loyalist Memory and Commemoration." Paper presented at *Féile an Phobail*. Belfast, 11 August.

Butler, J. 1990. *Gender Trouble: Feminism and the Subversion of Identity*. London: Routledge.

Cadwallader, A. 2013. *Lethal Allies: British Collusion in Ireland*. Cork: Mercier Press.

Callinicos, A. 1990. *Against Postmodernism: A Marxist Critique*. Cambridge: Polity Press.

Campbell, D. 2016. "Trevor Ringland Is Wrong about Loyalists." *News Letter* [Online], 25 May. www.newsletter.co.uk/news/your-say/trevor-ringland-is-wrong-about-loyalists-1-7400045.

Carr, E. H. 1990. *What Is History?* London: Penguin Books.

Carsten, J. 2000. "'Knowing Where You've Come From': Ruptures and Continuities of Time and Kinship in Narratives of Adoption Reunions." *Journal of the Royal Anthropological Institute* 6 (4): 698–703.

———. 2004. *After Kinship*. Cambridge: Cambridge University Press.

Cassell, J. 1988. "The Relationship of Observer to Observed When Studying Up." In R. Burgess, ed., *Studies in Qualitative Methodology*, vol. 1: *Conducting Qualitative Research*. Greenwich, CT: JAI Press.

Casserly, R. P. 2012. "The Snare Drum in the North of Ireland: Musical Instruments and Style in a Post-Conflict Era." PhD diss., Queen's University Belfast.

Century Ireland. 2014. "Redmond Urges Irish Volunteers to Join the British Army" [Online], 21 September. www.rte.ie/centuryireland/index.php /articles/redmond-urges-irish-volunteers-to-join-the-british-army.

Chatzipanagiotidou, E. 2012. "The 'Left-overs' of History: Reconsidering the 'Unofficial' History of the Left in Cyprus and the Cypriot Diaspora." In Y. Papadakis and R. Bryant, eds., *Cyprus and the Politics of Memory: History, Community and Conflict*, 94–117. London: I. B. Tauris.

Clark, C. 2012. *The Sleepwalkers: How Europe Went to War in 1914*. London: Penguin.

Clarke, R. 2014. "Archbishop of Armagh WW1 Service Address" [Online], 4 August. www.anglicannews.org/news/2014/08/archbishop-of-armagh-ww1 -service-address.aspx.

Cohen, A. 1989. *The Symbolic Construction of Community*. Abingdon: Routledge.

Cohen, S. 2007. "Winning While Losing: The Apprentice Boys of Derry Walk Their Beat." *Political Geography* 16 (8): 951–67.

Coleman, M. 2014. *The Irish Revolution 1916–1923*. London: Routledge.

Collingwood, R. G. 1961. *The Idea of History*. Oxford: Oxford University Press.

Community Relations Council (CRC). 2013. *Decade of Anniversaries Toolkit*. Belfast: CRC.

———. 2014. "Finish the Job, CRC Policy Conference 2014: Commemorations" [Online]. www.youtube.com/watch?v=wEYL3JqoUtc.

Community Relations Council (CRC) and Heritage Lottery Fund (HLF). 2011. *Guidance Notes for Funding Bodies—Funding Scheme on Marking Anniversaries: A Decade of Ideas 2012–23* [Online]. www.community-relations.org.uk /wp-content/uploads/2013/11/Remembering%20the%20Future%20 Funding.pdf.

Conference of Irish Historians in Britain. 2016. "Historians and the Stormont House Agreement: Report on a Workshop Held at Hertford College, Oxford, 19th October 2016" [Online]. irishhistoriansinbritain.org/?p=32.

Connerton, P. 1989. *How Societies Remember*. Cambridge: Cambridge University Press.

Cook, R. J. 2007. *Troubled Commemoration: The American Civil War Centennial, 1961–1965*. Baton Rouge: Louisiana State University Press.

Cramer, C. 2006. *Civil War Is Not a Stupid Thing: Accounting for Violence in Developing Countries*. London: C. Hurst & Co.

Cramer, C., and J. Goodhand. 2011. "Hard Science or Waffly Crap? Evidence-Based Policy versus Policy-Based Evidence in the Field of Violent Conflict." In K. Bayliss, B. Fine, and E. V. Waeyenberge, eds., *The Political Economy of Development: The World Bank, Neo-liberalism and Development Research*, 215–38. London: Pluto Press.

Creative Centenaries. 2017. "Resources" [Online]. www.creativecentenaries.org /resources.

Creative Ireland. 2017. "About Creative Ireland" [Online]. https://creative.ire
    land.ie/en/about.
Cubitt, G. 2007. *History and Memory*. Manchester: Manchester University Press.
Cunningham, S. 2016. "15,000 Loyalists Take to Belfast Streets to Remember
    Somme." *Irish News* [Online], 19 June. www.irishnews.com/news/2016/06
    /20/news/15-000-loyalists-take-to-belfast-streets-to-remember-somme
    -569993/.
Cusack, J., and H. McDonald. 2008. *UVF: The Endgame*. Dublin: Poolbeg Press.
Daly, M., and M. O'Callaghan, eds. 2007. *1916 in 1966: Commemorating the Easter
    Rising*. Dublin: Royal Irish Academy.
Davies, R. 2009. *Afrikaners in the New South Africa: Identity Politics in the Glo-
    balised Economy*. London: I. B. Tauris.
Davis, C. 2005. "Hauntology, Spectres and Phantoms." *French Studies* 59 (3):
    373–79.
Decade of Centenaries. 2016. "A Round-up of Online Resources for the Easter
    Rising Centenary" [Online]. www.decadeofcentenaries.com/a-round-up-of
    -online-resources-for-the-easter-rising-centenary/.
Deleuze, G., and F. Guattari. 1988. *A Thousand Plateaus: Capitalism and Schizo-
    phrenia*. London: Athlone Press.
Deloitte. 2015. "A New Story: Titanic Belfast: Evaluation of the First Three
    Years" [Online]. www.titanic-foundation.org/?download=file&file=1199.
Democratic Unionist Party (DUP). 2015. "East Belfast Somme Commemora-
    tion Parade Deserves Respect" [Online], 29 June. www.robinnewton.co.uk
    /press-releases/662-east-belfast-somme-commemoration-parade-deserves
    -respect.html.
———. 2016. "Our Plan for Northern Ireland: The DUP Manifesto for the 2016
    Northern Ireland Assembly Election" [Online]. www.mydup.com/images
    /uploads/publications/DUP_Manifesto_2016_v8_LR.pdf.
———. 2017a. *Our Plan for Northern Ireland: The DUP Manifesto for the 2017
    Northern Ireland Assembly Election* [Online]. www.mydup.com/images
    /uploads/publications/DUP_Manifesto_2017_v2_SINGLES.pdf.
———. 2017b. "Standing Strong for Northern Ireland: The DUP Manifesto for
    the 2017 Westminster Election" [Online]. http://dev.mydup.com/images
    /uploads/publications/DUP_Wminster_ManifestM_2017_v5.pdf.
Department of the Taoiseach. 2012. "Joint Statement by the Prime Minister,
    David Cameron and the Taoiseach, Enda Kenny" [Online]. https://www
    .taoiseach.gov.ie/eng/News/Archives/2012/Taoiseach%27s_Press
    _Releases_2012/Joint_Statement_by_the_Prime_Minister,_David
    _Cameron_and_the_Taoi seach,_Enda_Kenny.html.
Derrida, J. 1976. *Of Grammatology*. Trans. G. Spivak. Baltimore: Johns Hopkins
    University Press.

———. 1986. *MEMOIRES for Paul de Man*. New York: Columbia University Press.

———. 2006 [1993]. *Spectres of Marx: The State of the Debt, the Work of Mourning and the New International*. Trans. P. Kamuf. New York: Routledge.

Diprose, R. 2006. "Derrida and the Extraordinary Responsibility of Inheriting the Future-to-Come." *Social Semiotics* 16 (3): 435–47.

Doherty, G. ed. 2014. *The Home Rule Crisis 1912–14*. Cork: Mercier Press.

Dudley Edwards, R. 2016a. "Commemoration in Dublin of Easter Rising Very Fitting." *Belfast Telegraph* [Online], 28 March. www.belfasttelegraph.co.uk /opinion/columnists/ruth-dudley-edwards/commemoration-in-dublin-of -easter-rising-very-fitting-34576277.html.

———. 2016b. "There Are Harder Anniversaries to Come, But the Way We Marked 1916 Gives Me Hope for the Future." *Belfast Telegraph* [Online], 1 August. www.belfasttelegraph.co.uk/opinion/columnists/ruth-dudley -edwards/there-are-harder-anniversaries-to-come-but-the-way-we -marked-1916-gives-me-hope-for-future-34927027.html.

Dunne, T. 2004. *Rebellions: Memoir, Memory and 1798*. Dublin: Lilliput Press.

Edelman, M. 2001. "Social Movements: Changing Paradigms and Forms of Politics." *Annual Review of Anthropology* 30: 285–317.

Edkins, J. 2003. *Trauma and the Memory of Politics*. Cambridge: Cambridge University Press.

———. 2008. "The Local, the Global and the Troubling." In M. Zalewski and J. Barry, eds., *Intervening in Northern Ireland: Critically Re-Thinking Representations of the Conflict*, 21–34. Abingdon: Routledge.

Edwards, A. 2017. *UVF: Behind the Mask*. Newbridge: Merrion Press.

Edwards, A., and C. McGrattan. 2011. "Terroristic Narratives: On the (Re) Invention of Peace in Northern Ireland." *Terrorism and Political Violence* 23 (3): 375–76.

Eltringham, N. 2003. "'The Blind Man and the Elephant': The Challenge of Representing the Rwandan Genocide." In P. Caplan, ed., *The Ethics of Anthropology: Debates and Dilemmas*, 92–112. London: Routledge.

Enloe, C. 1988. *Does Khaki Become You? The Militarization of Women's Lives*. London: Pandora Press.

Etchart, J. 2008. "The Titanic Quarter in Belfast: Building a New Place in a Divided City." *Nordic Irish Studies* 7: 31–40.

Evans, R. J. 1997. *In Defence of History*. London: Granta Books.

———. 2014. "Michael Gove Shows His Ignorance of History—Again." *Guardian* [Online], 6 January. www.theguardian.com/books/2014/jan/06/richard -evans-michael-gove-history-education.

Farrell, M. 1980. *Northern Ireland: The Orange State*. London: Pluto Press.

Farrell, N. 2014. "Unique Memorial Unveiled in Woodvale Park in Tribute to World War One Soldiers." *Belfast Telegraph* [Online], 18 October. www

.belfasttelegraph.co.uk/news/northern-ireland/unique-memorial
-unveiled-in-woodvale-park-in-tribute-to-world-war-one-soldiers-3067
3208.html.

Faulkner, L. 2014. *Truth Recovery Revisited: A Contribution from within Loyalism*. Belfast: EPIC.

Faulkner, N. 2013. *No Glory: The Real History of the First World War*. London: Stop the War Coalition.

———. 2016. *Have You Forgotten Yet? The Truth about the Somme*. London: Stop the War Coalition.

Feeney, B. 2015. "Fine Gael Attitude to 1916 Changed Utterly." *Irish News* [Online], 25 March. www.irishnews.com/opinion/2015/03/25/news/fine-gael-attitude-to-1916-changed-utterly-119104/.

Feldman, A. 1991. *Formations of Violence: The Narrative of the Body and Political Terror in Northern Ireland*. Chicago: University of Chicago Press.

Fentress, J., and C. Wickham. 1992. *Social Memory*. Oxford: Blackwell.

Ferguson, J. 1990. *The Anti-Politics Machine: Development, Depoliticization and Bureaucratic Power in Lesotho*. Cambridge: Cambridge University Press.

Fielding, N. 1981. *The National Front*. Abingdon: Routledge.

———. 1982. "Observational Research on the National Front." In M. Bulmer, ed., *Social Research Ethics: An Examination of the Merits of Covert Participant Observation*, 80–104. London: Macmillan.

Finlay, A. 2001. "Defeatism and Northern Protestant 'Identity.'" *Global Review of Ethnopolitics* 1 (2): 3–20.

Finlayson, A. 1997. "Discourse and Contemporary Loyalist Identity." In P. Shirlow and M. McGovern, eds., *Who Are "the People"? Unionism, Protestantism and Loyalism in Northern Ireland*, 72–94. London: Pluto Press.

———. 2001. "Loyalist Political Identity after the Peace." *Capital & Class* 23 (3): 47–75.

———. 2008. "'What's the Problem?': Political Theory, Rhetoric and Problem-Setting." In M. Zalewski and J. Barry, eds., *Intervening in Northern Ireland: Critically Re-thinking Representations of the Conflict*, 63–80. Abingdon: Routledge.

Fitzpatrick, D. 2011. "West Belfast Exceptionalism: Richard S. Grayson's *Belfast Boys*." *Irish Economic and Social History* 38: 103–7.

———. 2014. *Descendancy: Irish Protestant Histories since 1795*. Cambridge: Cambridge University Press.

———. 2016. "Instant History: 1912, 1916, 1918." In R. S. Grayson and F. McGarry, eds., *Remembering 1916: The Easter Rising, the Somme and the Politics of Memory in Ireland*, 65–85. Cambridge: Cambridge University Press.

Focal Point. 2016. Television program, Northern Visions. Belfast, 20 June.

Ford, R., and M. J. Goodwin. 2014. *Revolt on the Right: Explaining Support for the Radical Right in Britain*. London: Routledge.

Foucault, M. 1980. *Power/Knowledge: Selected Interviews and Other Writings*. Ed. C. Gordon. Trans. C. Gordon, L. Marshall, J. Mepham, and K. Soper. New York: Pantheon Books.

———. 2002. *The Archaeology of Knowledge*. Trans. A. M. Sheridan Smith. London: Routledge.

———. 2004. *Society Must Be Defended*. Trans. D. Macey. London: Penguin.

frankryanswhiskey. 2016. *@BBCTalkback yes it does, getting it right implies that they actually care about the history, rather than bigotry* [Twitter] 3 June [Online]. https://twitter.com/frwhiskeyblog/status/738681410848993280.

Frawley, O., ed. 2011a. *Memory Ireland*, vol. 1: *History and Modernity*. Syracuse, NY: Syracuse University Press.

———. 2011b. "Toward a Theory of Cultural Memory in an Irish Postcolonial Context." In O. Frawley, ed., *Memory Ireland*, vol. 1: *History and Modernity*, 18–36. Syracuse, NY: Syracuse University Press.

———, ed. 2012. *Memory Ireland*, vol. 2: *Diaspora and Memory Practices*. Syracuse, NY: Syracuse University Press.

———, ed. 2014. *Memory Ireland*, vol. 3: *The Famine and the Troubles*. Syracuse, NY: Syracuse University Press.

Frawley, O., and K. O'Callaghan, eds. 2014. *Memory Ireland*, vol. 4: *James Joyce and Cultural Memory*. Syracuse, NY: Syracuse University Press.

Fritsch, M. 2005. *The Promise of Memory: History and Politics in Marx, Benjamin, and Derrida*. Albany: State University of New York Press. Kindle ed. [Online].

Fukuyama, F. 1992. *The End of History and the Last Man*. New York: Free Press.

Furedi, F. 2014. *First World War: Still No End in Sight*. London: Bloomsbury.

Gable, E. 2014. "The Anthropology of Guilt and Rapport: Moral Mutuality in Ethnographic Fieldwork." *HAU: Journal of Ethnographic Theory* 4 (1): 237–58.

Gallaher, C. 2007. *After the Peace: Loyalist Paramilitaries in Post-Accord Northern Ireland*. Ithaca, NY: Cornell University Press.

Gallaher, C., and P. Shirlow. 2006. "The Geography of Loyalist Paramilitary Feuding in Belfast." *Space and Polity* 10 (2): 149–69.

Garland, R. 2001. *Gusty Spence*. Belfast: Blackstaff Press.

Garry, J., and J. Coakley. 2016. "Brexit: Understanding Why People Voted as They Did in the Choice of a Lifetime." *News Letter* [Online], 15 October. www.newsletter.co.uk/news/brexit-understanding-why-people-voted-as -they-did-in-the-choice-of-a-lifetime-1-7630272.

Geertz, C. 1973. *The Interpretation of Cultures*. New York: Basic Books.

———. 1974. "'From the Native's Point of View': On the Nature of Anthropological Understanding." *Bulletin of the American Academy of Arts and Sciences* 28 (1): 26–45.

———. 1990. "History and Anthropology." *New Literary History* 21 (2): 321–35.

———. 1998. "Deep Hanging Out." *New York Review of Books* [Online]. www.ny books.com/articles/archives/1998/oct/22/deep-hanging-out/.

Giddens, A. 1996. *In Defence of Sociology*. Cambridge: Polity Press.

Giesen, B. 2006. "Performing the Sacred: A Durkheimian Perspective on the Performative Turn in the Social Sciences." In J. C. Alexander, B. Giesen, and J. L. Mast, eds., *Social Performance: Symbolic Action, Cultural Pragmatics and Ritual*, 325–67. Cambridge: Cambridge University Press.

Gillis, J. 1994. "Memory and Identity: The History of a Relationship." In J. Gillis, ed., *Commemorations: The Politics of National Identity*, 3–26. Princeton, NJ: Princeton University Press.

Gilroy, P. 2005. *Postcolonial Melancholia*. New York: Columbia University Press.

Girard, R. 1977. *Violence and the Sacred*. Trans. P. Gregory. Baltimore: Johns Hopkins University Press.

———. 1996. "Mimesis and Violence." In J. G. Williams, ed., *The Girard Reader*, 9–19. New York: Crossroad.

Gkotzaridis, E. 2001. "Revisionism and Postmodernism." Études Irlandaises 26 (1): 131–57.

Godden, A., and C. Palli. 2016. *Constitutional Questions, No. 6 of 6: Ethics and Commemoration*. Dublin: Royal Irish Academy.

Goffman, E. 1972. *Interaction Ritual: Essays on Face-to-Face Behaviour*. London: Allen Lane.

Gordon, A. 2008. *Ghostly Matters: Haunting and the Sociological Imagination*. Minneapolis: University of Minnesota Press.

———. 2011. "Some Thoughts on Haunting and Futurity." *Borderlands* 10 (2) [Online]. www.borderlands.net.au/vol10no2_2011/gordon_thoughts.pdf.

Gordon, G. 2017. "Crocodiles, Alligators and the Irish Language." *BBC News* [Online], 7 February. www.bbc.co.uk/news/election-northern-ireland-2017 -38892198.

Gove, M. 2014. "Why Does the Left Insist on Belittling True British Heroes?" *Daily Mail* [Online], 3 January. www.dailymail.co.uk/news/article-2532923 /Michael-Gove-blasts-Blackadder-myths-First-World-War-spread-tele vision-sit-coms-left-wing-academics.html.

Graeber, D. 2013. *The Democracy Project: A History, a Crisis, a Movement*. New York: Spiegel & Grau.

Graff-McRae, R. 2007. "Forget Politics! Theorising the Political Dynamics of Commemoration and Conflict." In M. Daly and M. O'Callaghan, eds., *1916 in 1966: Commemorating the Easter Rising*, 220–40. Dublin: Royal Irish Academy.

———. 2010. *Remembering and Forgetting 1916: Commemoration and Conflict in Post–Peace Process Ireland*. Dublin: Irish Academic Press.

Graham, B. 1997. "Ulster: A Representation of a Place Yet to Be Imagined." In P. Shirlow and M. McGovern, eds., *Who Are "the People"? Unionism, Protestantism and Loyalism in Northern Ireland*. London: Pluto Press.

Graham, B., and P. Shirlow. 2002. "The Battle of the Somme in Ulster Memory and Identity." *Political Geography* 21 (7): 881–904.

Grayson, R. S. 2009. *Belfast Boys: How Unionists and Nationalists Fought and Died Together in the First World War*. London: Continuum.

———. 2010. "The Place of the First World War in Contemporary Irish Republicanism in Northern Ireland." *Irish Political Studies* 25 (3): 325–45.

Greenlaw, D. 2004. *Borders of Mourning: Remembrance, Commitment and the Contexts of Irish Identity*. Dublin: Maunsel & Co.

Greenwood, P., M. Heywood, A. Healey, R. Sprenger, M. Browne, and M. Khalili. 2016. "Bands of Brothers: Could Brexit Bring the Troubles Back to Northern Ireland? – video." *Guardian* [Online], 20 October. www.the guardian .com/uk-news/video/2016/oct/20/bands-of-brothers-could -brexit-bring-the-troubles-back-to-northern-ireland-video.

Grundlingh, A. 2004. "Reframing Remembrance: The Politics of the Centenary Commemoration of the South African War of 1899–1902." *Journal of Southern African Studies* 30 (2): 359–75.

Guardian. 2012. "David Cameron Reveals First World War Centenary Plans" [Online], 11 October. www.guardian.co.uk/world/2012/oct/11/david -cameron-first-world-war.

———. 2016. "Arlene Foster Hails DUP's Performance in Northern Ireland Assembly Election" [Online], 7 May. www.theguardian.com/politics/2016 /may/07/arlene-foster-northern-ireland-assembly-election-dup-stormont.

Halbwachs, M. 1950. *The Collective Memory*. Trans. F. J. Ditter and V. Y. Ditter. London: Harper Colophon Books.

Hall, M. 1994. *Ulster's Protestant Working Class: A Community Exploration*. Island Pamphlets 9. Newtownabbey: Island Publications.

———. 2007. *A Shared Sacrifice for Peace*. Island Pamphlets 84. Newtownabbey: Island Publications.

———. 2015a. *A Process of Analysis (1): The Protestant/Unionist/Loyalist Community*. Island Pamphlets 108. Newtownabbey: Island Publications.

———. 2015b. *A Process of Analysis (2): The Catholic/Nationalist/Republican Community*. Island Pamphlets 109. Newtownabbey: Island Publications.

Hammersley, M. 2000. *Taking Sides in Social Research: Essays on Partisanship and Bias*. London: Routledge.

Hammersley, M., and P. Atkinson. 2007. *Ethnography: Principles in Practice*. 3rd ed. London: Routledge.

Hanley, B. 2015. "Whose History? Commemorating the 'Great' War in an Age of Shock and Awe." Cumann Stair Lucht Oibre Bhéal Feirste/Belfast Working Class History Group [Online]. www.bwchg.com/.

———. 2016. "'Moderates and Peacemakers': Irish Historians and the Revolutionary Centenary." *Irish Economic and Social History* 43 (1): 113–30.

Harrison, S. 1995. "Four Types of Symbolic Conflict." *Journal of the Royal Anthropological Institute* 1 (2): 255–72.

Hayes, B., and I. MacAllister. 2000. "Sowing Dragon's Teeth: Public Support for Political Violence and Paramilitarism in Northern Ireland." Paper presented at U.K. Political Studies Association Conference, London, 10–13 April.

Heartfield, J., and K. Rooney. 2015. *Who's Afraid of the Easter Rising? 1916–2016*. Alresford: Zero Books.

Heritage Lottery Fund (HLF). 2016. "Our Projects" [Online]. www.hlf.org.uk /our-projects/search-our-projects/search_api_combined_1/10011/field _programme/10053#12.

Higgins, R. 2012. *Transforming 1916: Meaning, Memory and the Fiftieth Anniversary of the Easter Rising*. Cork: Cork University Press.

———. 2016. "'The Irish Republic Was Proclaimed by Poster': The Politics of Commemorating the Easter Rising." In R. S. Grayson and F. McGarry, eds., *Remembering 1916: The Easter Rising, the Somme and the Politics of Memory in Ireland*, 43–62. Cambridge: Cambridge University Press.

Hinson, E. 2015. "50 Shades of Northern Ireland: Artworks and Identities in Loyalist Ex-Prisoner Narratives." Paper presented at Explorations of Northern Irishness, Belfast, 12 March.

Hirsch, M. 2008. "The Generation of Postmemory." *Poetics Today* 29 (1): 103–28.

History Hub Ulster. 2016. "Belfast Somme 100 Events Guide" [Online]. www .livinglegacies1914-18.ac.uk/FileStore/PDFs/2016/Filetoupload,674063 ,en.pdf.

Hobbs, R. 2001. "Ethnography and the Study of Deviance." In P. Atkinson, S. Delamont, A. Coffey, J. Lofland, and L. Lofland, eds., *Handbook of Ethnography*, 204–19. London: Sage.

Hobsbawm, E. 1983. "Mass-Producing Traditions: Europe, 1870–1914." In E. Hobsbawm and T. Ranger, eds., *The Invention of Tradition*, 263–308. Cambridge: Cambridge University Press.

Hobsbawm, E., and T. Ranger, eds. 1983. *The Invention of Tradition*. Cambridge: Cambridge University Press.

Hobsbawm, J., and J. Lloyd. 2008. *The Power of the Commentariat*. London: Editorial Intelligence.

Hocking, B. T. 2011. "Transforming the Stone: Reimagining Derry's Diamond War Memorial in the New 'Post-Conflict' Northern Ireland." *Irish Journal of Anthropology* 14 (2): 19–25.

———. 2015. *The Great Reimagining: Public Art, Urban Space and the Symbolic Landscapes of the 'New' Northern Ireland*. Oxford: Berghahn.

Hollan, D. 2014. "Empathy and Morality in Ethnographic Perspective." In H. L. Maibom, ed., *Empathy and Morality*, 230–50. Oxford: Oxford University Press.

Home Office. 2015. "Proscribed Terrorist Organisations" [Online]. www.gov.uk
/government/uploads/system/uploads/attachment_data/file/417884
/Proscription-20150327.pdf.

Hughes, B. 2014. "NIHE Apologies over UDA/UFF Commemoration." *Irish
News* [Online], 2 August. www.irishnews.com/news/nihe-apologises-over
-uda/uff-commemoration-1371075.

Hughes, J. 2009. "Peace, Reconciliation and a Shared Future: A Policy Shift or
More of the Same?" *Community Development Journal* 44 (1): 22–37.

Hume, D., ed. 2005. *Battles Beyond the Boyne: Orangemen in the Ranks 1798–2000.*
Belfast: GOLI.

Humphrey, C., and J. Laidlaw. 1994. *The Archetypal Actions of Ritual: A Theory of
Ritual Illustrated by the Jain Rite of Worship.* Oxford: Oxford University Press.

Humphreys, H. 2016. "Address by Ms Heather Humphreys TD, Minister for
Arts, Heritage, Regional, Rural and Gaeltacht Affairs at the NUIG Conference Ireland 1916–2016: The Promise and Challenge of National Sovereignty, Friday November 11th, 2016" [Online], 11 November. www.chg.gov
.ie/speech/speech-by-heather-humphreys-td-minister-for-arts-heritage
-regional-rural-and-gaeltacht-affairs-at-the-nuig-conference-ireland
-1916-2016-the-promise-and-challenge-of-national-sovereignty-f/.

Hutton, P. 1993. *History as an Art of Memory.* Hanover, NH: University Press of
New England.

Iles, J. 2008. "Encounters in the Field: Tourism to the Battlefields of the Western
Front." *Journal of Tourism and Cultural Change* 6 (2): 138–54.

Impartial Reporter. 2014. "Gerry Adams in Enniskillen: The Full Transcript and
Audio" [Online], 25 November. www.impartialreporter.com/news/138688
75.Gerry_Adams_in_Enniskille_the_full_transcript_and_audio/.

Ingold, T., and J. L. Vergunst, eds. 2008. *Ways of Walking: Ethnography and Practice on Foot.* Aldershot: Ashgate.

International School for Peace Studies (ISPS). 2007a. "Fellowship of Messines"
[Online]. www.schoolforpeace.com/content/article/fellowship-of-messines
/48.

———. 2007b. "In the Beginning" [Online]. www.schoolforpeace.com/content
/article/in-the-beginning/11.

In Thiepval Wood: Somme 90th Anniversary. 2006. DVD. Belfast: Ballymacarrett
Somme Festival.

Invisible Committee. 2009. *The Coming Insurrection.* Los Angeles: Semiotext(e).

Ipsos MediaCT. 2009. *Social Grade: A Classification Tool* [Online]. www.ipsos
-mori.com/DownloadPublication/1285_MediaCT_thoughtpiece_Social
_Grade_July09_V3_WEB.pdf.

Ipsos MORI. 2013. "BBC Good Friday Agreement Survey" [Online]. http://
downloads.bbc.co.uk/tv/nolanshow/BBC_Good_Friday_agreement
_survey_tabtab_FINAL.pdf [accessed 18 January 2014].

Ireland 2016/Éire 2016. 2016. "What's Next for Ireland?" [Online], 28 December. www.ireland2016.gov.ie/news/whats-next-ireland.

Jameson, F. 1999. "Marx's Purloined Letter." In M. Sprinker, ed., *Ghostly Demarcations: A Symposium on Jacques Derrida's Spectres of Marx*, 26–67. London: Verso.

———. 2004. "The Politics of Utopia." *New Left Review* 25: 35–54.

———. 2005. *Archaeologies of the Future: The Desire Called Utopia and Other Science Fictions*. London: Verso.

Jansen, S. 2003. "'Why Do They Hate Us?': Everyday Serbian Nationalist Knowledge of Muslim Hatred." *Journal of Mediterranean Studies* 13 (2): 215–37.

Jarman, N. 1997. *Material Conflicts: Parades and Visual Displays in Northern Ireland*. Oxford: Berg.

———. 1999. "Commemorating 1916, Celebrating Difference: Parading and Painting in Belfast." In A. Forty and S. Kuchler, eds., *The Art of Forgetting*, 171–95. Oxford: Berg.

———. 2003. "From Outrage to Apathy? The Disputes over Parades, 1995–2003." *Global Review of Ethnopolitics* 3 (1): 92–105.

Jeffrey, K. 1993. "The Great War in Modern Irish Memory." In T. G. Fraser and K. Jeffrey, eds., *Men, Women and War*, 136–58. Dublin: Lilliput Press.

———. 2000. *Ireland and the Great War*. Cambridge: Cambridge University Press.

———. 2013. "Irish Varieties of Great War Commemoration." In J. Horne and E. Madigan, eds., *Towards Commemoration: Ireland in War and Revolution 1912–1923*, 117–25. Dublin: Royal Irish Academy.

———. 2015. "Commemoration and the Hazards of Irish Politics." In B. Ziino, ed., *Remembering the First World War*. Abingdon: Routledge. Kindle ed. [Online].

Johnson, N. C. 2007. *Ireland, the Great War and the Geography of Remembrance*. Cambridge: Cambridge University Press.

Jones, O. 2011. *Chavs: The Demonization of the Working Class*. London: Verso.

The Junction. 2015. "About the Junction" [Online]. www.thejunction-ni.org /index.php/about.

Kaufman, M. 2001. "The Construction of Masculinity: The Triad of Men's Violence." In M. S. Kimmel and M. A. Messner, eds., *Men's Lives*, 4–16. Boston: Allyn and Bacon.

Kaufmann, E. P. 2004a. "The Decline of the WASP in the United States and Canada." In E. P. Kaufmann, ed., *Rethinking Ethnicity: Majority Groups and Dominant Minorities*, 61–83. New York: Routledge.

———, ed. 2004b. *Rethinking Ethnicity: Majority Groups and Dominant Minorities*. New York: Routledge.

———. 2007. *The Orange Order: A Contemporary Northern Irish History*. Oxford: Oxford University Press.

Keena, C. 2017. "Paint Thrown over 1916 Rising Remembrance Wall in Glasnevin." *Irish Times* [Online], 9 April. www.irishtimes.com/news/crime-and -law/paint-thrown-over-1916-rising-remembrance-wall-in-glasnevin -1.3042478.

Kelly, F. 2015. "An Post Gives Cold Shoulder to Sinn Féin 2016 GPO Spectacular." *Irish Times* [Online], 8 October. www.irishtimes.com/news/politics /an-post-gives-cold-shoulder-to-sinn-f%C3%A9in-2016-gpo-spectacular -1.2383147.

Kennedy, D. 2016. "Pride in 'Inclusive' 1916 Commemoration Rings Hollow." *Irish Times* [Online], 7 November. www.irishtimes.com/opinion/pride-in -inclusive-1916-commemoration-rings-hollow-1.2856808.

Kenny, E. 2016. "Speech by An Taoiseach at the National Academic Conference 1916–2016, NUI Galway, 10 November 2016" [Online], 10 November. www .taoiseach.gov.ie/eng/News/Taoiseach's_Speeches/Speech_by_An_Taoi seach_at_the_National_Academic_Conference_1916-2016_NUI _Galway_10_November_2016.html.

Kertzer, D. I. 1988. *Ritual, Politics, and Power*. New Haven, CT: Yale University Press.

Kilpatrick, C. 2014. "'Disgrace' as UDA Accused of Hijacking Memorial to War Heroes." *Belfast Telegraph* [Online], 2 August. www.belfasttelegraph.co.uk /news/local-national/northern-ireland/disgrace-as-uda-accused-of -hijacking-memorial-to-war-heroes-30478365.html.

Kirkby, J. 2006. "Remembrance of the Future: Derrida on Mourning." *Social Semiotics* 16 (3): 461–72.

Knox, C. 2001. "Establishing Research Legitimacy in the Contested Political Ground of Contemporary Northern Ireland." *Qualitative Research* 1 (2): 205–22.

Kramer, A.-M. 2011a. "Kinship, Affinity and Connectedness: Exploring the Role of Genealogy in Personal Lives." *Sociology* 45 (3): 379–95.

———. 2011b. "Mediatizing Memory: History, Affect and Identity in 'Who Do You Think You Are?'" *European Journal of Cultural Studies* 14 (4): 428–45.

Kvale, S. 1996. *InterViews: An Introduction to Qualitative Research Interviewing*. Thousand Oaks, CA: Sage.

Lacan, J. 1982. "Le symbolique, l'imaginaire et le reel." *Bulletin de l'Association Freudienne* 1: 4–13.

Lawler, S. 2008. *Identity: Sociological Perspectives*. Cambridge: Polity Press.

Lawther, C. 2011. "Unionism, Truth Recovery and the Fearful Past." *Irish Political Studies* 26 (3): 361–82.

———. 2014. *Truth, Denial and Transition: Northern Ireland and the Contested Past*. Abingdon: Routledge.

Lee, R. M. 1993. *Doing Research on Sensitive Topics.* London: Sage.

Leersen, J. 2001. "Monument and Trauma: Varieties of Remembrance." In I. Mc-Bride, ed., *History and Memory in Modern Ireland*, 204–22. Cambridge: Cambridge University Press.

Lefebvre, H. 2009. *State, Space, World: Selected Essays.* Trans. G. Moore, N. Brenner, and S. Elden. Minneapolis: University of Minnesota Press.

Leonard, J. 2003. *World War Commemorations at Belfast City Hall: A Report Submitted to Belfast City Council.* Belfast: Belfast City Council.

Lévi-Strauss, C. 1978. *Myth and Meaning.* London: Routledge and Kegan Paul.

Linstead, S. 1993. "From Postmodern Anthropology to Deconstructive Ethnography." *Human Relations* 46 (1): 97–120.

Little, A. 2006. "Theorizing Democracy and Violence: The Case of Northern Ireland." *Theoria* 111: 62–86.

———. 2008. *Democratic Piety: Complexity, Conflict and Violence.* Edinburgh: Edinburgh University Press.

Long, S. 2015. "Soapbox: Is it Time to Consider Giving Loyalists Special Group Rights?" *Slugger O'Toole* [Online], 17 November. https://sluggerotoole.com/2015/11/17/soapbox-is-it-time-to-consider-giving-loyalists-special-group-rights/.

Longley, E. 1994. *The Living Stream: Literature and Revisionism in Ireland.* Newcastle-Upon-Tyne: Bloodaxe.

———. 2001. "Northern Ireland: Commemoration, Elegy, Forgetting." In I. McBride, ed., *History and Memory in Modern Ireland*, 223–54. Cambridge: Cambridge University Press.

Loughlin, J. 2002. "Mobilising the Sacred Dead: Ulster Unionism, the Great War and the Politics of Remembrance." In A. Gregory and S. Pašeta, eds., *Ireland and the Great War: "A War to Unite Us All"?*, 133–54. Manchester: Manchester University Press.

Lowenthal, D. 1985. *The Past Is a Foreign Country.* Cambridge: Cambridge University Press.

———. 1994. "Identity, Heritage and History." In J. Gillis, ed., *Commemorations: The Politics of National Identity*, 41–60. Princeton, NJ: Princeton University Press.

Loyalist Communities Council (LCC). 2017. "Statement on the General Election Issued by the Loyalist Communities Council" [Online], 5 May. www.lcc-ni.com./index.html.

LucidTalk. 2016. April 2016 LucidTalk Monthly Tracker Poll (Northern Ireland) Results: NI Party Leader Ratings, NI Political Party Ratings, NI Assembly Seat Predictor, and UK EU Referendum Poll Results [Online], 3 May. https://lucidtalk.co.uk/images/News/AprilTrackerPollRslts-General Report.pdf.

Lundy, P., and M. McGovern. 2008. "A Trojan Horse? Unionism, Trust and Truth-Telling in Northern Ireland." *International Journal of Transitional Justice* 2: 42–62.

Mackie – Built to Last. 2012. Television program. BBC Northern Ireland. Belfast, 9 July.

Madigan, E. 2011. "Commemoration and Conciliation during the Royal Visit." *History Ireland* 19 (4) [Online]. www.historyireland.com/20th-century -contemporary-history/commemoration-and-conciliation-during-the -royal-visit/.

Manley, J. 2016. "Arlene Foster: Easter Rising Was a 'Violent Attack on the United Kingdom.'" *Irish News* [Online], 8 January. www.irishnews.com /news/2016/01/08/news/republicans-disappointed-over-foster-rising -commemoration-remarks-375953/.

Margalit, A. 2002. *The Ethics of Memory*. Cambridge, MA: Harvard University Press.

Martin, F. X. 1967. "1916—Myth, Fact and Mystery." *Studia Hibernica* 7: 7–126.

Marx, K. 1852. "The Eighteenth Brumaire of Napoleon Bonaparte." *Marxists Internet Archive* [Online]. www.marxists.org/archive/marx/works/1852/18th -brumaire/.

McAleese, D. 2015. "'Property of the UVF': East Belfast Caught in the Grip of the Racketeers." *Belfast Telegraph* [Online], 4 February. www.belfasttele graph.co.uk/news/northern-ireland/property-of-the-uvf-east-belfast -caught-in-the-grip-of-the-racketeers-30962426.html.

McAuley, J. W. 2005. "Whither New Loyalism? Changing Loyalist Politics after the Good Friday Agreement." *Irish Political Studies* 20 (3): 323–40.

———. 2010. *Ulster's Last Stand? Reconstructing Unionism after the Peace Process*. Dublin: Irish Academic Press.

———. 2013. "Ulster Loyalism and Extreme Right Wing Politics." In M. Taylor, P. M. Currie, and D. Holbrook, eds., *Extreme Right Wing Political Violence and Terrorism*, 85–104. New York: Bloomsbury.

———. 2016. *Very British Rebels? The Culture and Politics of Ulster Loyalism*. London: Bloomsbury.

McBride, I. 1997. *The Siege of Derry in Ulster Protestant Mythology*. Dublin: Four Courts Press.

———, ed. 2001a. *History and Memory in Modern Ireland*. Cambridge: Cambridge University Press.

———. 2001b. "Introduction: Memory and National Identity in Modern Ireland." In I. McBride, ed., *History and Memory in Modern Ireland*, 1–42. Cambridge: Cambridge University Press.

McCabe, C. 2013. *The Double Transition: The Economic and Political Transition of Peace*. Belfast: ICTU.

McCaffery, S. 2017. "Brexit, Theresa May, and the Ulster Plantation." *The Detail* [Online], 9 June. www.thedetail.tv/articles/brexit-theresa-may-and-the-ulster-plantation.

McCormick, J., and N. Jarman. 2005. "Death of a Mural." *Journal of Material Culture* 10 (1): 49–71.

McDaniel, D. 1997. *Enniskillen: Remembrance Day Bombing*. Dublin: Wolfhound Press.

McDonald, H. 2011. "Sectarian Clashes Erupt Again in East Belfast Following Orange Order March." *The Guardian* [Online], 2 July. www.theguardian.com/uk/2011/jul/02/riots-belfast-sectarian-violence.

———. 2014. "UDA Parade: Relaxed Spirit of Ormeau Road Won't Be Broken by This." *Belfast Telegraph* [Online], 2 August. www.belfasttelegraph.co.uk/opinion/news-analysis/uda-parade-relaxed-spirit-of-ormeau-road-wont-be-broken-by-this-30478367.html.

———. 2015. "Riot Police Called over Anti-Refugee Protest in Belfast." *The Guardian* [Online], 5 December. www.theguardian.com/uk-news/2015/dec/05/riot-police-called-over-anti-refugee-protest-in-belfast.

———. 2016a. "Easter Rising Centenary Honours Irish Rebels and Cherishes 'a New Peace.'" *Guardian* [Online], 27 March. www.theguardian.com/world/2016/mar/27/peace-easter-rising-centenary-dublin-gpo-honours-irish-rebels.

———. 2016b. "Prison Officer Injured in New IRA Car Bomb Attack in Belfast Dies." *The Guardian* [Online], 15 March. www.theguardian.com/uk-news/2016/mar/15/belfast-prison-officer-dies-targeted-new-ira-car-bomb-attack-adrian-ismay.

———. 2016c. "Teenager Arrested in Dublin as Fights Break out over 1916 Rising Memorial." *Guardian* [Online], 3 April. www.theguardian.com/world/2016/apr/03/man-arrested-dublin-1916-easter-rising-memorial-dissident-republicans-ireland.

McDowell, J. 2017. "Social Media Attacks on UDA Gang Resulted in Second Feud Killing." *Belfast Telegraph* [Online], 29 May. www.belfasttelegraph.co.uk/news/northern-ireland/jim-mcdowell-social-media-attacks-on-uda-gang-resulted-in-second-feud-killing-35764840.html.

McDowell, S., and M. Braniff. 2014. *Commemoration as Conflict: Space, Memory and Identity in Peace Processes*. Houndmills: Palgrave Macmillan.

McEvoy, K., and P. Shirlow. 2013. "The Northern Ireland Peace Process and 'Terroristic Narratives': A Reply to Edwards and McGrattan." *Terrorism and Political Violence* 25 (2): 161–66.

McGarry, F. 2010. *The Rising: Ireland, Easter 1916*. Oxford: Oxford University Press.

McGarry, J., and B. O'Leary. 1995. "Five Fallacies: Northern Ireland and the Liabilities of Liberalism." *Ethnic and Racial Studies* 18 (4): 837–61.

McGaughey, J. G. V. 2012. *Ulster's Men: Protestant Unionist Masculinities and Militarization in the North of Ireland 1912–1923*. Montreal: McGill-Queen's University Press.

McGovern, M., and P. Shirlow. 1997. "Counter-Insurgency, Deindustrialisation and the Political Economy of Ulster Loyalism." In P. Shirlow and M. McGovern, eds., *Who Are "the People"? Unionism, Protestantism and Loyalism in Northern Ireland*, 176–93. London: Pluto Press.

McGuinness, F. 1986. *Observe the Sons of Ulster Marching Towards the Somme*. London: Faber & Faber.

McGuire, S. 1987. "Expanding Information Sets by Means of 'Existential' Interviewing." *Oral History Review* 15 (1): 55–69.

McKevitt, G. 2015. "On the Runs—Key Questions and Enquiry Findings." *BBC News NI* [Online], 24 March. www.bbc.co.uk/news/uk-northern-ireland -26359906.

McLaughlin, G., and S. Baker. 2010. *The Propaganda of Peace: The Role of Media and Culture in the Northern Irish Peace Process*. Bristol: Intellect.

McNeill, W. H. 1986. "Mythistory, or Truth, Myth, History and Historians." *American Historical Review* 91 (1): 1–10.

McVeigh, R. 2002. "Between Reconciliation and Pacification: The British State and Community Relations in the North of Ireland." *Community Development Journal* 37 (1): 47–59.

———. 2015. "No One Likes Us, We Don't Care: What Is to Be (Un)Done about Ulster Protestant Identity?" In T. P. Burgess and G. Mulvenna, eds., *The Contested Identities of Ulster Protestants*, 113–33. Basingstoke: Palgrave Macmillan.

Meagher, K. 2016. "Brexit Is the Beginning of the End for Northern Ireland." *New Statesman* [Online], 27 July. www.newstatesman.com/politics/staggers /2016/07/brexit-beginning-end-northern-ireland.

Meredith, R. 2016. "Irish Gaeltacht Scheme for Young 'Cut by £50,000.'" *BBC News* [Online], 23 December. www.bbc.co.uk/news/uk-northern-ireland -38422550.

Miller, D. 1978. *Queen's Rebels: Ulster Loyalism in Historical Perspective*. Dublin: Gill and Macmillan.

Misztal, B. 2010. "Memory and History." In O. Frawley, ed., *Memory Ireland*, vol. 1: *History and Modernity*, 3–18. Syracuse, NY: Syracuse University Press.

Morrow, D., and P. Mullan. 2011. "Remembering the Future?" In *Remembering the Future*, 7–8. Belfast: CRC and HLF.

Mouffe, C. 1979. "Hegemony and Ideology in Gramsci." In C. Mouffe, ed., *Gramsci and Marxist Theory*, 168–204. London: Routledge and Kegan Paul.

———. 2005. *On the Political*. London: Routledge.

Mulvenna, G. 2015. "Labour Aristocracies, Triumphalism and Melancholy: Misconceptions of the Protestant Working Class and Loyalist Community." In

T. P. Burgess and G. Mulvenna, eds., *The Contested Identities of Ulster Protestants*, 159–76. Basingstoke: Palgrave Macmillan.

———. 2016. *Tartan Gangs and Paramilitaries: The Loyalist Backlash*. Liverpool: Liverpool University Press.

Mycock, A. 2014a. "The First World War Centenary in the UK: 'A Truly National Commemoration'?" *Round Table* 103 (2): 153–63.

———. 2014b. "The Politics of the Great War Centenary in the United Kingdom." In S. Sumarjato and B. Wellings, eds., *Nation, Memory and Great War Commemoration: Mobilizing the Past in Europe, Australia and New Zealand*, 99–118. Oxford: Peter Lang.

Myers, J. R. 2013. *The Great War and Memory in Irish Culture, 1918–2010*. Palo Alto, CA: Academica Press.

Nadai, E., and C. Maeder. 2005. "Fuzzy Fields: Multi-Sited Ethnography in Sociological Research." *Forum: Qualitative Social Research* 6 (3) [Online]. www .qualitative-research.net/index.php/fqs/article/view/22/47.

———. 2009. "Contours of the Field(s): Multi-Sited Ethnography as a Theory-Driven Research Strategy for Sociology." In M.-A. Falzon, ed., *Multi-Sited Ethnography: Theory, Praxis and Locality in Contemporary Research*, 233–50. Farnham: Ashgate.

Nash, C. 2008. *Of Irish Descent: Origin Stories, Genealogy and the Politics of Belonging*. Syracuse, NY: Syracuse University Press.

Navaro-Yashin, Y. 2009. "Affective Spaces, Melancholic Objects: Ruination and the Production of Anthropological Knowledge." *Journal of the Royal Anthropological Institute* 15 (1): 1–18.

Neill, W. J. V. 2006. "Return to Titanic and Lost in the Maze: The Search for Representation of 'Post-Conflict' Belfast." *Space and Polity* 10 (2): 109–20.

Neill, W. J. V., M. Murray, and B. Grist, eds. 2014. *Relaunching Titanic: Memory and Marketing in the New Belfast*. London: Routledge.

News Letter. 2014. "'Drumcree Was No Accident': Recollection" [Online], 26 November. www.newsletter.co.uk/news/drumcree-was-no-accident -recollection-1-6438948.

———. 2016a. "Incredible WWI Story of Catholic and Protestant from Same Street" [Online], 20 September. www.newsletter.co.uk/news/incredible -wwi-story-of-catholic-and-protestant-from-same-street-1-7586885.

———. 2016b. "Loyalists Get It Right in Left Red Hand Debate" [Online], 3 June. www.newsletter.co.uk/news/loyalists-get-it-right-in-left-red-hand -debate-1-7415542.

Ní Dhonnchadha, M., and T. Dorgan, eds. 1991. *Revising the Rising*. Derry: Field Day.

Nixon, K. 2016. *1: not another flag 2: in what way is this news. 3: yet again the PUP associate with terrorists 4: see point 1* [Twitter], 12 May [Online]. twitter.com /belfastbarman/status/730704767178166272?lang=en-gb.

Nolan, P. 2014. *Northern Ireland Peace Monitoring Report*, 3. Belfast: CRC.

Nolan, P., D. Bryan, C. Dwyer, K. Hayward, K. Radford, and P. Shirlow. 2014. *The Flag Dispute: Anatomy of a Protest*. Belfast: ISCTSJ.

Nora, P. 1989. "Between History and Memory: Les Lieux de Mémoire." *Representations* 26: 7–24.

Nordstrom, C., and J. Martin. 1992. "The Culture of Conflict: Field Reality and Theory." In C. Nordstrom and J. Martin, eds., *The Paths to Domination, Resistance, and Terror*, 3–17. Berkley: University of California Press.

Northern Ireland Equality Commission. 2014. *Fair Employment Monitoring Report No.25* [Online]. www.equalityni.org/ECNI/media/ECNI/Publications /Delivering%20Equality/FETF%20Monitoring%20Reports/No25/Mon ReportNo25-HighLevelTrends.pdf.

Northern Ireland Executive (NIE). 2012. "Executive Statement on Decade of Centenaries" [Online]. www.northernireland.gov.uk/index/media-centre /executive-statements/executive-statement-on-decade-of-centenaries.htm.

Northern Ireland Office (NIO). 2015. "Paramilitary Groups in Northern Ireland: An Assessment Commissioned by the Secretary of State for Northern Ireland on the Structure, Role and Purpose of Paramilitary Groups Focusing on Those Which Declared Ceasefires in Order to Support and Facilitate the Political Process" [Online]. www.gov.uk/government/uploads /system/uploads/attachment_data/file/469548/Paramilitary_Groups_in _Northern_Ireland_-_20_Oct_2015.pdf.

———. 2016. "The Somme and 1916 Centenaries" [Online]. www.gov.uk /government/speeches/the-somme-and-1916-centenaries.

Northern Ireland PUL Community Info, Politics and Debates. 2015. "The Big Lie" [Facebook], 10 February [Online]. www.facebook.com/Northern IrelandPulCommunityInfoPoliticsAndDebates/posts/410759522415841;0.

Northern Ireland Statistics and Research Agency (NISRA). 2015. Northern Ireland Quarterly Employment Survey September 2015 [Online]. www .economy-ni.gov.uk/sites/default/files/publications/economy/20161%20 QES%20publication%20v2.pdf.

Northern Ireland Youth Forum (NIYF). 2013. *Sons of Ulster: Exploring Loyalist Band Members' Attitudes towards Culture, Identity and Heritage*. Belfast: NIYF.

Novosel, T. 2013. *Northern Ireland's Lost Opportunity: The Frustrated Promise of Political Loyalism*. London: Pluto Press.

O'Brien, C. C. 1972. *States of Ireland*. London: Faber & Faber.

O'Callaghan, M. 2016. "Reframing 1916 after 1969: Irish Governments, a National Day of Reconciliation and the Politics of Commemoration in the 1970s." In R. S. Grayson and F. McGarry, eds., *Remembering 1916: The Easter Rising, the Somme and the Politics of Memory in Ireland*, 207–23. Cambridge: Cambridge University Press.

Ó Corráin, D. 2018. *The Irish Volunteers, 1913–1919*. Dublin: Four Courts Press.

O'Doherty, M. 2016. "Daithí McKay Resignation over Jamie Bryson Coaching Claims: Whatever the Truth, Losing MLA Is Body Blow Sinn Féin Will Struggle to Recover From." *Belfast Telegraph* [Online], 19 August. www .belfasttelegraph.co.uk/news/northern-ireland/daithi-mckay-resignation -over-jamie-bryson-coaching-claims-whatever-the-truth-losing-mla-is -body-blow-sinn-fein-will-struggle-to-recover-from-34978004.html.

O'Donnell, C. 2007. "Pragmatism versus Unity: The Stormont Government and the 1966 Easter Commemoration." In M. Daly and M. O'Callaghan, eds., *1916 in 1966: Commemorating the Easter Rising*, 239–71. Dublin: Royal Irish Academy.

O'Driscoll, S., and C. O'Boyle. 2017. "Sinn Féin's Michelle O'Neill in Firing Line over RHI as Role of Her Department in Hyping Faulty Scheme Revealed." *Belfast Telegraph* [Online], 28 January. www.belfasttelegraph.co.uk /news/rhi-scandal/sinn-feins-michelle-oneill-in-firing-line-over-rhi-as -role-of-her-department-in-hyping-faulty-scheme-revealed-35404342 .html.

Office for National Statistics (ONS). 2014. "Regional Gross Value Added (IncomeApproach)NUTS3 Tables"[Online].www.ons.gov.uk/ons/rel/regional -accounts/regional-gross-value-added--income-approach-/december -2014/rft-nuts3.xls.

Office of the First Minister and Deputy First Minister (OFMDFM). 2013. *Together: Building a United Community* [Online]. www.executiveoffice-ni.gov .uk/sites/default/files/publications/ofmdfm_dev/together-building-a -united-community-strategy.pdf.

———. 2014. *2013 Labour Force Survey Northern Ireland Religion Report* [Online]. www.executiveoffice-ni.gov.uk/sites/default/files/publications/ofmdfm _dev/labour-force-survey-religion-report-2013.pdf.

Officer, D. 2001. "'For God and Ulster': The Ulsterman on the Somme." In I. McBride, ed., *History and Memory in Modern Ireland*, 160–83. Cambridge: Cambridge University Press.

O'Leary, B., and J. McGarry. 1996. *The Politics of Antagonism: Understanding Northern Ireland*. 2nd ed. London: Athlone.

Olick, J. K. 2008. "'Collective Memory': A Memoir and Prospect." *Memory Studies* 1 (1): 23–29.

Ó Murchú, N. 2005. "Ethnic Politics and Labour Market Closure: Shipbuilding and Industrial Decline in Northern Ireland." *Ethnic and Racial Studies* 28 (5): 859–79.

Onta, P. 1996. "Ambivalence Denied: The Making of *Rastriya Itihas* in Panchayat Era Textbooks." *Contributions to Nepalese Studies* 23 (1): 213–54.

Orr, P. 2008. *The Road to the Somme*. Belfast: Blackstaff Press.

———. 2012. "The Great War, the Somme and the Ulster Protestant Psyche." Paper presented at Remembering the Future, Belfast, 26 July.

———. 2013. "Remembering the Somme." In *Remembering 1916: Challenges for Today*, 20–25. Belfast: CRC.

———. 2014. "The Great War and Unionist Memory." Paper presented at *Féile an Phobail*. Belfast, 6 August.

Ó Seaghdha, B. 2011. "Problematising Undecidability." *Dublin Review of Books* [Online]. www.drb.ie/essays/problematising-undecidability.

O'Toole, F. 2016. "In 2016, Official Ireland Trusted Artists. Please Do It Again." *Irish Times* [Online], 29 October. www.irishtimes.com/sponsored/in-2016 -official-ireland-trusted-artists-please-do-it-again-1.2845647.

Owen, W. 1917. "Anthem for Doomed Youth" [Online]. www.bbc.co.uk/poetry season/poems/anthem_for_doomed_youth.shtml.

Palys, T., and J. Lowman. 2012. "Defending Research Confidentiality 'To the Extent the Law Allows': Lessons from the Boston College Subpoenas." *Journal of Academic Ethics* 10 (4): 271–97.

Panel of Parties in the NI Executive. 2013. "Proposed Agreement 31 December 2013: An Agreement among the Parties of Northern Ireland Executive on Parades, Select Commemorations and Related Protests; Flags and Emblems; and Contending with the Past" [Online]. www.northernireland.gov .uk/sites/default/files/publications/newnigov/haass-report-2013.pdf.

Papadakis, Y. 1993. "The Politics of Memory and Forgetting in Cyprus." *Journal of Mediterranean Studies* 3 (1): 139–54.

Pearse, P. 2012 [1915]. "Ghosts." In *The Coming Revolution: The Political Writings and Speeches of Patrick Pearse*, 173–202. Cork: Mercier Press.

Perry, R. 2010. "Revising Irish History: The Northern Ireland Conflict and the War of Ideas." *Journal of European Studies* 40 (4): 329–54.

Petersen, R. 2002. *Understanding Ethnic Violence: Fear, Hatred, Resentment in Twentieth Century Eastern Europe*. Cambridge: Cambridge University Press.

Phoenix, É. 2011. "'Remembering the Future': Some Thoughts on a Decade of Commemorations." In *Remembering the Future*, 14–17. Belfast: CRC and HLF.

Pilkington, H. 2016. *Loud and Proud: Passion and Politics in the English Defence League*. Manchester: Manchester University Press.

Pine, E. 2014. "Irish Memory Studies." Paper presented at conference Commemoration: Contexts and Concepts, Cork, 10 October.

Polsky, N. 1971. *Hustlers, Beats and Others*. Harmondsworth: Penguin.

Posel, D. 2008. "History as Confession: The Case of the South African Truth and Reconciliation Commission." *Public Culture* 20 (1): 119–41.

Postill, J., and S. Pink. 2012. "Social Media Ethnography: The Digital Researcher in a Messy Web." *Media International Australia* 145 [Online]. http://blogs

.bournemouth.ac.uk/research/files/2013/04/Postill-Pink-socialmedia-ethnography.pdf.

Progressive Unionist Party (PUP). 1985. *Sharing Responsibility*. Belfast: PUP.

———. 2002. *The Principles of Loyalism*. Belfast: PUP.

———. 2015. *Firm Foundations, Education: Getting It Right for Every Child*. Belfast: PUP.

PUL Media. 2015. "Protestant Unionist Loyalist Culture & PUL Cultural Events" [Facebook], 22 February [Online]. www.facebook.com/pulmedia/posts/927656893945896.

Purple Standard. 2015a. "At Bugle Call My Darling, I Must Go." Issue 58, p. 19.

———. 2015b. "Centenary of the 36th (Ulster) Division, Belfast City Hall March-Past and Review." Issue 57, p. 10.

Purvis, D., M. Langhammer, M. Andrews, P. Bryson, C. Gray, K. Harland, J. Harrison, J. Keith, S. McCready, A. McMorran, J. Poots, C. Robinson, and P. Shirlow. 2011. "Educational Disadvantage and the Protestant Working Class: A Call to Action" [Online]. www.amazingbrains.co.uk/static/uploads/media/pdfs/A-Call-to-Action-FINAL-March2011_0.pdf.

Quigley, G., and B. Cowen. 2011. *A Decade of Centenaries: Commemorating Shared History*. IBIS Working Papers No. 108. Dublin: Institute of British-Irish Studies.

Quinault, R. 1998. "The Cult of the Centenary, c. 1784–1914." *Historical Research* 71 (176): 303–23.

Racioppi, L., and K. O'Sullivan See. 2000. "Ulstermen and Loyalist Ladies on Parade." *International Feminist Journal of Politics* 2 (1): 1–29.

Ramsey, G. 2011. *Music, Emotion and Identity in Ulster Marching Bands: Flutes, Drums and Loyal Sons*. Bern: Peter Lang.

Reed, R. 2012. "Researching Ulster Loyalism: The Methodological Challenges of the Divisive and Sensitive Subject." *Politics* 32 (3): 207–19.

———. 2015. *Paramilitary Loyalism: Identity and Change*. Manchester: Manchester University Press.

Regan, J. M. 2013. *Myth and the Irish State: Historical Problems and Other Essays*. Sallins: Irish Academic Press.

Review of the 36th – Ulster Division – Belfast 2015. 2015. "Please note that this tweet is wrong" [Facebook], 6 May [Online]. www.facebook.com/376697822454970/photos/a.377271409064278.1073741829.376697822454970/395997843858301/?type=3&theater.

Reynolds, D. 2013. *The Long Shadow: The Great War and the Twentieth Century*. London: Simon & Schuster.

Ricoeur, P. 2004. *Memory, History and Forgetting*. Trans. K. Blamey and D. Pellauer. Chicago: University of Chicago Press.

Ringland, T. 2016. "Loyalists and the Somme Memory." *News Letter* [Online], 23 May. www.newsletter.co.uk/news/your-say/trevor-ringland-loyalists-and -the-somme-memory-1-7397489.

Robinson, H. 2010. "Remembering War in the Midst of Conflict: First World War Commemorations in the Northern Irish Troubles." *Twentieth Century British History* 21 (1): 80–101.

Rodham, A. 1998. "The Ouch! Factor: Problems in Conducting Sensitive Research." *Qualitative Health Research* 8 (2): 275–82.

Rolston, B. 2010. "'Trying to Reach the Future through the Past': Murals and Memory in Northern Ireland." *Crime, Media, Culture* 6 (3): 285–307.

———. 2012. "Re-imaging: Mural Painting and the State in Northern Ireland." *International Journal of Cultural Studies* 15 (5): 447–66.

Rowthorn, B., and N. Wayne. 1988. *Northern Ireland: The Political Economy of Conflict.* Cambridge: Polity Press.

Ruane, J., and J. Todd. 1996. *The Dynamics of Conflict in Northern Ireland: Power, Conflict and Emancipation.* Cambridge: Cambridge University Press.

Runia, E. 2007. "Burying the Dead, Creating the Past." *History and Theory* 46 (3): 313–25.

Rushkoff, D. 2013. *Present Shock: When Everything Happens Now.* New York: Penguin.

Rutherford, A. 2016. "Veterans Plan Somme Boycott If Sinn Féin's Martin McGuinness Attends." *Belfast Telegraph* [Online], 17 May. www.belfasttele graph.co.uk/news/northern-ireland/veterans-plan-somme-event-boycott -if-sinn-feins-mcguinness-attends-34721304.html.

Saar, M. 2002. "Genealogy and Subjectivity." *European Journal of Philosophy* 10 (2): 231–45.

Sales, R. 1997. "Gender and Protestantism in Northern Ireland." In P. Shirlow and M. McGovern, eds., *Who Are "the People"? Unionism, Protestantism and Loyalism in Northern Ireland,* 140–57. London: Pluto Press.

Santino, J. 2001. *Signs of War and Peace: Social Conflict and the Use of Public Symbols in Northern Ireland.* New York: Palgrave.

Scheper-Hughes, N. 1995. "The Primacy of the Ethical: Propositions for a Militant Anthropology." *Current Anthropology* 36 (3): 409–40.

Scheper-Hughes, N., and P. Bourgois. 2004. "Introduction: Making Sense of Violence." In N. Scheper-Hughes and P. Bourgois, eds., *Violence in War and Peace: An Anthology,* 1–32. Malden, MA: Blackwell.

Schinkel, W. 2010. *Aspects of Violence: A Critical Theory.* Houndmills: Palgrave Macmillan.

Schwartzman, H. B. 1989. *The Meeting: Gatherings in Organisations and Communities.* New York: Plenum Press.

Scott, J. C. 1990. *Domination and the Arts of Resistance: Hidden Transcripts*. New Haven, CT: Yale University Press.

Shah, A. 2010. *In the Shadows of the State: Indigenous Politics, Environmentalism and Insurgency in Jharkhand, India*. Durham, NC: Duke University Press.

Shankill Historical Society. 2015. "Notice for Anyone Coming to Belfast for the Parade This Saturday" [Facebook], 6 May [Online]. www.facebook.com /376697822454970/photos/a.377271409064278.1073741829.37669782245 4970/395997843858301/?type=3&theater.

Shirlow, P. 2012. *The End of Ulster Loyalism?* Manchester: Manchester University Press.

Shirlow, P., and K. McEvoy. 2008. *Beyond the Wire: Former Political Prisoners and Conflict Transformation in Northern Ireland*. London: Pluto Press.

Shore, C., and S. Wright, eds. 1997. *Anthropology of Policy: Critical Perspectives on Governance and Power*. Abingdon: Routledge.

Sinnerton, H. 2002. *David Ervine: Uncharted Waters*. Dublin: Brandon.

6th Connaught Rangers Research Project (6th CRRP). 2011. *The 6th Connaught Rangers: Belfast Nationalists and the Great War*. Belfast: Ulster Historical Foundation.

Skinner, J. 2012. "A Four-Part Introduction to the Interview: Introducing the Interview; Society, Sociology and the Interview; Anthropology and the Interview; Anthropology and the Interview—Edited." In J. Skinner, ed., *The Interview: An Ethnographic Approach*, 1–52. London: Berg.

Skocpol, T., and V. Williamson. 2013. *The Tea Party and the Remaking of Republican Conservatism*. New York: Oxford University Press.

Sluka, J. A. 1992. "The Anthropology of Conflict." In N. Nordstrom and J. Martin, eds., *The Paths to Domination, Resistance, and Terror*, 18–36. Berkeley: University of California Press.

———. 2000. *Death Squad: The Anthropology of State Terror*. Philadelphia: University of Pennsylvania Press.

Smith, A. 1996. "LSE Centennial Lecture: The Resurgence of Nationalism? Myth and Memory in the Renewal of Nations." *British Journal of Sociology* 47 (4): 575–98.

———. 1997. "The 'Golden Age' and National Renewal." In G. Hosking and G. Schöpflin, eds., *Myths and Nationhood*, 36–59. London: Hurst & Co.

Smith, M. L. R. 1999. "The Intellectual Internment of a Conflict: The Forgotten War in Northern Ireland." *International Affairs* 75 (1): 77–97.

Smithey, L. A. 2011. *Unionists, Loyalists and Conflict Transformation in Northern Ireland*. Oxford: Oxford University Press.

Sontag, S. 2003. *Regarding the Pain of Others*. New York: Picador.

Spence, A. 1977. "Remembrance Day Oration." *Combat*, November 1977.

Spencer, G. 2008. *The State of Loyalism in Northern Ireland*. Houndmills: Palgrave Macmillan.

Spivak, G. 1988. "Can the Subaltern Speak?" In L. Grossberg and C. Nelson, eds., *Marxism and the Interpretation of Culture*, 271–313. Basingstoke: MacMillan.

———. 1995. "Ghostwriting." *Diacritics* 25 (2): 64–84.

Standing, G. 2011. *The Precariat: The New Dangerous Class*. London: Bloomsbury.

Strauss, A. L. 1984. "Social Worlds and Their Segmentation Process." In N. K. Denzin, ed., *Studies in Symbolic Interaction*, vol. 5, 123–39. Greenwich, CT: JAI Press.

Sutton, M. 2002. "An Index of Deaths from the Conflict in Ireland." *CAIN Web Service* [Online]. http://cain.ulst.ac.uk/sutton/book/index.html.

Svašek, M. 2010. "Intersubjectivity, Empathy and the Workings of Internalised Presence." In D. Spencer and J. Davies, eds., *Anthropological Fieldwork: A Relational Process*, 75–99. Cambridge: Cambridge University Press.

Switzer, C. 2007. *Unionists and Great War Commemoration in the North of Ireland, 1914–1939: People, Places and Politics*. Dublin: Irish Academic Press.

———. 2013. *Ulster, Ireland and the Somme: War Memorials and Battlefield Pilgrimages*. Stroud: History Press.

Taylor, P. 1997. *Provos: The IRA and Sinn Féin*. London: Bloomsbury.

———. 2000. *Loyalists*. London: Bloomsbury.

Tedlock, B. 1991. "From Participant Observation to the Observation of Participation: The Emergence of Narrative Ethnography." *Journal of Anthropological Research* 47 (1): 69–94.

Tilly, C. 1985. "War Making and State Making as Organised Crime." In P. B. Evans, D. Rueschemeyer, and T. Skocpol, eds., *Bringing the State Back In*, 169–91. Cambridge: Cambridge University Press.

Tilmans, K., F. van Ree, and J. Winter, eds. 2010. *Performing the Past: Memory, History and Identity in Modern Europe*. Amsterdam: Amsterdam University Press.

Tonkin, E. 1992. *Narrating Our Pasts: The Social Construction of Oral History*. Cambridge: Cambridge University Press.

Tonkin, E., and D. Bryan. 1996. "Political Ritual: Temporality and Tradition." In Å. Bonholm, ed., *Political Ritual*, 14–36. Gothenburg: IASSA.

Trott, B. 2011. "Just Do It? A Review of *The Coming Insurrection*." *Social Movement Studies* 10 (1): 113–18.

Turner, V. 1995. *The Ritual Process: Structure and Anti-Structure*. Hawthorne, NY: Aldine de Gruyter.

Uachtarán na hÉireann [President of Ireland]. 2016. "Speech at Symposium entitled 'Remembering 1916'" [Online], 28 March. www.president.ie/ga/ilmheain-agus-oraidi/oraidi/speech-at-a-symposium-entitled-remembering-1916.

Ulster Political Research Group (UPRG). 1987. "Common Sense: Northern Ireland—An Agreed Process" [Online]. http://cain.ulst.ac.uk/issues/politics/docs/commonsense.htm.

Unionist Centenary Committee (UCC). 2009. "Our Mission Statement" [Online]. www.unionistcentenaries.com/dynamic_content.php?id=110.

———. 2015. "2016" [Online]. www.unionistcentenaries.com/dynamic_content .php?id=92.

Urwin, M. 2016. *A State in Denial: British Collaboration with Loyalist Paramilitaries*. Cork: Mercier Press.

Viggiani, E. 2014. *Talking Stones: The Politics of Memorialisation in Post-Conflict Northern Ireland*. New York: Berghahn.

#WakingTheFeminists. 2016. "About the Campaign" [Online]. www.wakingthe feminists.org/about-wtf/how-it-started/.

Wallis, J. 2015. "'Great-Grandfather, What Did You Do in the Great War?': The Phenomenon of Conducting First World War Family History Research." In B. Ziino, ed., *Remembering the First World War*. Abingdon: Routledge. Kindle ed. [Online].

Wenger, E. 1998. *Communities of Practice: Learning, Meaning and Identity*. Cambridge: Cambridge University Press.

Whyte, J. 1983. "How Much Discrimination Was There under the Unionist Regime, 1921–68?" In T. Gallagher and J. O'Connell, eds., *Contemporary Irish Studies*, 1–36. Manchester: Manchester University Press.

Wikan, U. 1992. "Beyond the Words: The Power of Resonance." *American Ethnologist* 19 (3): 460–82.

Willis, P. 1977. *Learning to Labour: How Working-Class Kids Get Working-Class Jobs*. New York: Columbia University Press.

Wilson, R. 2001. *The Politics of Truth and Reconciliation in South Africa: Legitimizing the Post-Apartheid State*. Cambridge: Cambridge University Press.

Winter, J. 1995. *Sites of Memory, Sites of Mourning: The Great War in European Cultural History*. Cambridge: Cambridge University Press.

———. 2000. "The Generation of Memory: Reflections on the Memory Boom in Contemporary Historical Studies." *Bulletin of the German Historical Institute* 27: 69–92.

Wood, I. S. 2006. *Crimes of Loyalty: A History of the UDA*. Edinburgh: Edinburgh University Press.

Wright, T. P. 2004. "The Identity and Changing Status of Former Elite Minorities: The Contrasting Cases of North Indian Muslims and American WASPs." In E. P. Kaufmann, ed., *Rethinking Ethnicity: Majority Groups and Dominant Minorities*, 31–39. New York: Routledge.

Yeates, P. 2014. "No Poppy Please." *Dublin Review of Books* [Online]. www.drb.ie /essays/no-poppy-please.

Yeats, W. B. 1916. "Easter 1916" [Online]. http://apoemforireland.rte.ie/shortlist /easter-1916/.

Yuval-Davies, N. 1989. *Woman-Nation-State*. Houndmills: Palgrave Macmillan.

Zalewski, M., and J. Barry, eds. 2008. *Intervening in Northern Ireland: Critically Re-Thinking Representations of the Conflict*. Abingdon: Routledge.

Zerubavel, E. 2003. *Time Maps: Collective Memory and the Social Shape of the Past*. Chicago: University of Chicago Press.

Zinn, H. 2005 [1980]. *A People's History of the United States: 1492–Present*. New York: HarperPerennial.

Žižek, S. 1999. *The Ticklish Subject: The Absent Centre of Political Ontology*. London: Verso.

———. 2005. *Interrogating the Real*. London: Continuum.

INDEX

JONATHAN EVERSHED is a postdoctoral research fellow in the
Department of Government and Politics, University College Cork, and
a visiting fellow at the Institute of Irish Studies, Queen's University
Belfast.

CPSIA information can be obtained
at www.ICGtesting.com
Printed in the USA
LVOW13*1914090518
576598LV00006B/24/P